FIFTY YEARS ON BRITISH BIKES

George J Hylands

MINERVA PRESS

LONDON
MONTREUX   LOS ANGELES   SYDNEY

FIFTY YEARS ON BRITISH BIKES
Copyright © George J Hylands 1997

ISBN 1 86106 606 6

First Published 1997 by
MINERVA PRESS
195 Knightsbridge
London SW7 1RE

Printed in Great Britain for Minerva Press

FIFTY YEARS ON BRITISH BIKES

Preface

This story is a true one, and it tells of my own fifty years on British bikes. Starting with my first motorcycle ride through to the last one. It tells how I first started as a motorcycle mechanic, and how I developed into a very experienced rider of many fine machines.

Time has been taken to explain the older bikes, and the alterations I made to various machines, including my thirty-two and a half year love affair with a Velocette, which I converted from a standard model into a very potent road racer, and which is now in a motorcycle museum. It is all explained: the conversion, the snags, the tests and the fabulous rides I got as a result. I also shook a few riders and their bikes on the Isle of Man, so if it's British bikes you are interested in, then this book is for you, and I feel sure that it will give you as much pleasure reading it, as it has given me writing it. I have also told in this book the true and remarkable rides and spills that make up this story. Things were so different in those days; an era of motorcycling never to be repeated, and I am pleased to have been a part of it.

So, if you care to browse through the chapters, I'm sure you'll soon see that you are in for some very interesting and exciting reading. Relive experiences with me on my beloved Velo, and thrill to the fascination of British bikes, motorcycling at its best. I know I wouldn't have missed it for the world, as it was my life on British bikes.

George J Hylands
British motorcyclist and mechanic for over fifty years.

Contents

Chapter One

The Lure of the Motorcycle

I was born in Coventry in 1922, and when I was thirteen my cousin Ruby (five years my senior) came to see us with her future husband, Al. He had a new motorbike, and I the first chance to have a little ride. The machine was an OK Supreme (make of the motorcycle, the transfer in gold letters, was on the petrol tank), a 248cc pushrod Over Head Valve (OHV) with a JAP (make of engine) engine and a four-speed Burman foot change gearbox. It was a lovely finished machine with a gleaming bright red tank with gold bands surrounding the red panels.

The first glimpse I got of this bike was as I came down our road with my old dog, Pip. It was leaning on the pavement edge on its nearside footrest. As I got closer to it, it slowly toppled over, as the weight of the shifting petrol in the tank overbalanced it. I ran to the machine and got it back on its footrest in a more stable position. I hadn't seen the bike before, but I'd heard Ruby speak about it, so I dashed in home to tell Al what had happened. Ruby told Al to show me the bike, as she knew very well that I was longing to have a ride on it. So Al showed me round the lovely new sports bike. There were only 1,082 miles on the clock. The registration number was BOM 401, and Al told me that it was the fastest bike at Bourneville where he worked.

I enjoyed sitting astride the bike. It felt great.

Al said, "Go on then, start it up for me, and I'll take you round the block."

There were no crash hats then, except of course for racing and speedway. Most chaps had either a tammy hat held on by a pair of goggles, or a posh headgear was a leather helmet. Long leather coats were also worn, as the two-piece suits came later.

After Al had half retarded the mag with a lever on the left-hand side of the handlebar, he showed me how to just feel the piston over compression, and then give a mighty push down on the kick-start lever. The engine fired instantly, and Al advanced the timing up again.

On most machines of that era, the ignition advance and retard was controlled by the lever, as I have described; the other similar lever on the right-hand side of the handlebar worked the air control to the carburettor, like a choke. The foot brake was on the left, and the foot gear shift was on the right, one up for first gear, and three down for second, third and fourth, neutral being between first and second.

The ride round the block was great. I loved the sensation of going round a bend, and the acceleration was breathtaking. On coming back to our house, I was very surprised when Al said, "Do you think that you could ride it?"

"I could if you showed me how to," I said, so Al, to my delight, quickly gave me my very first lesson in the handling of a motorcycle. I soon learned how to gently 'feel in' the clutch lever, and to catch the falling revs on the throttle. After doing this a few times Al could see that I was in control.

"That's very good, young George," he said. "Do you think you could go up the road and back in first gear?" (We lived in a cul-de-sac with very little traffic.)

"Yes, I'm sure I could," I answered.

"All right," said Al. "Only first gear, and pull in the clutch before you turn, and only dead slow."

"Thanks Al," I said. "Don't worry, I won't drop the bike." Very carefully I let in the clutch, and gave it just a bit of throttle, and the bike and I took off. I was delighted at how easily it pulled away, and how lovely and smooth it was. I soon found out how quickly the bike responded to the throttle. In the meantime, my mum and Ruby, hearing the bike's engine, came running out to see just what was going on. They saw me coming back down the road for the fifth time. My mum nearly had a fit, and I could see by her face that it had really shaken her up. Poor Al got a telling-off from Ruby. She was going on about the law, the insurance, how dangerous it was, the lot.

I really felt sorry for Al, but he took it all very well and said, "I'm sorry. I know I was wrong, but young George here is a natural. He'll make a great motorcyclist. I just let him get a feel of the

machine, and he did everything right. He was in control all the time."
Well, I was thrilled to bits. I couldn't thank Al enough. My very
first motorcycle ride! I wouldn't forget that in a hurry. I'd got the
bug, but as yet I didn't know it.

Chapter Two

School Leaver's Dilemma

In August, 1936, I was due to leave school and start a new era working in Coventry, but I was in a dilemma about what to do.

My school was Cheylesmore Senior Boys. It was an elementary school, but in those days discipline was paramount in all schools, this being sadly lacking today. The teachers did their best to teach the rough kids of my schooldays, and the cane was a big deterrent for the foolish ones. I remember Mr Holland, my woodwork teacher, picking up a piece of wood which one boy had worked on, and tossing it into the scrap corner.

He said, "Most of you will soon be leaving school, and judging by your work some of you might make dustmen or labourers, but unless you all pull your socks up hardly anyone here will make a craftsman." That remark has stayed with me all my life. How true it was, because it's impossible to get more out of any work than what is put into it. Mr Holland made that very clear. It made me very thoughtful as I left the woodwork class. Like most boys of my age it wasn't until we reached school-leaving age that we realised how much our last school report would mean to us. In those days only a good school report would get one a good job. Hence Mr Holland's harsh remarks. My position in class exams was usually fifteenth or seventeenth out of thirty pupils, but Mr Holland really impressed me, and during my last two years at school I really did pull my socks up, coming fifth in my final exam.

My teacher was very pleased, and commended the first eight of us for the effort we had made. "You have all got potential for holding down a good job," he said. "Go for it, and put your best into your work, and good luck." Cheylesmore School was only for working-class boys, but it produced some good results. I worked with one of them for twenty-four years, but I will deal with that event later on.

At fourteen years of age I wasn't sure which trade I would choose, however my father thought that electronics was the coming thing. He wanted me to be apprenticed to the British Thompson Houston, (BTH) in Hood Street, Coventry, manufacturers of heavy electrical goods. At this early stage in my life I didn't have a lot of say in the matter, so two weeks prior to leaving school I accompanied my father for an interview with the apprentice supervisor at the BTH. The initials stand for the British Thompson Houston works, but in Coventry it was well known as the British Torture House. My wife verified this later on, as she worked there all through the war.

I must say that I wasn't impressed by the dirty, dismal building where I was to work on electrical engineering, which I knew nothing about. The interview went well, my good report helped, and the supervisor said that he would sign me on, but I would have to wait for a vacancy to come up. My father agreed and the papers were signed. 'Well,' I thought, 'I'll have a good holiday until then.'

Two days later the man next door got me a job in the planning office at the Riley car factory. I was to start the next morning at 9 o'clock. My heart sank.

"But I haven't had any holiday." I moaned.

"Never mind that," my father said. "The factories have two days off in September, and getting a job is much more important." The next morning I went to the gatehouse of the Riley works in Dunbar Avenue. The commissionaire directed me to the planning office to report to a Mr Saunders.

Mr Saunders looked up from his books.

"You'll be Master George Hylands, I believe."

"Yes, sir," I said.

"Right, young man, here is your desk and chair, and this is Trevor, who will show you what you have to do. If you don't understand anything, just ask. We are dealing with wages here and we don't want any mistakes." I soon got settled into the job, which was quite easy once I got to know the system. The first week was mainly checking work tallies and putting them in order according to their duties. Gradually I was given more to do, and felt that I was at last earning my salt, which was the grand sum of ten shillings and sixpence, the equivalent today would be fifty-two and a half pence. A man's average wage in those days was two pounds fifty, with foremen getting between three pounds fifty to four pounds fifty according to their trade and ability.   My pocket money was two shillings and sixpence, twelve-and-a-half pence in today's currency.

It was at the Riley Motor Company that I got the first inkling as to what I wanted to become. About three thirty one Friday afternoon I suddenly heard the lovely sound of racing cars parked right outside the office window. The noise was terrific. I didn't know at that time why racing cars sit with the engines continually revving up and down, as this was the noise we could hear. It is done because for a start off they had hard type spark plugs in, so the engine is revved to prevent them from oiling up, also the wild camshafts which were fitted gave a large valve overlap, so any engine with this type of camshaft can't tick over in low revs. In those days 1500 to 1800 were the lowest they would run at. This information was given to me by one of the drivers whom I questioned the following Monday. They were beautiful cars in British racing green with black wings. They made a big impression on me, and I remember Mr Saunders saying that they were off to Donnington.

About six weeks later I received a letter from the BTH telling me to report to the labour office in three weeks time to start my probationary training in the tool stores. My father said that I should take the letter and show it to my boss, which I did. He wasn't very pleased, and I remember him saying, "Damn me, we've just got you doing nicely and off you go. Oh well, it'll be a better job for you in the long run." I wasn't too keen on office work, but I had put in a good effort. By this time I had taken up amateur boxing and weight training. I really liked this, and I was learning well. I had three cousins, Frank, Sid and Dick Ireland who were all interested as well. Some people may remember Sid Ireland, as he was on many a promoter's bill. He was a really classy boxer with a good straight left, so I was in a good school.

The day finally came to start at the BTH. I settled into my job in the tool stores. It was very large, with six men working there. Mr Hunt was the boss, and he made sure everyone knew it. I liked dealing with tools, and in a very short time I could be trusted to deal with almost any tool. I got to know the men who used different tools, and when I saw them coming, I would have the required tools ready for them, with half a dozen clean wipers. They liked that, and to my surprise I got a lot of tips at Christmas. After the two-day Christmas holiday my boss told me that I had been enrolled at the Technical

College for training in electrical engineering. I didn't like the idea, as I was just becoming aware that electrical engineering wasn't my cup of tea. I stuck it out for the first term, but all the time I was getting more interested in mechanics.

My father, bless him, bought me a new Royal Enfield sports racing bike. I used my pocket money to improve it. I bought a De Raillier three-speed gear, a close ratio Sturmey Archer hub wheel, black celluloid mudguards and other things which transformed my standard model into a very nice machine. I made friends with another apprentice who also had a sports racer, and helped him to get his in good order.

Chapter Three

Getting Sorted

Around this time one of our old neighbours had a son who was dead keen on motorcycles. He had a KTT (denotes model lettering) Velocette which was a 348cc Over Head Camshaft (OHC) racer. It was beautiful, and the lad knew his stuff. He entered the bike in the Junior TT race on the Isle of Man. He rode the bike there, did all his preparation and repairs, and finished third in the race, which was a commendable performance. I got this chap's permission to watch him working on the bike, and in a lot of cases arrived home with oil on my shirt, to my mother's disgust.

"Get used to it, Mum," I said. "I'm going in for a motorcycle as soon as I can afford it." At this time it was occurring to me that what I wanted to do most was to work on motorcycles. To work on them for a living was a very exciting thought.

A few days later an advert appeared in the *Coventry Evening Telegraph* for personnel to work on cycles and motorcycles at the Coventry Eagle Cycle and Motorcycle Factory in Foleshill Road. I hadn't finished my two-year probationary period to become an apprentice in electrical engineering, so I could still get out of it, as I hadn't signed myself to a commitment of bondage, but what would my dad say? He had gone to a lot of trouble to get me into the BTH, and I knew it would upset him if I left. Well, after a lot of thought, I made my mind up. All I ever thought of was mechanics. I'd be wasting my time doing anything else. I dropped my bombshell that evening, and my dad hit the roof.

"What are you on about, lad?" he yelled. "Throwing away an apprenticeship for a tuppenny to ha'penny job on bikes! You must be barmy." The debate lasted all evening, but in the end, to my father's regret, I'd managed, with Mum's help, to get him to see that I wouldn't be happy at the BTH, as it wasn't the job for me. My dad turned to me and said, "All right, lad, I can't run your life for you. I only hope you won't regret it."

The next morning I was off to the Coventry Eagle factory in the hope of getting a job. They were impressed by what I told them about myself, and by my school report. They were not very happy with my turning down an apprenticeship, but I explained that my interests were in mechanics. I was told that I could start on the cycle assembly, as one had to go through cycles first, and then on to motorcycles, but if I had a mechanic's aptitude at seventeen I could be on motorcycles from start to finish, which meant rectification, where the real work was done. On rectification one tested one's work on trade plates, wearing white overalls with 'Coventry Eagle' on the back. I felt over the moon. For the first two weeks I'd be on a standard rate of pay, which was fifteen shillings, (five shillings more than I was getting), and then I would be on piece work, and my wages could reach two pounds a week, which was very good money then. I was given a form for my father to sign, and they arranged for me to start in two weeks' time.

On giving in my notice at the BTH I got a telling off from the apprentice supervisor, who backed my father, and thought that a lad of my age couldn't know his own mind.

"With all respect, sir," I said, "I'm only happy when I'm working on bikes, and I do have my father's permission. I've already got another job." There wasn't a lot he could say except that my record from the tool stores was first class, and the men would be sorry to know that I'd gone. Like my father, he hoped I wouldn't regret it.

The day finally came to start my new job. I was introduced to the lads on the cycle assembly, and first given the job of fitting the front wheels. I'll concentrate on this for a moment, as this information could be very useful as regards safety for anyone who rides a cycle. On most cycles the cones have locking nuts for safety today. In those days the Brampton and Wyles hubs did not, only on the dearer sports and racing models. For safety the adjusting cone on the front wheel was always fitted on the nearside of the cycle, that is, on one's left when sitting astride the machine. The reason was that if the wheel nuts holding the wheel in the forks were to come loose, the cone on a right-hand thread would, with the forward run of the wheel, work loose and lock onto the fork. Now, if the wheel was in the other way round, and the nuts came loose, the cone, with the run of the wheel would lock up solid, and the bike and rider would roll over the wheel. A point well worth checking.

One evening after finishing work I was riding home on my bike when my neighbour and hero Arthur came alongside me on his Cammy Velo and said,

"If you can come round about 7.00 p.m. tonight I've got a treat for you."

"Thanks very much," I said. "I'll be dead on time."

At 7.00 p.m. I was at Arthur's garage. He lived only four houses away from us. He had just wheeled his Velo out of the garage.

"Right, young George," he said. "You're just about the same size as my young lady, so with your help I'm going to fit on this pillion seat and a pair of footrests," And he pointed to a new pillion seat and adjustable footrests on his work bench. "When I've fitted the pillion," he said, "I want you to sit on it so that I can put the footrests on in the correct place, and when they're right you'll be the first to test them, as I'll take you for a ride."

I was thrilled to bits. A ride on a racing Velo that had raced on the Isle of Man! I could hardly wait for the job to be done, but it was soon finished, and Arthur said,

"Put this leather jacket on, we're going for a ride." He started up the Velo and we both got on. Before we took off he said, "Just sit relaxed, put your arms round my waist, and don't fight the bike, just let it take you." He went slowly at first to make sure I was all right, and when I assured him that I was he gradually opened it up, and soon we were cruising at 70 m.p.h.. I loved it, and what a thrill it was through the bends. At one stage there was a left-hander and a right-hander close together, and the exchange from left to right at speed brought my heart into my mouth, but I settled down and enjoyed it. We did a forty-mile run and just for a burst Arthur took it to 90 m.p.h. just for me. I was so excited about all this that I had a job getting to sleep that night, and when I did it wasn't long before my dreams had put me back on the Velo.

I learned a lot about cycles, as there wasn't one mechanical part of a cycle that I didn't have professional knowledge of. I would soon be on motorcycles. Work was brisk, and it seemed that the factory had plenty of orders, but it was 1939, and war was just around the corner. We all thought that we would soon all be on war work making cycles and motorcycles for the military, so it came as quite a shock when Mr

Mayo called us into his office, and told us that the factory was closing down at the end of the month.

"Don't worry, lads," said Frank, the charge hand. "You'll soon all be in the forces." It was a blow, as the only thing I'd done on motorcycles was to fit rear wheels. I wondered what my parents would say. They weren't very pleased, and in the meantime the Riley Motor Company had also folded up. There was only one thing to do. I had to find another job. The end of the month soon came, and we all got double wages, as it was customary to keep a week in hand when a job was started.

Chapter Four

A Job of Love

I had been out of work for two days, when there was a knock on the door at about 5.30 p.m. My father answered the door, and soon came back.

"George, it's for you," he said. "It's Frank Elliott from the garage." Elliott's Garage was very well known in Coventry for its wonderful stock, and also for its repairs on motorcycles and cars. Apparently Frank had heard from someone that I had lost my job, and here he was offering me another one. I was delighted. He said that if I took on all cycle repairs, he and his mechanic would teach me all about motorcycles. I knew that both Frank and Tim, the mechanic, were very experienced men indeed. My father was very glad when I accepted the job. He had bought my Enfield cycle from Frank. Elliott's were the main Royal Enfield agents in Coventry. Frank told me that I would always have a job there if I was a good worker. I thanked him, and we shook hands on it. On Monday morning I became Mr Elliott's cycle mechanic. It was a start, and I'd be able to work on motorcycles and cars, for a bonus. I thought of Mr Holland's words, 'Some of you might make dustmen.' I grinned to myself. I wasn't doing too badly, and I think Mr Holland would agree.

Between all the jobs a garage mechanic had to do in those days, time was found for Frank and Tim to show me how to handle motorbikes. I was taught how to handle and ride our box combination. The 'box', as we called it, consisted of a 1926 1100cc V twin side valve, three-speed hand change motorcycle attached to a long sidecar chassis, with a long box attached to it, hence the name 'box'. It was used for transporting new Royal Enfield machines from the Redditch works, and also for collecting breakdowns and crashed motorcycles. After I had learned how to handle the box correctly it was I who rode it, as it was very much different from riding a solo machine. I had one or two dicey moments with it. With four motorcycles in, the braking was not very good. On one occasion the brakes wouldn't hold the load, and I had to slide into the ditch to avoid a crash. Another time the clutch cable gave out, and I rode over thirty miles without being able to control the clutch. At the time, I had a crashed Harold Ronald Davies (HRD) Vincent 500cc in the box. However, the experiences I had riding the box taught me to became a good combo rider. Later, I replaced the box's front wheel with an Enfield front wheel, which had a larger front brake, as front brakes designed in 1926 were a joke. I made an anchor plate, which Tim brazed across the fork legs in the correct position, and after four flats had been filed into the front spindle on the new wheel, with a new tyre and tube I finally got the wheel fitted. I then found that I had to make up a new front brake cable, but this was easy, as I had become good at making up and fitting cables.

The alteration was a huge success as the box would now stop in half the distance, with the result that I could open up the big V twin a bit, and believe me, the old devil would go. By now I was a well-known figure on the box in and around Coventry. I was still only seventeen when I got the chance to have my first solo motorcycle. A local lad, whom I'd been at school with, came in for oil and petrol on his motorcycle which was a 248cc OHV four-speed hand change Birmingham Small Arms (BSA), in very good condition, having done only 3,743 miles from new.

He said, "Do you know anyone who would like to buy this bike? I'm getting married, and I won't be able to run the bike. I need the cash." This was just what I was hoping for. Tim had told me that I could perhaps get a good bike this way.

Chapter Five

My First Bike

"What are you asking for it?" I asked, trying to hide my excitement.

"Twenty-five pounds," said Alan. "It's in good order. I've had it from new."

"It looks good," I said. "1936 model isn't it?"

"Yes," replied Alan. "But I must have cash."

"I could give you twenty, cash, but I'd have to borrow the rest," I said.

To my surprise Alan replied, "All right, if you can get the twenty pounds tomorrow night it's yours."

"Hang on," I said. "I'll give you five pounds deposit now."

Dashing up to Frank I told him the story.

"That's a nice machine" said Frank. "Here's the fiver, and get a receipt."

When I told my parents my mum seemed a little edgy, but my dad, who by this time had fully accepted the fact that I would become a true motorcyclist said,

"Is this machine in good order?"

When I explained the situation as to why Alan was selling it, he said, "It sounds as if it will be a good buy, are you sure that you want it?"

"Certain," I said. "It's in lovely condition."

"All right," said Dad. "Twenty pounds you said, well, I bought your cycle and because you look after it so well I'm going to give you the twenty pounds for your first motorcycle, but no speeding or showing off, we don't want to be visiting you in hospital."

I felt great. I couldn't thank my dad enough. So, the next day at around 5.30 p.m. Alan came on the bike with his young lady on the pillion.

"Here's your bike," said Alan. "And this is Jean, the reason I'm selling it, so you can thank her." It didn't take long to do the deal, and as Alan had used his quota of petrol for the month, two gallons, Frank let me fill the tank on the 'garage surplus', as he put it.

Tim said, "Frank must like you a lot. Keep your nose clean and you'll soon have my job, as I got my call-up papers today. I go in six weeks time, and you are the first to know. I'll go and tell Frank."

Naturally Frank wasn't too pleased to hear the news, and after discussing it with Tim, he turned to me and said,

"George, it's a good job you got stuck in and like the job. There's no way that I could replace Tim, so you and I will have to manage between us, but I'll advertise for a trainee to help out. It looks like I'm going to have to trust you." He said to Tim, "When you've finished the car you're working on, I'd like you to take George out in the Armstrong, and teach him how to drive. George, it's up to you now."

The Armstrong was a 1933 long fifteen model with a Wilson pre-selector gearbox, and was a pretty easy car to drive. In any case I'd been driving it in and out of the garage for weeks now, so I didn't think I would have any problems driving it on the road, and that's how it turned out. Now that Tim was off to war service I was going to be very busy. I was also at home now on BSA (Beezer, as I called it). It proved to be a good bike, not fast, only the Gold Star was fast in the BSA stable, but it was very strong and reliable. Not long after I bought it I'd given it a decoke, checked and reset the ignition timing, and put the correct plug in, a KLG50 (the make of the spark-plug). KLG's motto was 'Too good to miss'. This work livened it up a bit, with a lively take-off, and 85-90 m.p.g..

After Tim had gone I was getting bigger jobs to do. Frank, of course, was the key man, but I was learning fast, and was rewarded with a pay rise for all the extra work. The month after Tim had gone, we got a trainee by the name of Trevor. He took over the minor jobs, which left me more time for bigger jobs. By this time I could use the Armstrong well, and it was useful to collect stock in, and on some occasions to transport customers home if they left their cars for repair. I'd also become a confident motorcycle tester, which gave me good experience on all types of machines. Trevor wasn't a bike lad, he preferred cars, so the bikes were all left to me. Of course, I was very interested in Velos on account of my friend and neighbour teaching me about his own Velo, and already I was beginning to see just why a Velo was such a beautifully built machine. It was getting rare now for me to have to call Frank in on any bike job, as I was very keen to learn, and was learning fast. The Enfield of course took priority, as we were the main agents in Coventry, so at this early stage of my motorcycling career, it was the Royal Enfield that I got to know first. I could tackle almost any job on an Enfield, and a lot of other makes as well, for at Elliott's we were well blessed with lots of different bikes. It was not easy in wartime to get repairs done, as most mechanics were either in the forces, or in the factories. The result was plenty of repairs for me; I loved it. Two or three of our customers had Velos, one had a 350cc Cammy similar to my friend Arthur's, one was a 350cc MAC (make stamped on the nearside crankcase) OHV short pushrod, and the other one was a 250cc two-stroke with an outside flywheel. The Velo two-stroke was a very robust engine, and it was capable of a very long life and high mileages, the sort of machine one could completely trust.

In those days, the Velocettes were made at Hall Green in Birmingham, but originally, they started up in Wolverhampton. They were a family firm by the name of Goodman, and the company did a very nice range of machines. A very good feature that made the Velo engine so mechanically quiet, was the unique high camshaft, and the beautifully machined Helical gears in the timing chest. The idler gear between crankshaft and camshaft gear had ninety-three teeth on it to help the distribution of wear, and was adjustable for perfect gear meshing, hence the very accurate and silent gear train. The helical gear was invented by André Citroën of Citroën Cars, and the best way I can describe it, is that the gear teeth were in the shape of an inverted letter V, hence the Citroën emblem. This gear train was far superior to most other makes and never, as far as I know, gave any trouble if properly set up. The Velo wasn't a machine to be played with by the amateur, as not only was the gear train critical to set up correctly, so was the clutch; if the correct 'clutch drill' was carried out, many thousands of trouble-free miles could be enjoyed. My reason for mentioning Velos like this is because later on in this story, I will take you right through the love affair I had with a Velo for thirty-two and a half years.

Chapter Six

My First Crash

Dennis Jenkins, my bosom pal, and myself, were both lovers of physical fitness, with the result that it was a regular practice for us to both go on my Beezer every Sunday morning to the swimming baths at Leamington, as the Priory Street baths in Coventry, had been bombed by the Jerries. Now both of us were good swimmers, and youth-like, we liked to swim up and down the baths, showing ourselves off to the local talent. This particular morning, we had been picked out by two nice young ladies around our age of seventeen or so, and as we reached the shallow end of the bath, both came over to us, and one of them said,

"Did you know that you've just done forty lengths?"

My pal Den, as big-headed as usual said,

"Oh yes, ladies, we have just reached half-way." So the ice was broken, and we sat out with them and got into conversation. We found out that their names were Julie and Joan, and although they didn't go swimming every week, they both agreed to see us there next Sunday. They told us that they were impressed by our swimming and because they didn't swim very well, they would like us to help them improve, so the date was made. The next Sunday was nice and fine, and Den and I were full of beans at the thought of the two lovelies we were hoping to meet, but a little way into Leamington (we had come in the back way), as we came round a sharp left-hand bend, a car had at that precise moment, proceeded to pull away from the halt sign he had stopped at. The halt sign on our left, was only about twenty yards from the corner that we had just come round. The car driver, seeing the bike coming, put his foot down, but alas, his engine being cold, as he'd only travelled about a hundred and fifty yards or so, cut out, and the car stopped, blocking almost the width of the road. At the time, I was accelerating out of the bend in third gear, there was no room either in front or behind the car, as it was all across the road. I acted as best possible, and, bringing the bike upright, I hit both brakes hard. I knew we weren't going to make it, as it was too close for us to stop at the pace we were travelling.

At that moment, I felt a mighty push on my shoulders, as Den parted company from the bike. His effort got him clear of the crash, but he took the skin off both the soles of his feet on contact with the road. As soon as Den's weight was off the machine the rear brake locked up the wheel, the front brake, like most in the thirties being about thirty to forty per cent too small, only partly slowed the bike down, so I too, just a split second before impact, gave a big leap upwards and forwards. Yes, I cleared the roof of the car first, ripping off two buttons from my leather riding coat as I slid along. I turned a complete somersault in the air, and landed on my backside in the road on the other side of the car. It was as well that I did, for in those days, no crash helmets were worn, only leather ones similar to flying helmets, like the one I had on, but if I had stayed on the machine, I would no doubt have received either some bad injuries, or even been killed. Yes, I'd done the right thing, I'd learnt the lesson the hard way, and the lesson is: never hang on to a crashing machine, get clear. In that way, you can save yourself like I did. I was bruised and a bit stunned, but otherwise all right and no bones broken. The car driver jumped out and ran round the front of the car to me, and helped me up. He was a doctor, going out on a call, but this one seemed more urgent, as he was most concerned. He didn't have to worry, Den and I were all right, considering. I reckon our fitness saved our skins.

The car I had hit, was a 1937 Rover 10HP with a strong chassis and outside running boards between the front and rear wings, and although the Beezer had disintegrated the offside running board completely, the car suffered no panel damage. The bike wasn't too bad either, the front rim had caved in and so had the front guard. The inner tube in the front had burst when the wheel rim caved in. The head lamp rim, glass and bulb had gone, and one side of the handlebars had bent slightly, and that was about all. When I did a geometry check on frame and forks at home, neither had moved. I was very lucky. The doctor and I went to the local police station and made a statement, a sort of gentleman's agreement really, stating that neither of us blamed the other and we were both responsible for our own repairs. After a sergeant had checked our insurance covers and driver's licences we shook hands on it, and the doctor let Den and I put the busted Beezer alongside his garage and covered it with a large tarpaulin. He then took us back to Coventry. Back home, I had to convince my parents that I was okay and that there was nothing to worry about. I did have a big bruise on my backside, and somehow my left ankle had swollen up, but really, I was okay and so was Den. Back at work on Monday, Frank let me take the box on the Tuesday night, so, with Den, I went and collected the Beezer. I took it back home. For one thing, it was my baby, so to speak, and another, without asking Frank, I knew he'd let me take it back to the garage for repairs, but as we were so busy at work, I didn't think it would have been fair to do that. Besides, I could do it at home and take my time about it. So Frank wrote out a trade order for my bits and pieces, and the wheel was rebuilt with a new rim and spokes at Len Booth's, Coventry's leading motorcycle wheel builder at that time. The Beezer when finished, was even better with its new parts, and by this time, both Den and I were over our bumps and bruises. As for our lady friends, although we searched every week, we didn't see either of them again. I guess they thought that we had stood them up. Den moaningly said that fate had put that car there just so we wouldn't meet them. He reckoned that his luck with women was right down the pan!

Chapter Seven

Bigger and Better Things

One of the many regular customers that called at Elliott's Garage, was a chap on an Ariel Squarefour, which was known in the trade as a 'Squariel'. It had four 248cc cylinders in the shape of a square, all being fed by one Solex carburettor through one induction manifold. The exhausts were let out through two-finned manifolds on either side of the engine. Well, one day, I was just coming out of the garage on a 350cc Douglas for testing after repairs, when in came the chap on his Squariel. Out of politeness, I went across to serve him and while I was putting his fuel in his tank he said,

"This is the last time you'll see me on this bike, I'm picking up my new 350 Red Hunter tomorrow."

"What ever for?" I replied. "I should have thought that this bike was just right for the job." He was a dispatch rider between different aircraft companies and he was based in Bristol.

"Oh, the bike's fine," he said. "It's just me that's at fault. You see, I'm too small to reach the floor properly, so my boss is getting the 350 Hunter."

"I see." I said, with my brain racing. "What's happening to this one?"

"I guess they'll flog it or leave it in the garage. I don't really know, I didn't ask."

"I'd love it," I said. "Find out what they are asking for it."

"Right," said the young man. "Give me your name and address. I reckon you could get this."

Well, one week to the day, he came in on his new Hunter. It was a lovely bike and it sounded a treat.

"What do you think of this?" he asked proudly.

"It's beautiful," I said. "How does it handle?"

"Like a dream," he replied. "And by the way," he said. "This is for you," And he handed me a typed bill for the purchase of the Squariel. One hundred and twenty-five pounds all in; I could hardly believe my luck. What a bargain, and it had only done 5,118 miles from new. I felt myself going hot under the collar. At the age of eighteen, I was being offered a premier bike at a bargain price.

"Oh, that's madness," I said. "I'll give you a deposit now, and pay the rest when I collect it."

"That will be fine" he said. "My boss said if you want it, I can come in on it next week and bring the paperwork with me, but you'll have to take me to the railway station, for me to get back." Well, I was delighted; what a bit of luck! I had just under £300 in my Post Office savings account, so I could easily afford it. Boy, what would my parents say about this? A week to the day, I walked to work and the Squariel was brought in for me. Frank let me take our friend to the station in the old Armstrong we used at the garage, so that was that. I was the proud owner of a 1000cc four cylinder, quite something in those days.

Considering that a 250cc bike cost between fifty and sixty pounds new, I had got myself a very good bargain, and at such a low mileage, old Den would be green with envy. I was used to most types of bikes, having been tester of all the bike repairs, but I'd never ridden a Squariel, and the experience was breathtaking to say the least. Because of my experience with various machines, it didn't take me long to get used to this one, but, as with to the high-powered bikes of today, if you took off too fast, then you could easily burn rubber. The secret was, of course, to always take off nice and easy, and not accelerate hard under 50 m.p.h.. In that way, one could get a reasonable mileage out of the rear tyre. The tyre being a 4.00 x 18 Dunlop Fort, the best one made at the time. The front was a 3.25 x 19 ribbed, and both brakes were very good. The year of the bike was 1939, just pre-war.

One could reach 100 m.p.h. very easily, the top speed was about 110 m.p.h., economy running being 50-55 m.p.h. giving around 47 m.p.g. and altogether a very nice big road burner. Handling was good too, and the machine was very well-balanced, but being solo, I'd hardly call it an all-round weather machine, weighing over four hundred pounds. I loved riding it and I know that a lot of the motorcycle lads at that time would have loved to have owned one.

Chapter Eight

Combo Capers at Blackpool

One evening as I was locking up for the day at Elliott's, my pal Den, came flying in on his old push-bike with his rear mudguard waving in the breeze.

"What do you think of this?" he asked, thrusting an advert from the *Coventry Evening Telegraph* under my nose. The advert read, 'BSA 500 Blue Star & single seater Watsonian sidecar in excellent order throughout. Forty-five pounds.'

"Sounds very good if it's true," I said.

"Right," said Den. "How about going up to see it? We could go on the Beezer, then if it's any good, you can drive it back and I'll ride your bike."

"Getting ambitious aren't we?" I replied.

"Well," said Den, "I thought it would be better for a girlfriend!"

"Fed up with me, are you?" I asked.

"You know what I mean" said Den. "What about it?"

"Okay, you're on, but let me be the judge."

"I wouldn't do any other," said Den. So an hour and a half later found us knocking on the door where the bike was for sale.

To our surprise a speed cop opened the door, as it was his machine that was for sale. Without wasting time he took us round the back to his garage. There stood the Blue Star Combo, and I must say it was immaculate. It shone; it certainly had a very good owner. Speed cop Broomfield wheeled it out and started it up. It started first kick, as he'd run it up thirty minutes before in case anyone came up. Well, it sounded great, no rattles or oil leaks, and the sidecar was lovely too. It was indeed a very fine outfit.

After showing us round it he said,

"I've seen you somewhere before, but I can't place you."

"Elliott's Garage," I said. "I'm their motorcycle mechanic."

"Of course! I've seen you riding that lethal box combo of theirs, so feel free to take this one for a test run," he said.

"Thank you," I said. "Jump in, Den. This looks a very nice outfit." And although the bike stood upright, for it should have been leaning one inch out empty, the tyres showed no sign of it being out of line, or, if it was, then it wasn't by very much, which, when it was checked, proved to be so. The bike took off very smoothly and without any vibration, proving that it was in good condition generally; also, the interior of the sidecar was very clean. Just up the road was a steep hill, so up we went, and I was very pleased at the smooth and easy way it climbed the hill. On the straight, the outfit went very well. I took it up to 50 m.p.h. and it was still very smooth.

On the way back, Den yelled,

"What's your verdict? It seems very good to me." And indeed it was.

I yelled back, "It's a very nice outfit and a very good buy." It only remained for me, out of sheer curiosity, to find out why such a lovely outfit was for sale. We arrived back at Mr Broomfield's house, and Den was beaming all over his face, which really said it all.

"You like it then?" Mr Broomfield asked.

"It's a really nice outfit; it's a credit to you," I replied. "I don't think we need to look anywhere else."

"Right, lads," he said. "Now you've said you'll have it, I'll give you a bonus." With that he opened up the rear sidecar boot and brought out a very nice long all-weather motorcyclist's coat, a pair of black leather gauntlet gloves, and a good pair of Stadium goggles. "I've hung on to these for whoever bought the bike," he said. "They're all in good condition. The coat hasn't been worn much, as it's a bit small for me, so it'll save you a few quid." We were flabbergasted. Den, as he was buying the outfit, thanked him very much and he was delighted at the deal, for it was indeed a very good one.

After the deal was made, I rode Den's new love back to the house for him and he followed on my Beezer, which he was very familiar with. It turned out that it had been sold because his wife wanted him to buy a car instead.

"I suppose I'll have to show you how to handle it," I said. "Well, I'll retrack it first, so you can start off right." On the test, I'd detected a slight pull to the right, possibly caused by lack of any lean out on the part of the bike. So, Sunday morning found Den and I retracking the new outfit. As I thought, it wasn't much out, but the slight alteration that I made improved the overall handling quite a bit. It is critical to track and line up a combo correctly, for if it isn't right, it becomes a lethal weapon on cornering and braking. The general rule is, bike leaning one inch out, track at least three quarters of an inch in at front, and most important, the sidecar wheel needs to be at least one and a half inches in front of the rear wheel of the bike. This tracking is subject to alteration for handling and is of course different on machines and sidecars, but if my measurements are adhered to, you won't be far out.

Well, I soon got Den riding his combo. He was a very good pupil and after about a week of running me around as I gave him instructions, I put a large bag of sand in the sidecar as ballast. In this way, it kept the sidecar wheel down on left-handers, a very critical point in combo riding. After this, Den, on my instructions, reduced the amount of sand by about one stone a week, and in so doing, finally got complete control of his combo. By the time all the sand had been taken out, he could control the weight down to zero, or an empty chair. He could now lift up the chair wheel on left-handers without pulling out across the road. As any sidecar man will tell you, tracking and line up etc., is a must for stability and safety, either loaded or empty.

It looked as if Den had got his riding under control just in time for the Whitsun break, as he had plans for both of us to go to Blackpool for a couple of days in the combo. Quite a good idea as Frank, my boss, was closing the garage for Saturday, Sunday and Monday, as his wife hadn't been very well, so it would give us both a good chance to go. As Den remarked, we could both take a rest in the chair, and all our gear could go in as well, so we made plans to do this. Den had bought a new army bell tent and a very thick groundsheet and all the tackle, as it was going to be fun, or at least an adventure. So on Friday night, I went all over the outfit, oils, adjustments and did a nut and bolt check to make sure all was safe. I also packed up a large new puncture outfit and a full box of tools. At the time, Den complained about the weight, but as I pointed out, what's the good of a mechanic without tools? At six o'clock on Saturday morning, we set off. I drove first and we made good time and didn't meet much traffic. About five miles from Blackpool, Den was driving, when the cylinder head gasket blew. Poor old Den nearly had a fit, for we were pulling hard uphill when it went, and about a half-inch piece blew straight out of it. Immediately flames were shooting round Den's legs and the bike came to a halt.

"What now?" asked Den.

"Well," I said, "we can walk, it's only five miles, or the tools could come in very handy."

"Very good," said my pal, "but what do we use for a gasket?" Well, of course we hadn't got one but I didn't know bikes for nothing.

As I said to Den, "Fear not, mighty friend. All is not lost. George is here and if the valves clear the piston, then we'll grind on the cylinder head with grinding paste, to plough on to Blackpool where we can get a new gasket and slap it on."

"Go to it, mighty friend," said Den. "I'll give you all the help I can." We had made very good time and had conked out by a very wide pavement with nice slab paving stones.

"Right," I said. "Let's push the bike over there and I'll get started." It didn't take me very long to get the cylinder head off and scrape off the now scrap gasket and sure enough it cleaned up well. Then I lightly put the head back, loosened the tappets for clearance, then with the spark plug out, slowly turned the engine over on the kick-start lever, in order to ascertain whether the valves would clear the piston. They did, so I took off the head again to lap it onto the cylinder barrel top to seal it. As I said, I'd got plenty of tools, also a tube of jointing cement, grinding paste and a large tin of Chemico Hand Soap.

To grind on the head, I had to remove the carburettor in order to get a half twist on the head for grinding. So, having got the head ground on and gasket cement to help seal it, I carefully reset the tappets and rechecked to be sure the valves cleared the piston. They did, so now it was all done, and all I had to do was put in the spark plug and start it up. To our delight, it fired at once and started up. It sounded very sharp, for of course, the compression had gone up quite a bit. I had, before starting up, retarded the ignition by about three degrees to allow for it, and it wasn't far out. It was, as I told Den, that the compression must be at a critical high, so I would drive while it was like this, as going uphill I was going to move the advance and retard lever in order to find the correct setting for the engine. So, after we had packed our tools and washed our hands in a puddle, we set off. The engine seemed to leap forward on this high compression, it certainly went well and, best of all, there was no blow. We were just reaching Blackpool, when it started to rain, so, as we were near a common, we decided to stop and pitch our tent before we got soaked. I found an old piece of tarpaulin that covered the bike.

The tent was a beauty, and was warm and cosy and didn't let a drop of rain in, so we decided to have our sandwiches and coffee and have a rest, then find a phone to get a BSA gasket for the cylinder head. I didn't think that this would be a problem, but I was wrong, for this wasn't Coventry, as I was about to find out. I'd brought my old telescope with me and through the tent flap I could see a phone box way back down the road. After eating I put my gear on and set out. After ringing the main BSA dealer in Blackpool and quite a few other places, I was told no one had a gasket. I'd been on the phone for about half an hour now and I was really browned off, for in old Coventry, at least five dealers would have had one. When I got back and told Den, he too was down in the mouth, for I'd also found out that the holiday weather forecast was 'wet and windy' for four days. I wasn't too concerned about the gasket problem, for I reckoned it would hold up if it wasn't driven hard. I think at the time, it was the weather that got us down, too.

Well, at least we had a good dry tent, so we decided to stay put for the night and then, if it was still raining in the morning, pack up and go home. In the meantime we wanted some more food, so Den went out to the shops I'd spotted to see what he could get. He didn't do too badly for he brought back a large loaf, half a pound of butter that we had food coupons for, and the old shopkeeper let him have a large cheese coupon free, as no doubt Den had told him a sob story of how we were stuck. He also got two packets of biscuits, a small jar of jam, six packets of crisps and a ham bone with quite a bit of ham left, so at least we weren't about to starve. He rounded it off with two bottles of milk, so we had enough food for a couple of hearty snacks.

The rain came down all through the night, and all the next morning. It was so hard that to try and pack would have been folly. At about 1.00 p.m. the rain eased off, so we decided to pack up as fast as possible. We got everything stowed away into the sidecar and set off.

I retarded the ignition lever on the bike and lightly flooded the carburettor. The engine fired first kick, so after resetting the ignition lever I gave it a couple of minutes to circulate the oil and get rid of any dampness. We had only been on the road about ten minutes or so, when it started to rain very hard and I knew I was in for a soaking. Before we had packed our stuff away I'd found two big sheets of brown paper in the sidecar, so I put one under my pullover across my chest and the other between my jacket and pullover. This I knew would help to keep the cold out, for with all this rain, the temperature had dropped considerably.

The bike was running great and was barking away very nicely between 45 and 55 m.p.h. and the pulling power uphill had improved. We got about a third of the way back, and just as I was slowing down for a traffic island, there was a loud bang from the front tyre and down it went. It was all I could do to prevent the outfit from slipping into the island. I dared not use the front brake, but by pumping on the rear brake pedal, somehow we got round the island without hitting it and slowly pulled up about thirty yards or so past it. The front tyre although flat with the tube hanging out in ribbons, had somehow managed to stay on the rim.

"What now, mighty friend?" asked Den, as he heaved himself out of his nice cosy sidecar. "I doubt if even you can get us out of this, with no spare tube!"

"Don't bet on it, because I think you'd lose," I said with a big grin on my face. "I know a little trick to get us home, but as yet, I've never had the chance to put it into practice."

I was looking hard at the front tyre as I said this, for it had a slit about an inch and a half long in the nearside wall and it was this that had caused the blow-out.

Again we had stopped at a lucky spot. We were miles from anywhere, as Den pointed out, but all the better for the little trick I had in mind to work. We had stopped by open ground with a large grassy area on our left and fields and woods further down on our right.

"Now, old pal, what we have to do first of all is to go searching for a suitable piece of leather or thick lino, or even rubber, anything that will make a good gaiter to cover this split. It needs to be about ten inches square or bigger. We can cut it to size and we've got a good puncture outfit and a large tube of rubber solution, so let's get looking."

"Hang on," said Den. "I don't get it. How can that get us home without a tube?"

"That's the trick. We fill up the tyre with grass, then a few miles further on when it's all bedded down, we refill it and ride on."

Den's face was one of wonderment. "That's clever," he said. "Where did you learn that trick?"

"Frank Elliott, he's taught me well," I said. "He had to do it once on a 600cc Panther and rode it for eighty miles. Now it's our turn, so let's get searching, while it's still light."

About ten minutes later, Den called out, "What about this? I reckon this will do the trick." Den had found a good piece of leather and it was about twelve by nine inches, just about right.

"Very good," said I. "We'll clean it with petrol and check it for size." So, while Den cleaned up the leather, I took out the front wheel and got the tyre off. In those days most bikes had a front wheel stand as the bottom stay on the large front guard and the Blue Star was one of them. The leather was perfect. All we had to do was cut off the corners. Den soon had this done with his 'Bowie knife' as he called it. It wasn't a real Bowie, but it was a lovely big strong knife, all the same. While Den was applying rubber solution to the rough side of the leather, I had wedged the tyre open with two double-ended $^5/_{16}$" x $^3/_8$" spanners, and was carefully washing a large area around the split with the petrol rag. Then I covered the cleaned area with solution and a few minutes later stuck on the patch. It bonded very well.

"What about all this solution round the patch?" Den asked.

"Leave it," I said. "The grass will stick to it and stop the patch from moving." So, I got the tyre back on the rim, and we proceeded to pack in as much grass as we could. Now, normally, one would push the tyre on with one's thumbs to stop pinching the tube, but in this case, with no tube, we could safely use the tyre levers. The two levers we had were really heavy duty Dunlops, and they made it easy to get the tyre on with plenty of grass packed in it. We left the valve in place, as it would stop the grass from working its way out.

With the wheel back in place and all connected up again, we again got going. It wasn't too bad, and in fact I even dared to get up to 50 m.p.h. on the straight, but of course, I had to go steady round bends and islands. If anything, the front brake was better. I guess it was the front tyre having more rubber on the road. About ten miles further on, we again stopped to repack with grass. We got a lot in again, and this time the bike felt much more stable and we were able to get along very well. We got back about 7.00 p.m. with the rain still coming down, but the brown paper had kept me dry and quite warm. The gaiter hadn't moved and the tyre looked as if it would have done a lot more miles free of trouble.

The next weekend, I fitted on a ribbed Dunlop front tyre and tube, but not before drilling the rim five spokes from the valve hole, to fit a tyre security bolt. As I said before, it was sheer luck that the tyre stayed on the rim after a blow-out. This time we were prepared for it. The new gasket was no trouble, so, with the head off, I took the opportunity to decoke it and grind in the valves. The engine was great after this and the bike, to Den's delight, did very well on fuel. The acceleration was thirty per cent better and after this, the bike gave no further trouble and was a better bike for it.

Chapter Nine

Dennis and Passenger Take a Nosedive

Coming out of Woolworths one Tuesday afternoon, which was my usual half-day off, I met my cousin Francis and her friend Connie. I hadn't seen Francis for months, although like me, she lived in Coventry. After chatting for a bit, she asked me how Den was, so naturally, I told her about his combo and our Blackpool disaster. They both had a good laugh and both said that they would like to go for a ride on our bikes, so I said that I'd fix it up and let them know when. Den, of course, was delighted when I told him, so the arrangements were made for two weeks' time on a Sunday afternoon. We decided that I had better go on the Beezer rather than the Squariel, as Den would be rather hard put to if I went on the big bike, and as it turned out, it was as well that I did.

Francis and Connie were both ready when we got there. Francis was disappointed that I didn't go on the Ariel, as my mum had told my Aunt Lily, Francis's mum, all about it. However, it was a very nice day, so with Francis in the chair and Connie on my pillion, clinging very tight, we set off. We had decided to do about a hundred-mile trip, as I had been given several petrol coupons as tips at work. I was very lucky in this, and this time my tips added up to about seven gallons of petrol, so we had plenty of fuel. After about thirty-odd miles or so, Francis asked to ride on my pillion, as she had never been on a solo machine, so, pulling into the next lay-by, we swapped passengers. About twenty miles further on, we were passing an army convoy that had pulled in at the side of a grassy banked road. Den was leading on the combo, and about two-thirds of the way past the convoy a car approached from the opposite direction. The army lorries had parked very neatly with about three lorry lengths between them, making it safe for traffic to pull in between them if need be, such as right now. So Den did this, but unfortunately, at the gap he chose, the grass bank was more than half cut away with disastrous results. As be swung in, the sidecar wheel dropped over the edge of the bank, and the chassis of the chair dug into the soft turf. The bike shot round to the left and went careering down the steep slope only to be stopped by a strong young tree, as the down tube between bike and chair hit it. Both rider and passenger were catapulted forward. Den hit his handlebars with both thighs, bending both sides of the bars, and Connie's head hit the top of the chair's screen as the hood was folded down. The screen shattered and Connie received a nasty cut on her head which also laid her out. Den was rolling in agony on the grass where he had landed. I had stopped at once and Francis and I and half a dozen or so soldiers dashed down to give assistance. One of the lads was an army nurse, so he was able to attend to poor Connie. I dashed up to Den and tried to do what I could. The army nurse told me to remove his trousers so that I could attend to his very badly bruised thighs. Connie had come round and the nurse was putting a bandage on her cut head. He'd had to cut some hair away as the cut was in the front of her head, about five inches above her right eye. The scar wouldn't be noticeable, but she was in shock and was crying and shivering and the nurse told me to get her to a hospital and get the cut stitched. He said there was one about three miles down the road, and the sooner we got there the better.

Leaving Den to be attended to, Francis and I got Connie back to the Beezer, but she was too scared to ride pillion, so almost before she realised what was happening, I'd put her on my saddle, started up the bike and rode with me on the pillion behind her. It was a bit awkward, but it wasn't far and we got there safely and Connie was treated straight away. I was allowed to stay with her, which I did, and I held her hand and comforted her as best I could. I think I must have done a fair job, for Connie was shouting my praises for weeks afterwards. After about an hour, when Connie had taken tablets for her headache and had a lie down, we went back to the disaster spot. This time Connie was much steadier and rode correctly on the pillion, but I felt sorry for her, as she was terrified, and I knew in my heart that this very nice young lady had been put off bikes for ever. It was a real tragedy.

When we arrived, Francis was sitting in the sidecar, while Den was leaning heavily half on and half off the bike. The outfit was now on the road again, as the army had winched it up, but the convoy had moved on, so Francis and Den were relieved to see us back. The two girls hugged each other and Connie began to cry again, but this time it was with relief as she felt a lot better and by now her colour was rapidly coming back. Den on the other hand was worse. His thighs were wrapped up but very swollen, and also, it was as much as he could do to stand up. The combo was a wreck. The tree that stopped it had also wrecked it, and the sidecar chassis was scrap. How were we to get back? That was the question. It was very lucky that the sidecar body itself wasn't damaged; neither, as I could see, was the bike, except of course for the bent bars. They were bent forward by about one foot on both sides. Whether it would be possible to ever ride this wreck back, I was about to find out. It was obvious to all, that if we were to ever get the combo mobile, that it would be me who have to get it back, and that would mean that I should have to ride it with one girl in the chair, and one pillion. Not a very happy thought, for I knew from my experience with the old box, that when I'd got four motorcycles in it, the strain on the rider was very severe, but with a wrecked chassis, well, the question was, was it possible? And if so, could Den ride my bike?

The first thing to do was to get Den on my bike to see if he could ride it. Once he was on he was okay, so that was one problem solved, and I now set about the wrecked combo chassis. I wasn't looking forward to this, as I needed welding equipment to heat up the bent chassis and reset it. As it was, all I could hope to do was loosen off all the chassis joints and try to pull the bike upright. After a lot of hard pulling and loosening and re-tightening the chassis joints we had got it into a rideable state. Den did his very best to help. As you can imagine, he felt terrible about this, so he leant his weight on the chassis while I did the pulling and tightening. I'd got the sidecar body off to make it easier to get at. This helped a lot and we made better progress. The bent handlebars weren't a problem, for all I did was loosen off the twistgrip, front brake lever, clutch lever, advance and retard lever, air lever and finally the exhaust lifter lever for stopping the engine, then, with the four bolts holding the bars onto the top fork leg, I was able to twist the bars backwards so that instead of being bent forwards they were now bent upwards making the riding position a lot better.

After this I couldn't do any more. I refitted the body and took it on a test run up the road. It was horrible, but with care, I felt sure I could get it back. The distance back was just forty-two miles, as I had set my trip to zero before we set out. If we took it easy, we should make it. When all was ready, Connie got in the sidecar with a cushion for her head and Francis got on the pillion. Den, on my bike, would follow, as obviously it was to be a slow painful journey for all of us except Francis. By the way, Francis's maiden name was Barnett, and her dad, my Uncle Bert on my mother's side, named her Francis after the motorcycle he used to ride. So our slow journey got under way. The outfit was pulling right, so I had to be very careful as it was a big pull on left-handers, but for all that, we were doing around 30 m.p.h. on the flat, but slower downhill as the pull increased. It was easier going uphill as the weight came off the steering. After about ten miles, I pulled in for a rest by a large grass verge as my arms were really aching. Den, too, was ready to get off and ease his legs as he said that they felt as if they were locking up. Connie, to my surprise, had gone to sleep and only awoke when the engine stopped. Apart from her headache she was feeling quite good. Francis of course had no aches or pains, but she was concerned for Connie.

After about twenty minutes we carried on. We had about four stops in all and by the time we reached Francis's house my arms felt as if they were dropping off. My Aunt Lily was horrified and after it had all been explained to her, she rang up Connie' s house to break the news.

"This is it," remarked Den. "I shall now get slaughtered. I've been dreading this." About twenty minutes later, Connie's dad arrived in their car, and as soon as he saw Connie, hugged her close.

"I'm all right, Dad," said Connie.

As I'd been sitting next to her, I guess he thought I was to blame for the accident, for he said in a very harsh tone,

"I hope your bike's a wreck. It's a pity you didn't break your neck."

"Stop it, Dad!" yelled Connie in horror. "It wasn't George. He was the one who got us back." So it all came out, and Connie's dad shook my hand and apologised for blaming me. By then he had cooled off and was very nice about the whole affair.

The following week Den sent Connie a lovely bunch of flowers and a letter wishing her a speedy recovery. My pals in the trade, Bernard and Geoff Holland, who ran a motorcycle spares and repairs business with their father at the top end of Hearsall Lane in Coventry, got us a very good second-hand chassis complete with wheel, tyre, tube and mudguard for twenty-seven pounds. The broken screen Den got replaced at the Coventry Moor Mart on London Road, but this he had to buy new for seven pounds and ten shillings (seven pounds fifty today). I soon got the other chassis on and the bars, when removed, were very easy to deal with and it wasn't long before the old combo was back to square one. Den's legs took about six weeks to heal and for about three weeks he could only get around with the assistance of a walking stick. This crash had shaken him up and he wasn't at all keen to meet any more young ladies for motorcycle rides. As for Francis and Connie, I don't think either of them were keen to go. I heard afterwards that Connie had said she didn't ever want to go on a bike again. It happens like that sometimes, after all – big dents in cars would mean very injured riders, if they had been on a bike!

Chapter Ten

Thrills, Frills and Spills

Just after the combo incident, I got a shock through the post, as it was an order from the government for me to be transferred to the Coventry Corporation Bus Depot in Harnall Lane to work on buses. I felt just devastated. Me, work on stinking buses! They had got to be joking! But it was no joke, it was an order from the government and during wartime, one had no option but to obey or go to clink; that was your only choice. 'They must be bloody barmy,' I thought. I was doing far superior work at Elliott's, and besides, Frank relied on me very much and most of the bikes and cars I repaired were owned by workers on the war effort, as we had about thirty-odd customers from Armstrong Siddley alone and there were also a lot from Baginton Airport and other factories, all on war work.

'Not to worry,' I thought. 'Frank will soon sort this out.' When I showed Frank the letter, he nearly took off. I'd never seen him so angry and upset. He went very pale and said he intended to get this stopped immediately.

He got up a petition among the customers, collecting about eight hundred signatures and sent it off, but alas, I had to go, and I remember him taking my hand and saying,

"God bless you, George. You're like a brother to me. I just don't know how we'll manage without you. It could finish the garage."

"I'll be back, Frank," I promised, and I was, but it wasn't until 1946 when the war was over. I'll mention my stay at the bus depot just for the record. I was only there for about ten months and to me it seemed a waste of time, but I did learn a bit, as, not being a fully qualified mechanic, I was classed as a second-class mechanic which meant I became a mechanic's mate. I was with a good chap, but he wasn't a bike man. In fact he didn't approve of bikes, as his younger brother was killed on a 350cc International Norton, so of course I didn't push the subject.

However, the pay was good and after the first three months my companion and I were both put on 'early starts'. This meant being there at 4.00 a.m. to get the engines running for the drivers. This gave me three pounds more a week, so altogether I wasn't too badly off. Every third week I got the Saturday off, and you can imagine how pleased Frank was when I spent it in the garage, so through all this, my Post Office savings book was looking a lot healthier.

It was while I was at the bus garage that I met my future wife. She was the daughter of a lady who worked there and it was this lady who came up to me one day and said,

"Please don't think I'm being rude, but are you courting at all?"

"I haven't got a girl," I said.

"Well, now," she replied, "what do you think of her?" And she pushed a lovely photo of her daughter into my hand.

"She's lovely," I said. "What's her name?"

"Ivy," her mum replied. "She's seventeen, but like you, she's rather shy, and she hasn't got a boyfriend." She went on to say that she had been watching me every day and she knew that I didn't drink or smoke, that I liked motorcycles and that I was a keep-fit lad.

"I like you," she told me, "so if you like the look of my daughter, maybe you'll let me have your picture to show her?"

"I'll bring one in tomorrow," I said.

"Good," said this lady. "You had better hang onto that one and see what happens," And she walked off with a twinkle in her eye.

'Wow! What a figure!' I thought as she walked away, and, although the lady was forty-five, as I found out later, her figure was stunning.

"Well, what did gorgeous want?" asked George Prew, my mechanic-in-charge.

"For me to meet her daughter," I said and showed him the photograph.

"You be careful, young George," said my mate. "She came up here once to meet her mum and she's gorgeous. She's got lovely legs, and, like her mum, she's got a cracking figure."

"She looks lovely," I said. "So we'll see what happens."

Well, what happened was that after I'd sent this young lady my picture with a message saying that I'd like to meet her, she fixed up a date and place, and so the lovebirds met. The first time we went for a long walk to get to know each other, but, on the second date, I went on the Squariel. I guess it was to impress her. Anyway, she had never been on a motorcycle, so I told her to sit close and hold tight. As we were going to the pictures, she was hardly dressed for the bike, and on the second corner we took, Ivy thought that the bike was toppling over and put her foot on the floor, with the result that the road ripped off the high heel of her shoe, which went flying into the air. We stopped and found the heel, and I promised I'd repair it for her and bring it round the following night, which I did. At the pictures Ivy gasped, for when we left the bike in the car park, I picked her up and carried her into the cinema, but it broke the ice and it was all lovey-dovey as time went on. Poor old Den was taking a back seat now, for I began to see more of Ivy. However, he understood, and said he'd be just the same if it was him. Ironically, because of one thing or another, I'd volunteered and passed my medical for the Royal Navy as a mechanic. Had I met Ivy before, I doubt very much that I would have done it, as Ivy, like my mate George had said, was a cracker and had been very well brought up with perfect manners, a truly lovely girl. I was a very happy and lucky chap.

It didn't take Ivy long to get used to the bike and she was enjoying it very much and was dressing accordingly. By now she had met my parents, and I, of course, knew her mum. Her dad had died when she was only two and a half years old, hence her mum going out to work. The following Sunday we had planned a long ride. By this time I'd taken the Beezer off the road, and was just using the Squariel. Well, this coming Sunday turned out fine and off we went. About twenty miles from home, I pulled in and stopped. Ivy smiled and said,

"Please don't stop here, it's too open."

I grinned and said, "It isn't for kisses and cuddles. Jump on my seat. I'm going to teach you how the bike works and how to ride it. This can be your first lesson."

Ivy flushed a little, but did as I asked, and, with me manipulating the controls from the pillion seat, we set off.

We covered about twenty miles like this, and when we came to a halt at a lovely spot, Ivy gave me a big kiss and said, "Darling, that was really wonderful. Oh, I do love motorcycling. It's so exhilarating, I feel really alive. I can see why you love it so much, and now, my darling, so do I."

At that moment, I knew this was the girl for me, and I let out a loud yell, and swung her round in a circle and gave her a big kiss. I knew that we were going to get on like a house on fire and we did.

I'd better explain this situation, as it's only people like me who have lived through the war, who would understand. For a start, the vehicles on the road in the 1940s were very few in comparison to today, also, petrol was very strictly rationed so it made for very clear roads. To give you an idea, a 250cc bike got two gallons of fuel a month in four half gallon units, my Ariel, being a 1000cc, got five gallons in one gallon units, so you can imagine that at that time, the roads were pretty clear. If one tried the things we did back then today, one would be killed or badly injured for certain. When I let Ivy control or partly control the bike, it was always when there was no other traffic around and if we met another vehicle, I would take over immediately. It appears too risky, and yes, it was still dangerous, as you will see a little further on.

After this, it was a regular practice for me to allow Ivy to control the bike. It was a laugh if we caught up with an army convoy, for I can remember saying to Ivy, "Go on, girl. Show 'em your legs!" For when she accelerated past, her skirt blew right up her thighs, and the whistles and horn blowing she got were out of this world!

However, all this would come to an end in a few weeks' time, as I would be in the Navy, but not before we had been taught a lesson, and almost landed up seriously injured. Ivy was gently controlling the Ariel down a quiet country road, when suddenly, a horse pulling a large old hay cart came into the road in front of us from a field on our left, about a hundred yards ahead.

"Shut off," I yelled at Ivy, but Ivy got 'flummoxed' as she put it later, and slammed the throttle wide open. The big bike shot forward before I could get control.

"Hang on!" I yelled and at the same time hit both brakes. But alas, one can't control a bike correctly from the pillion seat, with the result that I put too much pressure on the rear brake, which was a very good one. The 400 x 18 Dunlop tyre locked up solid and the bike gracefully slipped forward on its offside. At this precise moment, the horse and cart turned off into a field on the right, putting the cart sideways on. By this time we had reached the cart, and how we ever got away with it, I shall never know, but with the bike on its side, we shot under the hay cart and never even touched it. Out the other side, I must have let go of the brakes front first and then rear, for the bike slid round on a blip of the throttle and shot upright. I pulled up and stopped. As I did so I could bear the poor old horse whinnying and the farmer yelling, "Whoa! Whoa!" to stop its headlong gallop. Ivy and I looked at each other and both of us had gone deadly white. I grabbed her and we just stood there and held each other for a good five minutes or more.

I finally broke the silence, saying, "Darling, I don't know how, but we've just done the impossible. We've been under that hay cart and come out unscathed. I don't think we'll say anything because I don't think anyone would believe us."

Ivy was stunned and very slowly said, "I can't believe it – but I know we've done it." I speak the truth, as my Ivy will tell you today. After that, we were much better road users, and we never took such a dangerous risk again.

About two weeks later, Ivy said to me, "I do hope that your job will prevent you going into the forces. Do you think it will?" I hadn't told her yet that I'd already volunteered for the Navy, for by this time we were very much in love and I hadn't got the heart to tell her for fear of hurting her. Like a mouse with a snake, I was hoping that it would go away. But of course, it didn't, so I had to tell her and the sooner the better.

Chapter Eleven

A Crash and a Shock for Ivy

The only other incident that we had was about three weeks later, but it was a lot worse, even so. This one nearly did put us in hospital. It happened when we were on our way to Great Malvern, for we had not used the bike except for two short journeys and on top of that, a chap had given me a three-gallon petrol coupon for finding a fault on his van and putting it right. Frank had sent him to me as he was being swamped under with work. "They should never have taken me away from there," I told this man. "The bus garage didn't know what work was. They wouldn't last a day at Elliott's, the way they worked."

On the way to Malvern it started to rain. I told Ivy that we would be wiser to turn back as there was no shelter in the Malverns, but as I'd told her so much about them, and she had never been there, plus we were over halfway there before the rain started, she urged me to go on. I guess, like all lovers the world over, the urge to be alone together is far too strong to bother about a drop of rain, so on we went. If you have ever been in love yourself, then you'll know exactly what I mean, and if you haven't, then I hope that you'll soon have that pleasure. By the time we reached Worcester it was raining quite hard, and as you know, or may not know, rainwater brings the oil from vehicles and leaves to the road's surface, making it dicey in the wet. Well, through Worcester in those days was a steep hill. Just as we were starting down this hill, Worcester Hill we called it, a woman pushing a cycle, with a mac over her head, dashed straight across the road without stopping or looking, from an entry between the houses. I had no chance, as I was forced to hit the brakes or I would have killed her for certain as a big heavy bike at about 30 m.p.h. is a lethal weapon to someone in front of it. How we missed her I didn't really know for in an instant the bike shot to the left as the rear wheel locked up. Ivy shot off into the air, but really, she was very lucky, for on her back was my old Army rucksack and it swung round and dropped under her face as she crashed down onto the wet road surface. The road surface was tarmacadam and it was very smooth and slippery and Ivy, with my rucksack under her face came sliding down the road behind me and the bike. The next moment there was a bang made by the Ariel knocking a shop door in. I can still see in my mind's eye the door support sticking out from the wall at a crazy angle and the front wheel and forks of the Ariel halfway through the door. At almost the same moment, I hit the rear of the bike and shot off, hitting the low shop wall under the window, where, for a few moments, I blacked out. The next thing I recall was being pulled up by two ambulance men who then, half-carrying me, took me across the road to a pub and took me inside and sat me down.

By then I'd realised what had happened, so the first thing I said was, "Where's my girl?" The man looking at my damaged leg told me that she wasn't too badly hurt and was in the next room in a dazed and shocked condition, and that when he'd fixed me up, I could see her. I now found out that I had a badly cut right leg and knee, a cut right arm, a badly grazed right hand and a throbbing head with a big bump coming up.

Now, this came as a double shock for Ivy, for, unknown to us, about ten minutes prior to us coming off, an army dispatch rider had come off on the slippery road almost at the same spot. This chap was in the pub as well. The chap treating Ivy asked how this other chap was and, when a man replied, Ivy all but fainted, for, not knowing about the other accident, she thought it was me, when he said, "Any time now, he'll never make it to the hospital. I'm afraid he's had it." The ambulance man treating Ivy couldn't understand it, as she almost keeled over, and it wasn't until Ivy insisted on seeing me, then saw the dispatch rider, that she realised he had not been referring to me. Well, after this shock, Ivy was brought in to where I was being treated and of course, she could see that I was alive and kicking, and the next minute, a big hug of relief was taking place. Ivy's wounds weren't too bad, but her right thigh was badly grazed and all red, and a big bruise was rapidly coming up. Her other leg was bruised too, she had also got small cuts on her legs, and a bruised right shoulder, and a cut on the back of her right-hand, so between us, we were in a bit of a mess.

"Thank goodness for your rucksack," Ivy said, and, looking at the rucksack, I could see how the road had all but ground it away.

"You were very lucky, that could have been your face!" I said. So, after I had left my name and address with both the landlord of the pub and the ambulance men, we thanked them all very much because the landlord had opened his pub for the injured dispatch rider before we arrived. It was very lucky for us that the ambulance was already there before we came off. Back outside the pub, a small crowd had gathered despite the rain, and when Ivy and I appeared, gasps and 'Ohs!' were let out immediately. Looking down at Ivy as she walked by me, I could see the reason for this, for the clothes under her coat were all but in ribbons, even her pink panties were all shredded.

On realising this, Ivy quickly got her coat back on. Fortunately, her coat wasn't ripped, as it must have been folded up. 'Ah, of course; that is how her legs got so battered,' I thought. And speaking of battered, we were now faced with a very battered Ariel, but could I repair it enough to get us back home, and was it in a good enough state to do so? Someone had stood the Ariel up on the nearside prop stand, and I could tell at a glance that we were in trouble as the damage was as follows: a broken kickstart lever, broken foot-change lever, broken footrest, bent handlebars, bent front brake lever, badly knocked up front mudguard, smashed right head-lamp rim and glass and the offside silencer completely ripped off the bike. It was lying in the gutter, more oval than round, like it should be.

The frame, as I had hoped, hadn't bent, as it was a big strong heavy one, and the large all-chrome tank was unmarked. The forks too seemed okay and the front wheel wasn't buckled either. It could have been a lot worse. Again we had been fortunate in so much as there were no major breakages. I might just be able to fix it up enough to get us home.

"We've just got to find a blacksmith," I said, "because there are quite a few parts that need brazing and I shall need the use of a six inch vice." While we stood there, the pub owner came up to see the damage to the shop I'd broken into.

"Well," he said. "This is only fit for firewood. I've informed the owner, but he won't be down till after 2.00 p.m., and a chap is coming to plank it up." So I asked if he knew of a blacksmith. "You're in luck there," he said. "There's one just around the corner and he lives over the premises. I'm sure he'll help you." So, with me hanging on to Ivy for support, we went round to see the blacksmith and sure enough, he was more than willing to help. He'd got the biggest vice I'd ever clapped eyes on; it must have had a foot jaw on it. I reckon you could have got the bike in it! After about two to three hours I finally got the bike into a rideable state. I'd taken all the bent, damaged parts off and straightened them out. The huge vice and a three-foot tube was perfect for all these repairs and it made the job much easier.

The handlebars came up spot on, and the blacksmith allowed me to braze up all the broken parts. The correct way to do it, of course, was to file off one side square, and file the other side like the end of one side of a chisel, then when brazed up, the gap being filled up with brazing rod, it makes a very strong job. The blacksmith nodded his approval and said that I could work for him any time.

As for the silencer, well really it was scrap, as the side that had been dragged down the road surface had been rubbed away.

"Pass it to me, lad," said the blacksmith, "and I'll wrap a thin metal skin round it, and make a bracket for it. Don't you worry, lass," he said to Ivy, "you'll soon be on your way home." The blacksmith did a lovely job, and the bracket he made wouldn't have been out of place on a battleship, it held the silencer like a vice. No fuel or oil had been lost, so all I had to do was to knock out the dents in the huge front mudguard and fit it back on to the bike. The blacksmith took it off me.

"Sit down and rest, lad," he said. "This is my job. I'll soon make short work of this." And he sure did, he even put some primer on it to stop it going rusty, a very nice job. I was delighted.

"Many, many thanks," I said to the blacksmith. "I've got no doubts about this lot getting us back, how much do I owe you?"

"How about 2/6d," he said. "As you've done nearly all the work yourself." Half a crown in today's money is just twelve and a half pence, so I gave him double and thanked him again, after all, he had opened up for us, and helped in every way. We had been there about three and a half hours, and in all that time, no policeman had been to see us, for the pub landlord knew where we were, and strangely enough, I never heard any more about it, but then again, very strange things happened in wartime. Ivy, by now, had started to shiver. It was more through the shock coming out, so the sooner we got going the better, for the rain had now all but stopped. The bike started up first kick, which was as well, as my right leg was hurting like crazy, and looking down, and despite the dressing, I could see and feel that blood was running down into my boot.

So, saying goodbye to our friend the blacksmith, we set out on our way.

The bike ran very well and felt almost normal, even the repaired silencer sounded good, but Ivy and I had had enough, all we wanted was to get back home, and neither of us felt very well. We stopped just twice on the way back, to rest our battered bodies, and, looking over the bike, I could see that all was well, we'd got no more worries there. Back at Ivy's house, her mum was horrified, but after the initial shock, and when we'd had a couple of cups of strong sweet tea, of course, she attended to Ivy's wounds. I, for my part, thought it better if I left mine as they were until I got home, as I thought that to disturb the bandage would set them bleeding again; for at the moment, the bleeding had stopped. Funny really, sitting on the bike it didn't hurt, but it was a different story when I stood up.

"Well," I said, standing up, "my worst ordeal is over. I love you both, now to shock my mum and dad." I wasn't looking forward to this. On leaving Ivy's it started to rain again and by the time I got home it was pouring. On my arrival back home, my dad caught sight of me struggling with the bike in the rear garden, then noticed the damage and came running over.

I was surprised that he wasn't mad at all, he just said,

"Get your bike away and come in, you look terrible. What's happened to Ivy?" In the house, and with my mum bathing my leg which was now killing me, I told them the whole story. I rested all that day and on Monday, I went to work on my battered bike, as it was too painful to ride my push-bike, for I used this to save petrol.

Monday evening I went round to see my darling Ivy. She too had been to work, but her right thigh had gone black and I felt very upset about it all; and do you know, the woman who caused all this, didn't even come to see what she'd done, or maybe she did, and was too scared to own up. That evening, we sat at Ivy's house just cuddling and kissing, knowing that we could have both been lying in hospital. This accident wasn't our fault, but we were suffering and paying for it.

On the Tuesday, as I stood looking at the bike, I noticed a thin line of oil across the outer gearbox casing. A hairline crack had shown up that I didn't know about. 'Just a bit more expense,' I thought. 'I'd better get a list made for new parts,' for although the bike worked perfectly, I wasn't the sort of bloke to just make do, it had to be right, so I made my list. It was then that I thought of Frank, and was I glad I'd been in on my Saturdays off, for I felt sure that he would make me out a trader's order, and yes, he certainly did just that.

Brandish's in White Friars Street in Coventry, was the main agent for Ariel motorcycles; the manager, Mr Walter Brandish, was himself an ex TT rider. There is even a corner on the Isle of Man course named after him, and all of them at Brandish's knew me. When I went in with my trade order under Elliott's bill head, I was still limping quite badly, as my leg took about three weeks to get right, and when the chap behind the counter saw me, he burst out laughing,

"Sorry, old pal," he blurted out, "I just couldn't help it. Of all the bikes you've tested you had to do it on your own and with your young lady on the back as well. Shame on you!"

"It hasn't taken the word long to get round," I replied.

"Well, you know what they say, that bad news carries fast. How are you anyway?"

Well, after I'd explained it all, he said, "Don't worry. I'm going to Ariels tomorrow. I feel sure you'll be lucky as we don't use many Squariel parts." Well, that weekend, I collected all my bits and pieces. Den took me in on his combo, and the bill was just under twenty-eight pounds. Frank had saved me about ten pounds and I was very grateful. Two days later, the new parts were on the Ariel. It looked very smart, for I'd polished it all over as well.

When Den saw it, he said, "I'd love to buy that off you, what about it?"

I replied, "Not yet, but if ever I do sell it, you'll get first chance."

Chapter Twelve
A Motorcycle all at Sea

Three weeks later found me reporting at Chatham Docks for my six weeks physical training for the Royal Navy. I didn't know it then of course, but it was going to be four and a half years before I could marry my darling Ivy, because I didn't come out until 1946. I don't intend to write about my naval service, but as one part deals with a Norton motorcycle, then that part I'll relate to you. The war was all but over, and our squadron was at Singapore harbour where we were overhauling our engine rooms, at least, us Motor-Macs were; as for my engine room, at this particular time, I was about halfway through. My mate and I had been given a couple of days off, as our two skippers had decided we needed a rest. So, Bash and I, Bash being my pal, decided to go about forty miles inland, just for a look-see and rest. About a month before, Bash had bought a watch from a street trader, a 'Shines spiv'. I'd told him not to buy it at the time, but Bash knew best, and thought he'd got a bargain.

"You've got to be joking!" I said. "Those sort of people only sell duds to mugs."

"We'll see," said Bash.

Well, up to now, I must admit, the watch hadn't given any trouble, until today. Today, the liberty truck took us to where we wanted to go, and as he drove off, he shouted,

"Don't be late, 7.30 p.m. on the dot, I'll be pulling out," And believe me, service people in war time didn't mess about, he'd go dead on time.

As we were finishing our banana fritters in a better type of restaurant, I looked over at Bash and said,

"How's the time? Is it 7.00 p.m. yet?"

Bash, looking at his 'ten dollar' watch said, "No, it's only 6.40 p.m."

"Okay," was my reply. "I'm going to have some more fritters, then."

"Make it two lots," said Bash. "We've got plenty of time," So with that, we got stuck in to another plate of lovely banana fritters and believe me, they were delicious. So we took our time, and didn't rush to leave the eating house. Outside and on our way back to our pick-up point, Bash looked hard at his watch, then took it off and gave it a good shake.

"Don't tell me it's stopped," I said scornfully.

"It still says 6.45," replied Bash. "Let's find out what time it is." Just over the road was a small hotel, so we went over and found the time was 7.50 p.m. Bash was so wild about his watch, that when he saw a young lad approaching, he took it off and gave it to him. The lad was delighted and ran off beaming.

"Bash," I said, "I'm not letting a dud watch interfere with our chances of getting back home. We've got to get a lift."

Well, a taxi, if you could ever find one out there, would have cost a bomb, as we were a good forty miles or so from our base.

"What are we to do, pinch a couple of bikes?" said Bash.

"That's it!" I cried out. "A biker! Of course! There's an army depot about two miles down the road and they've got bikes there. I noticed it when we came in. I reckon I can bull my way to get the loan of a bike. We could bring it back tomorrow. We've got the day off, so let's go and see. It could just work." On reaching the depot, we had a word with the sentry at the gate and showed him our paybooks. He then directed us to the duty sergeant's office, as it would be up to him if we were going to be successful or not.

"Come in, lads," said the sergeant, when we got to the office. "What can I do for you?"

"I'm not sure that you can do anything, Sergeant," I said, "as I'm after the use of a motorcycle for just one day."

The sergeant looked hard at me and said, "I don't know about that. I don't think anyone has ever requested this before." Well, we told him our story, and he grinned. "Our Major likes people who show initiative. I reckon he'll like this. Be smart, peel him off a nice salute, and convince him that you can handle a bike and you might just get away with it. The best of luck." With that, he picked up the phone and rang up the Major, who in turn, told the Sergeant to send us to his office. On entering the Major's office, we both gave him a very smart salute and both of us stood stiffly to attention. The Major stood up himself and he too saluted us back.

"At ease, gentlemen," he said. "What can I do for the senior service?"

"I hope you can help us out of an embarrassing problem, Sir," I said and I poured out the whole story.

"I admire your initiative in this matter," he replied. 'The Sergeant was right,' I thought, 'so here goes.'

"Can you ride a motorcycle?" he asked.

"Since I was thirteen years old, Sir," I replied, and I went on and told him a bit about myself, in particular, all my repairs and testing, and did not forget to mention the Squariel, 'that might just do it,' I thought.

I was right too, for, looking me in the eye he said, "KRs and Is (King's rules and instructions as laid down in armed forces rule book) here, PO, but I'm going to trust you. Outside my office is my motorcycle. Start it up and ride it around the yard a bit. Let's see how you fare."

"Thank you, Sir." I said and went out to the Army Norton. Switching on the fuel and looking into the oil tank, just for the Major's benefit, for he stood by the window watching me, I then retarded the ignition, turned the engine over to just past the compression stroke, and gave the kickstart lever a mighty push. The engine fired at once, and giving the oil a minute to get round, I took off round the yard. There wasn't a lot of room to spare, so in second gear only, I did various tight manoeuvres and a couple of tight figure eights to show control. I then put the bike back on the same spot, switched off the fuel and closed the air lever.

"Very good, PO," said the Major. "I can tell you're at home on a bike, but tell me, why did you close the air lever when you parked it?"

"To keep dust out of the induction, Sir." I answered.

"Excellent, PO. I'm going to lend you a bike. Let me have your paybook, as you will be responsible for it when it leaves here." With that, he made out a transfer chit, stamped it and signed his name on it. Turning to Bash, he said, "Go and fetch my duty sergeant, PO. He should be in his office."

"Sir," replied Bash, and with a real bull of a salute shot out to fetch the Sergeant. When the Sergeant came in the Major said, "Find a spare bike for them to use, Sergeant. I'm breaking all the rules and I need your signature to make it legal." So, after thanking the Major and his Sergeant very much, I very carefully put my motorcycle document in my paybook and we went with the Sergeant into their workshop to find us a bike. A bike was found, and the Sergeant filled the tank with fuel, and topped up the oil tank. In the meantime, I'd found an oil can, and went all over the cables on the bike and also oiled the chain. All that remained now was to find a pillion seat for Bash, for, as you most probably know, army bikes weren't fitted with pillions.

The Sergeant was a good friend, as he came up with an old pair of pillion footrests, a large very thick lump of sorbo rubber, a square canvas bag to put it in, and four webbing straps to clamp it on with, and this we were fixed up. The Sergeant and I soon got the footrest on, while Bash strapped on the makeshift pillion seat; I say makeshift, but it turned out to be a lot better than most pillions at that time, for it was twice as thick and twice as big. The bike fired up on the third attempt and the Sergeant said that it was a spare bike and hadn't run for about four months, so to use it would do it good, and of course, I said how right he was.

The journey back was great, the bike ran very well as it had only done just over four thousand miles and it had a nice sweet engine. Bash loved it, he didn't let on to me at the time, but he'd only been on a pillion once, and that was only for a couple of miles, but by the time we got back to base, he was ready to go and he was all smiles. Our skipper just stood and looked.

"I might have known you'd get yourself a bike. How the hell did you manage that?" After telling him our story, he grinned and said, "Better get it on board, PO, for if you leave it there, it'll be gone by morning and you'll be charged for a motorcycle." So with that, I rode the bike up the gangplank with the crew cheering its arrival. The next day, we didn't take the bike back until midday, as our skipper got me to take him on a short journey to collect some papers from the CO regarding our pending run from Singapore to Subic Bay, Manila. We were going to pay back our all-American craft to the Yankee Navy and then, we hoped, we could go home, and this is how it worked out. So, after lunch, Bash and I took the bike back to its base. At the base, we got a shock, as they were moving out, with the bikes being

loaded up onto three-ton army trucks. The sentry let us go through to
the Major, who grinned all over his face.

"This is your lucky day, lads," shouted the Major. "I can't take
the bike back as it hasn't been assessed for transport."

"That means we have to hang on to it then, Sir" I said.

"Correct, PO," said the Major. "You'll have to hang on to it till
the next battalion arrive, for it's this base which it must be returned
to."

"No problem, Sir. It'll be well looked after and I'm delighted.
Thank you very much, Sir. As you said, it's our lucky day."

The Major replied, "It will be about five weeks before you'll need
bring it back, as the next lot here are still in Worcester, England, and
we are going home. Good luck and happy motorcycling."

"All the best, Major, and a good journey home." So, with a salute
all round, we restarted the bike and made our way back to base.

"What are we to do with the bike?" yelled Bash, as we rode along.

"I'll have to keep it. The skipper can hardly refuse me now." So,
even in the Navy, I'd got a motorcycle and I still have a picture of
myself on it.

The outcome of this story, is that when Bash and I took the bike
back six weeks later, and gave it back to the new Major in charge of
bikes, he took one look at the Norton and turning to the duty sergeant
said,

"This bike makes ours look like scrap machines. This is what a
bike should look like. I want it on display so all can copy it, for if the
Navy can do it, then so can we." But, of course, I had really cleaned
the bike up before taking it back, also I'd improved it a lot. I had a
little chuckle to myself. I bet they had the same fun trying to better
that, but then, I'd advanced the valve timing by about 3° and moved
the exhaust silencer to suit, and retuned the carburettor. It went quite
well after that, as it had jipped it up considerably.

Chapter Thirteen
Back to the Grindstone

Exactly eight weeks to the day found the remnants of our flotilla aboard the *Glen Roy*, a former luxury liner, now an LCA carrier and parent repair ship. LCA was short for Landing Craft Assault, of which the *Glen Roy* carried twelve, and they were all there. The *Glen Roy* was to take us all back home, and in the last eight weeks, we had been taking our LCILs (Landing Craft Infantry Large) back to the Yankee fleet at Subic Bay, Manila, so you can imagine how happy we all were, going back to dear old England after three or four years away, for that is the time that the flotilla had been out there. The very next day, we were bound for almost a world tour and a passage home.

There is just one incident I will mention, it was this. On the evening prior to us setting sail for England, the *Glen Roy* was slowly swinging round her anchor chain with the ebb of the tide, and as she settled, Bash and I were leaning on the deck rail talking of our plans for when we arrived home. It may be difficult for you to believe this, but we had a real longing for some fish and chips as we couldn't get any out there. As we stood I noticed a metal tool box on the sea bed, as the tide at this point was just on the ebb.

"That's a tool box," I said. "Fetch a heaving line. I'm going down for that." So Bash ran and fetched a heaving line and as we were only wearing shorts all I had to do was remove my shoes and socks.

Bash dropped the line over and I dived in. The weight lay about three feet clear of the box. It was about twenty-five to thirty feet down, however I got there and tied the weight to the tool box, which was very full and very heavy. I tied the heaving line to one of the metal handles and surfaced. To my surprise there were about thirty of our lads on the rail, yelling and waving their arms wildly. They were yelling to me to get back quickly and Bash, cupping his bands round his mouth yelled,

"Shark! Move! Move!" And believe me, I moved. The lads had dropped a Jacob's ladder over the side for me to get back aboard. About halfway up, I looked down at where the lads were pointing and then I saw it; a huge tiger shark slowly cruising across the seabed and coming right across the spot I had just emerged from.

As I climbed over the ship's rail, a lieutenant of the ship's crew came up and said,

"What's going on lads? No bathing I hope."

Bash told the officer what had just happened and he grinned and said, "Now you know why the Yanks didn't bother to get it up. Good luck to you, but this is not the time to feed the sharks!"

Well, the box was full of chrome vanadium AF tools from $1/8$ AF to $1^1/2$ AF, also box spanners and ring and open end spanners, six screwdrivers and two large and two small hacksaws, several punches of various sorts, two sets of Allen keys, two steel rulers, a leather pouch of taps, dies and holders, a very good find indeed, for according to Naval law, I claimed it as bounty, spoils of war. Bash and I shared it out, but as it was I who spotted it and risked my neck, I got the lion's share; the box and any tools left over. I still have most of them to this day, and the box.

I arrived home to find that my mother was very ill, and I could tell that she wouldn't last long. After seeing my parents and giving them both a present I couldn't wait for Ivy to come home. So, without delay, and still in uniform, I went to the BTH, the same factory where I used to work as a kid, and asked to see Miss Ivy Jeffreys. The commissionaire wasn't going to fetch her at first; he said that she would be 'knocking off' in two hours.

However, I said to him, "I'm going to marry that young lady, and I haven't seen her for three and a half years, so if you don't fetch her, I will." He could see that I meant every word of it. Five minutes later, a very red-faced Ivy came into the reception.

I remember the moment very well, she just looked at me for a moment, then said, "Darling," and flung herself into my arms. She didn't speak for quite some time, as she was sobbing with joy. On looking up, all her workmates were watching through the windows and when they knew that I'd seen them, they all started to clap and cheer. It was a very emotional moment and the feeling of relief we both felt was just indescribable. I'd made it home and the bloody war was behind us. The next day, I dropped in to see Frank at the garage, he was delighted to see me and I told him that I was taking about two week's leave, then back to the Navy to be demobbed.

Frank said, "Just what do you intend to do?"

"Well," I said, "I was hoping to start work at a place called Elliott's Garage, because I don't break my promises." Frank was too full to speak, he just gripped my hand very tightly, and gave me a big hug. He was never a man to make a fuss, but me saying I was coming back had knocked him sideways and I know that it made him a very happy man.

My old pal Den had been demobbed about three months before me, and he'd been up to see Ivy a couple of times. Apart from viewing this as a courtesy visit, Ivy said, "I feel sure that Den is about to ask you to sell him the Ariel. I think he is hoping you will before our marriage, as he knows we'll need the money for a house."

"Well," I said, "I know he'd like it, but I don't think he'd be safe on it. The previous owner was about Den's size, and it was too big for him. I'll have a word with him tomorrow night, and we'll get it settled, and if he still wants it, we'll sort out a price."

I was a mug really at this time, for I had a golden opportunity to start up on my own. I couldn't have failed and we could have put a deposit on a small garage business with living accommodation, for by now, with the money I got from my time in the forces, and with my bank account and by letting the Ariel go, we could have done it easily. However, I didn't and, as I could see later, opportunity only knocks once and I didn't answer the knock. I guess really, that my mother's poor health and our impending marriage was as much as I could think of at the time. So, on talking to Den about the Ariel, I got him across it to see how he felt. It was obvious to me and Ivy that it was too big for him: with one foot on the ground holding the bike up, his other foot was at least two or three inches clear of the ground, but despite this, Den insisted he wanted it, and that was that, and besides, "I've got plenty of cash," said Den. "I don't want you to let it go cheap. I want to pay the right price; it's only fair. You'll need the cash when you're married."

I turned to Ivy and said, "What's it to be, love? If you say 'keep it', I will, for I think now that it belongs to us both."

Den looked hard at Ivy and dropped down on his knees.

"Dearest Ivy," pleaded Den. "Please say I can have it and I'll be your slave forever."

Ivy replied, "Rise, oh slave of the bike. Your wish is granted."

Den got up, and looking at me said, "This is special," And he gave Ivy a big hug and a kiss. "You can borrow it back any time, when I'm not using it," said Den, and indeed we did have it for one or two outings as you will see.

It was a laugh, the first time Den rode the Ariel. I had taken it round to him with all the paperwork and put it alongside his house, when he came out to try it. I offered to get it on the road for him. "No, I'll manage it okay," said Den, so I turned the bike round for him to ride it up onto the road, as it was quite a slope from the road to the house. Den started the bike with difficulty, due to his short size, for although the bike wasn't that tall, it was a wide machine, which also made starting up awkward.

Well, not having got the feel of a four cylinder, he gave it too much throttle, and with me yelling, "Steady, steady!" Den shot off, losing his balance as he did so, and, by losing his balance, he also lost control of the clutch, with the result that, with far too many revs up, the weight proved too much for him to hold, and the bike, pulling sideways, went through the wooden fence, through his dad's tulip bed and into the hedge where it stopped. We got the bike out, and neither Den nor the bike were damaged, but Den's dad was really wild when he saw the garden and the fence. Over the next two weeks while I was on leave, Den had his shoes built up with very thick soles, only to find that now, he couldn't feel his back brake lever properly. We also had to move the foot change lever up a spline, so that he could get his foot under it. He then tried to lower the seat, but it looked horrible. Then he tried altering the footrests, but got into all kinds of problems.

In the end, I said, "There is one sure answer and that is to fit a chair."

"But I want it solo," moaned Den, but after I'd shown him a picture of a German Stieb sidecar and we saw one outside Elliott's shop, Den was most impressed. "What a beauty!" he remarked. "What a lovely outfit it would be. I must get one. You're right; it's the only answer."

My leave ended, I went back to Scotland for demob. Three weeks later I was back home in civvy street and it wasn't long before I was in my world of motorcycles and all the problems that go with them.

A week later, Den got his Stieb side-car, and it was an unmarked beauty in olive green with gold stripes and a gold disc on the sidecar wheel. For safety reasons I went to fetch it, for I knew that Den wasn't able to fit it like I could and I didn't want anyone else to do it; also, I wouldn't risk Den doing an eighty-mile journey to get it home, for I had to collect it from Hertfordshire. Before I went, I paid a visit to my friends at Alf Holland's, who only too willingly lent me a load of chair fittings so I wouldn't be struggling when I got there.

The chap who owned it was a good motorcyclist himself, and between us we got it on in about forty minutes, and it looked a picture. It cost Den forty-five pounds plus five pounds for fittings, but it made that bike. With so much power there was no need to change the sprocket like you would on a smaller bike, for the outfit simply flew along, and at 70 m.p.h. it was lovely.

When Den saw it, he was really happy about it, and sitting in the chair when I got back with it, he said,

"Carry on, James, and take me for a spin." And spin we did as the bike was lovely and warm and I'd got the feel of the chair. We went about thirty miles. I could see Den holding onto the fitted hand bar in the chair's cockpit. It shook him the first time, but after that, he just loved it; no – he wasn't as mad as me, but it gave him the confidence to see how safe it was and I think all combo riders should be able to lift the chair as I did, for in my opinion, it could mean life or death in an emergency.

After a couple of weeks or so, Den got it all under control and it was certainly a handsome outfit. People used to look and stand and admire it when it was parked. Dennis took his dad for a trip in the chair when he'd mastered it all, and I can still see his dad's face when they got back.

Poor old chap, he said, "I think our Den's gone mad, as he all but killed me," And indeed, it had shaken him up, as I felt obliged to help him into the house. Of course, by now, I'd got my old Beezer together again and on the road, quite a light bike to handle after the Ariel, but a cheap bike to run for a couple about to get married.

Chapter Fourteen

Don't Trudge It – 'Rudge' It!

After my demob, Frank, my old boss said that it would be marvellous for me to get the bike side of the business going well again. Frank had done his best to keep it going, but with the shop and the rest of the garage to run, not forgetting the nuisance of the petrol coupons, he admitted that he had just about kept it ticking over, but he'd been able to sell every push-bike he could get. However, Frank realised that the motorcycle side was at a low, and needed a boost to get it going again. Although there were two mechanics working for Frank, both were car men, and it had only been Frank who had tackled the bikes. The Monday when I started back, there was only one bike in for repair. It was an Enfield that had got clutch trouble and required a new chain and sprocket. The sprockets had arrived two or three days before, but poor old Frank hadn't had time to bother with it. So I soon got it out of trouble, and Frank rang up its owner to come and collect it.

I heard him say on the phone, "No sir, you'll be out of trouble now. I've got George back and your bike is his first job and it's all ready for you." I got on well with both of the other chaps, Bill and Harold. Bill was about Frank's age, around forty-five, but Harold was a young chap like me, and was an RAF fitter first class.

Because Frank was forced to allow the bike business to run down, we were at that time having quite a lot of cars and light vans to repair, with the result that Frank though he'd better explain the situation. I told him not to worry as I wouldn't mind working on cars. It would be a doddle to what I'd been doing.

"And don't forget, Frank, I can weld, braze, in fact the lot. I'd have got my Chief's rate had I stayed in the Navy so take the lot. We'll soon get this lot moving." It wasn't long before work was coming in thick and fast. Frank put an advert in the *Coventry Evening*

Telegraph to say I was back for all motorcycle repairs of any make or model, with all sidecar fittings.

A couple of days later, bikes slowly started to come in and slowly, over the next couple of months, I gradually did less cars and more bikes. It took just two months and bikes were flooding in again. I was just putting an engine back in a Triumph that I'd overhauled, when Frank dashed into the garage.

"Go home, George. It's your mum."

I felt it instantly. My poor mum had gone after a long illness. I was twenty-four at the tine, and because of my mum's illness, Ivy and I had postponed our wedding arrangements, as we all knew that this was inevitable. After the funeral, Ivy and I made plans to be married in the February, for Mum had died in early November, so that sufficient time would pass to ease the sadness.

About two weeks before the wedding, one of our customers said to me, "I know where you could pick up a TTRudge cheap, for cash. Would you be interested?" Well, I'd just completed a decoke and new piston rings on his car and he was delighted with it. He'd already tipped me well, but I think he wanted to do me a good turn as well, for he said that he didn't know the man who owned the Rudge, but his wife worked alongside the other chap's wife and she had told her that her husband had been gambling and was deep in debt and was hoping to sell the bike to pay off his debts. The only problem was, he couldn't start it.

"I should be able to strike a bargain, then," I said.

"That's how I see it," he said. "I don't know him, but here's his address, only don't mention I told you, as I shouldn't officially know."

When I knew this, I was in a dilemma. Here was a very rare bike and I had a chance to get it a bargain price, but the wedding – and what would Ivy say? In my heart I knew what she would say, then I thought of the Ariel. Den had paid me its market price, so I'd still be in pocket if I bought the Rudge. This dilemma was gnawing at me all day. In the end, I knew that I'd have to go and see the Rudge, even if I didn't get it, to satisfy my curiosity. So, after work that night, I went to see it. It was in Coventry and it only took me about fifteen minutes to get there.

The man's wife opened the door, and I told her that I'd heard her husband had got a TTRudge for sale.

"That's right, he has, but I don't know who told you. You see, he was hoping to advertise it, but there's something wrong with it. He can't get it going."

"Yes, I was told that" I said. "I don't know if I can help, but it's quite possible, as I'm a motorcycle mechanic." So this lady took me through to her husband, who was busy repairing a puncture in what looked like his wife's cycle.

Like his wife, he too was surprised, but he took me into his large bike shed and, pulling an oily sheet off the bike said,

"That's the beast. It's nearly ruptured me trying to start it. It's racing you see, no kickstart, you have to run and bump it." Well, I was very impressed with the bike. It was one big racing beast and it looked that it was. Rudges, like Velos, were very well made.

"Have you any idea as to why it won't start?" I asked.

"It could be the carb," he said. "It keeps wetting the plug."

"More like spark," I said. "Or rather the lack of it. Mind if I have a look?"

"I'd be very pleased if you would. As I said, it's worn me out." So I used a couple of large wooden blocks that were lying on the bench, and between us we lifted the bike onto them, leaving the rear wheel about four inches clear of the ground.

"Give me your plug spanner," I said, "and a dry plug if you've got one."

"There's a boxful there," he said, putting a biscuit tin with about twenty different types of plugs onto the bench. As he handed me the plug spanner he asked, "How do you know about bikes, then?"

"I'm George, Elliott's motorcycle mechanic," I told him.

"Blow me," he said. "I would have liked it to have gone there, but I haven't got the cash."

"Don't worry," I told him, "this is for free. I'll soon find the trouble."

By this time I'd got the wet plug out. The plug was right in the centre of the four-valved radical allum bronzed cylinder head, a real racing job.

"I bet it's a pig to change the plug when it's hot," I said.

"Yes, it sure is," said its owner. "I have to do it with a glove on. You can't do it without." I'd now got the lead on the plug and, holding the plug flat on the head finning, I put the bike in second gear and told its owner to turn the wheel sharply in a forward motion.

"Dead," I said, and after trying two more dry plugs and the lead itself a fraction away from the head and then finally holding the high tension lead in my hand. "Your trouble is in the mag," I told him. "There is absolutely no spark whatsoever. The mag more than likely needs an overhaul, but I will check the points first." I did this and the points were clean and dry, but no spark.

"What do you reckon?" he asked.

"Well, as I said, the mag needs overhauling. You could be looking at about thirty pounds as this is a BTH racing mag, and they don't come cheap."

"That's it," he said. "I was hoping to get about ninety pounds for this, but now," and he raised his hands up in a gesture of despair.

"I'll take it as it is for sixty," I said, "and risk the cost of the mag."

"I can't let it go for that. I need sixty-five pounds at the very least."

"Sixty-two pounds ten shillings," I said. "I can't go any higher, as I'm getting married a week on Saturday, and my future wife doesn't even know I'm looking at this."

At me saying this, his wife, who was just bringing us in a cup of tea said,

"My God! Your poor wife! I hope she likes bikes. It looks as if you two are as bad as each other." She meant of course, her husband and I. "Let it go," she said. "This chap will get it done and there'll be no extras if he takes it on. It could cost you a lot of money, and we haven't got it. Let it go!"

"Okay," he said. "Sixty-two pounds ten shillings and you're getting a bargain."

"Done!" I said, and we shook hands on it. I put twenty pounds down as a deposit. "I'll collect it on Tuesday," I said.

"My wife will be in," he said. "She gets home about 2.30 p.m."

"I'll be there for 3 o'clock."

So I'd bought the Rudge – but I felt so guilty, even though I knew it was a bargain. My conscience told me if it wasn't right I should refuse it, but I didn't have the guts, and I didn't like myself for it. Frank let me fetch the Rudge in the old box on Tuesday afternoon, which was my half-day off, as I worked all day Saturday. The Enfield that was on the box had been replaced by a 570cc single cylinder Enfield, and the box shortened. Now only one big bike could be carried, or two small ones, or six cycles, enough to do the job, as Frank put it, for now Enfield were delivering the bikes to us, when we could get them. Frank allowed me to take the mag off the Rudge in the garage, and it was done as a spare job, for of course, our customers came first, as it was our living. By Saturday the mag was off, and to my delight, the fault was only a stuck carbon pick-up brush which, when freed and lightly greased, allowed the mag to work beautifully, and one could get a cracking deep blue spark to jump to earth by just flicking the mag over by hand, but of course, now I'd got it off, I very carefully checked it over before refitting it.

On the Saturday afternoon, when only Frank and I were left at the garage, Frank came down to see how I was doing, and looking at the Rudge said,

"George lad, that's one killer of a bike. A beast on wheels if ever there was one. It was only designed for racing. What does Ivy think of it?"

"She hasn't seen it yet," I answered, "and when she does, I don't think I shall want to hear."

"Get it right and get rid of it," said Frank. "Don't let a bike come between you and Ivy. It isn't worth it, and that's a lethal weapon." As he was saying this, the alarm bell went in the garage, letting us know that someone had just gone into the shop.

'Yes, Frank,' I thought, 'I'll do that, because I know in my heart that you're right, but first, I must go right over it and get it right, have a few runs and then sell it.'

Frank came back to me and the bike. "When you're ready to sell it, you can use the forecourt to get the sale. I'll print a nice 'For Sale' notice for it, with the price on, so you needn't pay out on adverts."

"Thanks, Frank. I'll do that, because I know you're right. Ivy isn't going to like this bike one bit. I've been thinking; a little car might help."

Frank grinned and said, "Welcome to the realms of married men. You'll be doing the right thing. Besides, how are you going to start that brute, after your honeymoon!" and grinning, he went back to the shop to make us both a cup of tea.

The Rudge was a machine built solely with speed in mind. It had a five-gallon fuel tank, half a gallon more than the Ariel's tank. The filler cap on the Rudge was huge, about five inches in diameter, with a big heavy chrome snap-shut cap like that on a Bentley's fuel tank, the cap opening forward for safety. The oil tank was a wrap round affair, wrapping round the rear down tube of the frame with a turn press, for quick release. On either side of the large oil tank, I believe it held either five or even six pints of oil. The handlebars were one inch and short, almost straight bars, with a very short turn for steering. As Frank had said, it wasn't designed for the road. The front wheel was a 300 x 21 with a ribbed front tyre which was nearly new and a very nice large front brake to with it. The rear wheel was 3.50 x 19 with a Dunlop racing tyre on it, this too had a very nice brake on it and both brakes had thick, chrome brake plates. Now, on road Rudges, they bad a unique interlocking braking system whereby, if correctly adjusted, whichever brake was applied, the other one followed on just a fraction lighter in poundage. You see, the correct way to brake on a bike is: bike upright and both brakes on together, but priority being put on the front brake for this is the real stopper. As the front wheel brakes, the weight of the machine and rider tend to press down onto the front wheel, so you can see why the front brake is the real stopper. So, with this in mind, Rudge developed their own braking system, which, if adjusted correctly, was very safe and effective. But this Rudge was purely a racer, so both brakes were separate in action, for when racing, it may be necessary to slide the bike by using the rear brake only, either to miss another machine, or even a fallen rider. At any rate, the coupled braking system wouldn't be practical for racing. The spokes in the wheels were 'double-butted' spokes, that means that they were thicker where they laced through the brake drum, giving extra strength in hard braking. The drive chain to the rear wheel was a heavy $5/8$" chain that should have been endless, in other words, with no connecting link, as a connecting link is usually the weakest part of a chain, and from the crankcase was a breath tube made of copper, which was run to blow oil mist onto the chain for lubrication. There was also a breather to the primary chain from the same source. The forks were heavy girder type, with a huge steering damper to tighten or loosen the steering according to one's requirements. There was also a large damper at the offside on the bottom fork shackle to damp the up and down movement on the forks. The frame was a heavy cradle frame, and the whole machine was very well made. The engine was a single cylinder 498cc OHV pushrod, with a four-valve head and an Amal GP carburettor with a large bell mouth. A new counter cable ran from the timing chest; driving the huge rev counter which was about six inches in diameter no speedo, but a very strong, short fly screen in front of the rev counter. The clutch and front brake levers were huge and easy to handle, there was no air control, for it was a Grand Prix carb, but there was an advance and control lever for the mag, and its former owner warned me to be sure that it was set at halfway before attempting to start the engine, as he forgot at one time, the result being a locked-up rear wheel which threw him over the front of the bike with the bike landing on top of him. He showed me the cuts on his head and hand, the one to his head needed four stitches. I won't say much more about the bike, except that the sprung saddle was well back; there was no pillion for on this lay out, there just wasn't room. The heavy rockers in the cylinder head were mounted in needle roller bearings, all beautifully oil pressure fed. The gearbox too had needle rollers in it and it was a foot change four-speed close ratio and the bike was very high geared, 40-50 m.p.h. in first not being a problem.

Frank came down again with a mug of tea for me.

"Let's see," said Frank. "You finished Mr Bell's bike, didn't you?"

"All done," I said. "The ticket is waiting for you to price it."

"Well done, George," said Frank. "You may as well finish your bike. I don't suppose it'll take you too long," Then with a grin, he said, "You can then get your first telling off, as there's no way Ivy is going to give you a big welcome on that."

Well, three-quarters of an hour later the bike was ready to run. I think Frank too was keen to hear it run, for he said, "Just get it running and see if everything is okay." So, following the drill for starting a racing machine, I pushed off. I'd better tell you the drill. It's as follows. First, half retard the ignition control lever, next switch on both fuel taps, one on either side of the tank, and both feeding one large swill pot, so that on long slopes either left or right, the carburettor gets fed alternately. Next open the throttle wide and, wait a minute or so to allow time for the swill pot to fill up as there is no tickler or primer on a Grand Prix Amal carburettor. Now put the bike in bottom gear and heave hard to pull the bike backwards in order to 'suck in' a petrol vapour charge. Now close the throttle, having got the charge into the cylinder, and all that remains is to pull the clutch lever tight into the bar and hold it there very tight, then, with a little throttle on, not too much, one runs with the bike as hard and fast as one can, and then, when you've got up to a fair speed, let the clutch in sharply and at precisely the same moment, throw yourself across the saddle sideways on and hope for the best.

Now, Elliott's Garage was at the top of Gulson Road, a fairly steep hill, so the problem wasn't really starting a bike here, the problem came later, if it didn't start, but of course, with a big bike like the Rudge, we could always bring it back in the old box. But in this case, the Rudge fired up immediately, there was a mighty roar and a cloud of black smoke that denotes a rich mixture. Black means unburnt fuel, but of course, with a Grand Prix carburettor it's designed with this start in mind. Well, I let it go steadily down Gulson Road and it was evident that right from the start, one only had to look at the throttle and it was away. So I went to the bottom of the hill and turned round. The steering circle was so close that I could only just get it round. However, I opened up the throttle fairly easily, even so, I shot up the road like a dart, still in bottom gear. At the garage I put it in neutral and blipped it up a bit. It was like a TT bike all right, for although there were two good silencers on it, as it was a two-port head, the noise was far louder than a road bike; people walking by were looking across, but the engine sounded very good and the oil was pouring back into the oil tank.

Frank said, "I don't envy you, George. Ivy's going to do her nut when you turn up on that. Hell! It'll bring half the neighbours out! You're going to have to be extremely careful on that." I advanced the ignition up and blipped the throttle again and it was really something; just one lethal bomb. I could hardly wait until I knocked off to try it. Placing my hand flat against the carb bell mouth, I stopped the engine, switched off the two fuel taps and wheeled my new toy into the garage. Now to show it to Ivy – and I wasn't looking forward to it.

After I left the garage for home, I thought I would give it a run as I hadn't even changed gear on it yet. Again it fired on the first turn over, so, advancing the mag up again, I shot off and shoot off I nearly did. I had a few too many revs up because of a cold engine and when I took off it caught me unawares. When the multi-plate clutch bit home, the Rudge took off with the front wheel lifting into the air! There was a couple walking along Gulson Road and they both stopped to look. The lady had her hands over her ears. I must have been doing around 30 m.p.h. when I changed into second gear and I soon found out that about four to five thousand revs were best for a nice smooth gear change. In top at around 100 m.p.h., about 5,500 r.p.m., the engine wasn't even taxed so I increased the revs to 6,500. I was really going now, this gearing must be on maximum for, on coming up through the gears, I estimated about 40 m.p.h. in bottom, 60-65 m.p.h. in second, around 80 m.p.h. in top and at six thousand five r.p.m. on this gearing, I must have been doing about 115 m.p.h.. It was flying along, much faster than the Squariel and a lot more stable. One could feel the power. It was a real motorcycle. I felt elated and on shutting off I punched the air in sheer delight as I had never ridden a racer like that one. It was brilliant and on pool petrol too, the octane was about eighty-five. This was terrific! I didn't care what anyone said, for I was on a high.

I had ridden down the old London Road, the old A5 as it was known, and at Rytonon-Dunsmore I turned and rode back at about 90 m.p.h. all the way. The Rudge didn't falter and when I got back, our old dog Pip, we still had him, he was now fourteen, started to bark. He knew it was me and my dad let him out as I came in through the gate. When I first saw Pip when I got home from the Navy, my mum had told him I was coming, and when he saw me, he went barmy. What a pal. No wonder they say a dog is a man's best friend; it just has to be true. That night, I showed Ivy the Rudge. I could tell that she wasn't happy about it and although it hurt to say it, especially after my very fast ride, I promised Ivy what I'd told Frank.

"All right, if you'll do that, I'll forgive you," she said. "Because, be honest, I'd be worried sick every time you went out on it. Promise me?" Then she gave me a big hug and that was it. I knew my new love was only for a short time. Den thought it was great but said he wouldn't ride it for a pension, and our Den was Dennis Walter Jenkins 'BEM', as he had saved a wounded sergeant by going out on his Norton dispatch bike and bringing him in whilst under machine-gun fire. A good lad was Den.

Chapter Fifteen

I Take a Very Hard Knock

I still had the Beezer of course, so we weren't stuck for a cheap run around. On the Sunday, after I'd tested the Rudge the day before, the weather turned very cold and so, on Monday, I had to go to get fixed up with a gas cooker for our new house. I went on the Beezer and, having got everything arranged, as I was coming back I hit a patch of ice. I saw it too late, and the next moment the bike just shot away as both tyres lost their grip on the road, and I was thrown forward, where I landed on my head and one shoulder. I didn't even have my beret on at the time and the blow was a severe one that split my skull from front to back. I was out for about forty minutes. By a remarkable coincidence, Ivy had just seen me go by, as she had taken the day off work to do wedding shopping. She saw me crash and ran over to where I lay in the road. It was by the entrance to the General Electric Company (GEC) works in Ford Street and the gateman, who had also seen it, rang for an ambulance.

The next thing I remember was looking up at two skylight windows in the hospital, then a nurse came in and looked at me.

She took my hand and said,

"Lie still and the doctor will be with you in just a minute." I then heard her say, "Doctor, the head patient has come round. Do you want to see him now?" I felt the bandage on my head. I'd done it this time. I felt terrible and yes, I lay still all right and I tell you; for the next five hours or so I thought I was going to die. In a few moments the doctor and two nurses came in. The doctor shone a light into both my eyes then asked me if I had any sharp pains other than a very bad headache. I couldn't feel any and told him so.

"That's a good start and also your speech is good, but you've had a nasty crack on your head, so for the next forty-eight hours you must stay here in bed and the nurses will keep you monitored during this time." He then asked me to repeat what he had said, which I did and then said, "That's very good. Word perfect. You're going to be okay, but the next two days will be crucial. You must lie still, but for the next few hours there will be a stream of various nurses coming in to check on you as I don't want you to sleep for at least ten hours. Right. Your young lady is here. I'll send her in to you." A few minutes later Ivy came in to see me.

"Oh darling, I'm so, so sorry," is what I think she said, for at that moment, I felt queer and I knew that it was my head wound that was causing it. Well, I can't remember much more of the next two days as every time I tried to sleep, the nurses would come in and tell me not to.

They were very good and this seemed to go on for hours, but at last, I was unable to keep awake, and it was then that the sister came in and after taking my temperature and pulse she said,

"That's better, George. We thought that you might be in trouble, but you're fine now and the doctor is coming to see you again." After seeing the doctor, I was allowed some soup and bread and it was only then that I realised what had really happened. I'd hit ice on the bike and here I was in hospital and I was all undressed in a nightshirt.

"How did I get here, Nurse?" I asked. "Was it in the ambulance?"

"Yes, and you've been here about eight hours."

"But who undressed me and got me into bed?" I asked.

"Who do you think?" she said, with a cheeky grin. "We are nurses, you know. You're in good hands. Eat your soup then I'll come back and have a chat with you, because you've got another three hours to go before I can let you sleep." This nurse had no doubt been assigned to me kept me awake for the next three hours after which I was again examined by the doctor.

Once again he shone his torch in my eyes, took my pulse, temperature and blood pressure and said, "You are a fit and lucky chap. You appear to be back to normal but with a blow like you've had, it's rest and sleep for the next seven days. No bending down, no work and definitely no motorcycling. We'll keep you here for the next two days then, if you're well enough, you can go home.

"Thank you, Doctor" I replied. "Just how bad is it?"

"Well, your skull is cracked from front to back on the left side of your head. That will only heal in time, but the good part is that there is no internal bleeding so, as long as you keep quiet, you should be okay. By the way, no alcohol of any sort." So, at last, I knew the worst. Well, I knew that Ivy would be in to see me, so till then I had better sleep.

My nurse got me a lovely meal, and tucked me up in bed, and now that I was feeling better, I could see what a nice young lady she was. I was going to enjoy this.

Well, I slept till 10.00 a.m. the next morning. I think Ivy came, but I was dead to the world and they wouldn't wake me, but Ivy was assured that I was out of danger. She must also have told them of our marriage a week on Saturday, for when I woke up the next morning, my nurse said to me,

"I've got to get you fit. Your special day isn't far off, you lucky thing. I wish I had a nice young man."

"You will," I told her. "You make sure he's the right one. I think you're lovely." This pleased her very much and five minutes later she brought in a wash bowl and washed my face for me.

"I could have got up and done that" I said.

"That's just it, you can't," she said. "No bending down remember, so lie back and enjoy it." And indeed I did. That night Ivy came in again, and my nurse winked at me, and pulled the curtain right round the bed.

"Be good," she said and with a delightful chuckle kindly left us to it. Ivy told me of her horror and fears when my head hit the road; she also said that the bike slid on the ice for about twenty yards and the gateman at the GEC had taken it into the gatehouse for me and that Frank sent his regards and was going to collect my bike for me that day.

"Was the bike badly damaged?" I asked.

Ivy said that at the time she wasn't bothered, but she didn't notice any damage.

"What a pig! If I'd gone on the Rudge, I bet this wouldn't have happened. I'd have been extra careful," I remarked, and indeed, that was more than likely correct.

Naturally Ivy was concerned about the wedding, but I assured her that I was feeling fine, then, just as I was enjoying a big kiss, in came the doctor to check me over.

"I hadn't better check you yet," he said. "Your blood pressure will be too high!" My nurse, who was with him, was laughing, and pulled back the curtain again. I slept for most of that day. I completely refused a bedpan and insisted on going to the toilet.

"All right," said my nurse, "but I insist that I take you and I'll be outside. If you get dizzy or feel ill call me, and remember, I am a nurse." I didn't have any ill effects and I ate all my meals and slept like a log. By morning my headache had gone and the nurse washed my head and rebandaged it, then, after taking my pulse, temperature and blood pressure, she told me I was doing fine and I'd be okay for the wedding. About four that afternoon I scrounged a pen from another patient and left a note and a couple of pounds for my nurse to drink my health and when she had gone to take her break I quickly got dressed and sneaked out by the rear entrance. I'd been walking about twenty minutes or so when an ambulance pulled up alongside me and my nurse came dashing out.

"You naughty boy! I can see your poor wife's going to have trouble with you!" Anyway, after she had made sure I was okay, I kissed her cheek and thanked her very much. So, I was out and although I looked awful I didn't feel too bad. A few minutes later I found a two shilling piece on the path, so of course, I bent to pick it up, but as I straightened up I felt very dizzy and just for a moment I was glad to hold onto the railings of a football field I was passing, but it reminded me not to bend down. I went to see Frank on my way home and of course he was surprised to see me.

"George," he said, "you look awful, lad. You shouldn't be here. Go home and go to bed."

"I will," I told him, "but first I'll just see Bill and Harold and have a look at my bike."

"Its okay," said Frank. "I've repaired what little there was to do," And sure enough, apart from a couple of minor scratches, the bike was fine. The icy road of course, would give no resistance, hence very little damage.

I was at home for the rest of the week. I did as instructed and sat around a lot and rested. I took old Pip for a couple of short walks and by Saturday, I was able to bend down without feeling dizzy. Of course, my head was still sore, but I took the dressing off to let the air get to my wound which had started to heal nicely. I was back at work on Monday and Frank was very surprised to arrive and find the garage already open. In fact I was actually serving a customer when he came in.

"Well done," said Frank. "But please take it easy. Just do what you think you can and don't push it." So I did and by Friday I was a lot better.

The wedding took place as planned on 22nd February 1947, one of the worst winters this country has ever known, and it was a cold and battered George John Hylands who married a cold and lovely Miss Ivy Jeffreys. We were now man and wife. But the run of bad luck hadn't yet finished, for when we got back to our new house, the snow was about three feet deep and the taxi had to stop in the middle of the road, for deep snow was everywhere. I carried my lovely bride through the deep snow. I remember her wedding dress trailing in the snow and me having to blow through my cupped hands to thaw out the frozen lock to get in. Once inside, the priority, for by now we were frozen, was to get a fire going, for in those days, most houses were heated either by gas fire or open coal fire heating. About ten minutes later, after soaking wood in paraffin, I got the fire started and soon piled on the coal. We had plenty, as I'd been stocking up for weeks. It was after we had got warmed up a bit, that Ivy went into the kitchen.

"Oh, darling!" she shouted. "Its all frozen!" Sure enough every pipe in the kitchen was solid with ice. "What shall we do?" asked Ivy.

"Don't worry," I said. "I got Den to take my home tool box up last week, and he locked it in the coal house. I'll get it." There was the tool box with a note from Den saying:

'Happy honeymoon. I hope you won't need these tools. Den.' The pipes in the kitchen were modern copper ones so I gently thawed out the stop tap and turned it off and got the pipes dismantled. Being new I didn't have any trouble. Ivy, by this time, had got three burners on the new cooker going for warmth and it wasn't long before we were out of trouble.

Two days later trouble struck again. When we got up at about 10.00 a.m. on Tuesday morning we found a note had been delivered marked 'Very Urgent'. It was from Frank. His father, Mr J W Elliott, the founder of the firm, had been rushed into hospital with cancer of the throat.

"I can hardly believe this," I said, as I handed the note to my wife. The note was full of apologies, asking me if I could possibly take over the garage as Frank wouldn't be able to be there for at least a week, but would explain everything when he saw me.

I remember Ivy almost in tears saying, "This is awful, darling. Have you really got to go?"

"Yes, I'm afraid I have," I said. "You see, I have all the keys. Safe keys as well. I may as well tell you now. Frank is making me foreman as a sort of wedding present. It was supposed to happen after our honeymoon." So fate struck again. There are very few things in life if any, sweeter than a lovers' honeymoon and I was having to walk out on mine, but I had no choice. I had all the keys, I had to cash up both shop and garage. I was the only one other than Frank who could deal with all the petrol coupons and order petrol, and I could run both shop and office. Frank had put me in charge and I couldn't let him down, for right now he was relying on me to keep everyone's livelihoods rolling, and this I faithfully did. Frank's father got through the terrible agony of radium needles in his throat and slowly got better, but as for Ivy and I, it wasn't all love and kisses after the honeymoon, for, about a month after the wedding, I started to suffer mental blackouts. I've never really remembered much about them even to this day, the only thing that I do remember is seeing Ivy sitting in the armchair crying her eyes out.

"What are you crying for?" I asked.

"Oh, thank God you've come round." said Ivy, as she threw her arms around me. "You've been like that for thirty minutes or more." You see, I was now suffering from the blow to my skull. Years later I found out that a part of my skull had been pushed in, pressuring my brain, hence these terrible blackouts. But gradually, as time went on, the blackouts got fewer and further apart, but it was a couple of years according to Ivy, before I was finally free of them. But Ivy was a great wife. She loved me dearly, and I feel sure this made all the difference.

Chapter Sixteen
Four Wheels for Two – Almost

Married life suited me fine. As I said, Ivy was a great wife and it was lovely to come home to a piping hot dinner instead of kippers and beans like I'd been having with my dad. We were still rationed of course, but Ivy was a good cook and she fed me very well, and now I was almost my former self. When I first came home on the Rudge it caused a bit of a sensation, for my new neighbours had never seen, let alone heard a bike like this, and when I got it home, dogs were barking and curtains were twitching. It really caused a stir. But it wasn't a nuisance, for no sooner had it fired than it was off, and when I got back a couple of gear changes were all that was heard as I used to stop the engine and arrive the last hundred yards on freewheel.

A spiv I knew who lived near Elliott's had an Austin 7HP saloon. The body was good, no dents or scratches and would clean up well. There were two nearly new motorcycle Dunlop 3.50 x 19 tyres on the front, an excellent model, the rear had two 400 x 19 Dunlops and on the spare was a 350 x 19 Dunlop with plenty of tread on it. The interior, such as they were in those days, wasn't bad, and the engine, although sluggish, wasn't noisy mechanically. So, bearing in mind my promise to Ivy, to part exchange the Rudge for a small car, I went round to see him. I went on the Rudge, as he was a motorcycle lad at heart.

Before I went, I decided to have one last run on the old Rudge. So, off I shot to Ryton-on-Dunsmore and back, a distance of around thirty miles. On the way back, just prior to reaching the hill past the Talbot works, I was doing well over 110 m.p.h. and shut off when going downhill. At the bottom of the hill, I speeded up again, only to hear the engine revs scream up and no drive. I pulled over and stopped as I could hardly do anything else. On examination of the bike, it didn't take long to see why there was no power arriving at the rear wheel. The chain was no longer there! Leaving the machine leaning on the grass verge, I walked back up the hill in an endeavour to find the drive chain. The chain should have been endless (riveted solid) but I knew I hadn't replaced the connecting link (always a weak point on a fast bike). However, on reaching the top of the hill, about one hundred and twenty yards further on, a lorry had stopped and its driver was going back to it with my chain dangling from his right-hand. I ran up to him, and seeing me coming up in motorcycling gear, he realised that it was obviously my chain that he had stopped to pick up. He was smiling as he held it out to me.

"You're just in time, lad," he said. "I'd have been off in another few seconds. Where's your bike?" I told him and he gave me a lift back to it. As we went along, he told me that his spotlights had picked up the chain lying in a dead straight line, as if someone had stretched it out by hand, but it was as I told him; at 100 m.p.h. plus, I wasn't at all surprised. I was only very grateful that it hadn't wrapped itself around the rear wheel and locked it up, as it could have been a very different ending. As it was, knowing the chain wasn't riveted, I'd had the good sense to keep a cranked link, a connecting link in my tool kit, along with a chain cutter, so, with the new connecting link, and about ten minutes work, I'd got the chain back on and readjusted, and shot off to make my latest deal.

When I arrived, as soon as he saw the Rudge, his face lit up, and I knew he'd like it, for by this time I'd got it all cleaned up with no oil leaks. I'd already viewed the Austin a few days before, as he used Elliott's for oil and petrol. It was then that I told him that I'd drop round on the Rudge, so there I was.

"What are you asking?" he asked.

"I was going to put a ticket on it at the garage for £110," I said, "but if we can strike a deal, it's ninety pounds to you." He eagerly looked over the Rudge and sat on it.

"There's no problem there," I told him. "I've been right through it and you won't even have to put a rag on it. It goes like a bomb."

"Let's hear the Austin," I said. "Start it up."

"Oh!" he exclaimed. "That's the trouble. It won't start. I don't know why, but it'll go with a good fast push."

"What's the battery like?" I asked.

"I thought about that," he said, "so I got a heavy duty one on it, but apart from the lights being brighter, it hasn't made any difference."

"Would you like me to take a look?" I asked.

"I wish you would. You know more about them than I do," he said. So I quickly checked the spark and the timing. The spark was good and the timing only slightly retarded.

"Nothing much wrong there," I said, as I helped myself to a couple of spanners from his tool box to advance up the distributor a couple of degrees. I then felt the compressions on the handle. It was like turning over a sewing machine as the compressions were non-existent.

"Here's your trouble, there's no compression."

"The valves have gone then," he said.

"Could well be, but whatever it is, you're not going to get much for it like that." I didn't say so at the time, but the only way you would get all exhaust valves burnt at the same time, is if all the clearances had been set up too close when fitted.

"Have you got any feeler gauges handy?" I asked.

"I'll get you some," he said and tipped out the contents of his tool box. Having tested the clearances and putting the two right that were at fault, I checked the compressions again.

"Useless," I said. "The engine will have to come down."

"I was asking sixty pounds for this," he said. "I gave forty-five pounds for it and then changed the front tyres and put another battery on. What do you think?"

"I think that if the engine had been any good, it would have been worth sixty pounds, but not like this. If the engine needs new exhaust valves that's sixteen pounds and another five pounds for gaskets and that's to me, but if you add on labour charges on top," And I held out my hands in a hopeless gesture. "Look," I said. "You gave forty-five for this. Here is a bike in very good condition, which I'm sure will fetch its price, so if I said ninety pounds for the bike, you give forty pounds and the car, you've got fifty pounds for a sick car and as well, you've got yourself a very healthy bike!" He thought for a few minutes. You could almost hear his brain working.

"Will you stand the cost of the engine repair?" he asked.

"I will take it on that deal, just as it is." He grinned and held out his hand. "You've got your wife a car," he said, and in doing so, brought out a large bank roll from his back pocket and counted me out forty pounds. We changed the paperwork, no receipts were exchanged, as he lived by his wits, and the less he wrote, the more he could get away with. So, after the deal was over, I told him to be very careful with the bike, as it was something special. So, having been given a push start, I set off for home.

To me it was like driving a car with an elastic band for an engine, and I couldn't help thinking what a 'bloody lame duck' I'd bought. Oh, well, I guessed I'd get it right. I had a theory about that engine and it proved to be correct. Back home, I drove the Austin into our garden and switched it off.

When I went inside, Ivy said, "You're very late and I didn't hear the bike. Did it break down?"

"The bike is fine," I said, "but I would like you to put on your coat and come outside. I'd left the lights on in the car, so Ivy could see a bit of it, as the car was black in colour, and by now it was dark.

Ivy was delighted when she saw it, and sitting inside she said, "Darling, this is lovely. Oh, I'm so proud of you!" Of course, a big kiss followed. I walked to work the next morning, so I could use the Beezer, and I took my bike gear with me. So, until Sunday, the car would have to stay where I'd left it.

There was new antifreeze in it, as I'd noticed a nearly new radiator and a new top and bottom hose and clips. Sunday was fine and the weather was getting much better, so after breakfast I checked out my theory as to why there was such a loss of power. Draining off the coolant from the engine I removed the bonnet and radiator in order to get at the timing chest. After I'd got the cover off, I set up number one piston on top dead centre compression stroke, and yes, there it was. The valve timing was one tooth in the retarded position; that is why there was hardly any compression. This I quickly put right and when I'd put the radiator back and the coolant, the engine fired up immediately. At once, Ivy came running out, smiling all over her face.

"That sounds lovely," she said. "Is it ready to run yet?"

"Give me an hour," I said, "and I'll give you your first ride in it." And indeed, after I'd weakened and reset the carburettor, the engine was lovely and quiet and was purring like a cat. Ivy liked the Austin very much and we did a lot of miles in it and had a lot of fun. The body came up well and three months later I got a spare engine out of an abandoned car and it turned out to be a brand new engine with 'std' on the piston: 'standard size' and not a rebore. Other marks and parts all indicated that this engine was 'genuine works engine'. I also obtained the clutch and gearbox and four good wheels with tyres and tubes in usable order, the tyres all being 400 x 19 Dunlop Universal, all for five pounds, as the chap who sold it to me thought he was selling a load of scrap. After fitting this engine the little car ran like a new one and, what is more, I got fifteen pounds for the old engine in working order.

A month or so later, I sold the Beezer after giving it a decoke and fitting two new tyres and it paid off, for I got a very good price for it. I think it was about eighty-five pounds. Two weeks later, a chap called in at the garage to have his cycle repaired, and in the garage was a James motorcycle that I'd just finished a rebuild on.

When this chap saw the James he said, "There's one like that in my neighbour's shed, but this one is almost new. My neighbour's husband got killed on it. He braked for a child that ran into the road and he landed on his head and it proved fatal."

"I know the feeling," I replied. "Is it badly damaged?"

"Just a small dent on the rim of the headlamp. It didn't even break the glass and I know the lady would like to be rid of it, but doesn't know what to advertise it for."

"Tell her that if she would like me to go and see it, I might be interested, as I could do with a bike for work," I said.

"I'll tell her," he replied. "And I'll let you know when I collect my cycle, tomorrow night." Sure enough, when he came for his cycle, he gave me his neighbour's name and address, and told me that she would be very pleased if I was to see it, as she didn't even like going into the shed while it was there. So, I sent her a message saying I would call on my way home from work, about 7.10 p.m., which I did.

The bike was as he said. It was all but new, and there were only 857 miles on the clock.

"It's lovely," I said. "What do you want for it?" The bike was only ten months old and as the cycle man said, the only damage was a one inch dent on the headlamp rim and the outside footrest was slightly bent, but that was all.

"Well," replied the lady, "my brother says I should get about fifty pounds for it, as it's hardly been used."

"Its a lovely bike," I said. "Here's ten pounds as a deposit. Could I call and pick it up tomorrow afternoon?"

"Thank you, I'll be in all day tomorrow," was her reply. Her house was only just off Gulson Road, about a quarter of a mile from Elliott's so I knew I could pop down on the box and pick it up. This I did and on examining the bike at the garage, and with Frank looking on, I found the reason that had more than likely caused his death. The fulcrum on the front brake hadn't been greased, most probably an assembly fault at the factory. The water had started to seize up the pin, and when the front brake was applied, it just stayed on.

As Frank said, "Only using it for work, he probably only used the front brake in the emergency." And he was most probably right, as it's essential to get into the habit of using front brakes. Anyway, a nearly new machine for fifty pounds hardly made sense. The reason was that people are superstitious, generally speaking, and a bike that some poor devil got killed on makes it taboo, but to me, it's not taboo; it's a mechanical or a practical reason and in this case I was sure I'd found it. So, having eased off the seized fulcrum pin and having had a quick check round, the bike started second kick and it went like new. A beautiful little machine. When Ivy saw it, and knew how much it cost, she was delighted. After all, it was just like new, and a more reliable bike for work would be very hard to come by.

Chapter Seventeen

A New Hand and Two Unusual Occurrences

A few weeks later, Harold left. He'd been offered a job in Bristol, his home town, and a house went with it. The job was a good offer as it would put him back into aero fitting, which is what he really wanted. This of course meant a lot more work for Bill and myself at this time. A lot of work was coming in as it was now springtime and people were slowly getting themselves sorted and looking for cars and bikes. Elliott's of course, was a very well-known garage, known for good repairs and service, and a wonderful stock in the shop. I'd heard it said that if Elliott's hadn't got it, then you're lucky if you can find it, and as for the motorcycle repairs, well we even did jobs for other garages. One of the lads from the Antelope Motorcycle Club used to call in regularly and he was always trying to get me to ride trials and scrambles for them. I remember saying at the time,

"Get me a bike and I might just have a go."

Well, as I said, we were very busy, so much so that I forgot dinner on Saturday, as I never got time to eat it. It was the same with Frank. He used to take about two hours to eat two sandwiches and an apple, while I used to take a bar of chocolate, for now, we were on bigger and better rations. One Saturday afternoon a chap came into the garage on a very well kept Enfield 500 twin combo. Frank had sent him to me as he'd been in the shop for a few parts and had got a problem on his bike.

"Yes, sir," I said. "What can I do for you?"

"I hope you can do something," he said. "Frank has just told me how very busy you are."

"That's very true," I said, "but I'm not too busy to help if I can. That's what we are here for, so tell me your problem."

"I reckon I've got a big end going," he said. "And the trouble is that I do forty miles a day to and from work and without the bike I'm stuck as I live at Brandon." Brandon was a few miles out of Coventry.

"Okay," I said. "Start it up. Let's have a listen." He kicked it up and sure enough on full advance when the throttle was blipped there was a definite knock. So I got a pair of insulator pliers and pulled off first one plug lead and then the other.

"Its the offside big end," I said. "What's the betting that the feed cork is in trouble?" On the Enfield timing cover was a $^{7}/_{16}$" plug. It was the oil feed plug being controlled by a hollow cork fitted on the feed stem, the cork sealing the oil to direct it down the feed.

"The cork should be fine," he said. "It was replaced three months ago."

"Oh," I said, "but was it soaked in oil first?"

"No, it wasn't," he answered.

"Then it's quite possible that it's damaged." By now I'd taken out the plug and there it was; the cork was damaged. "Here's the cause," I said. "You see, fitting it dry has scuffed a lump out of the cork and that has prevented the full oil flow from reaching the big ends."

"Bloody hell!" exclaimed the man. "All for a drop of oil!" "Don't worry," I told him. "I'll fit you in the latest oil-proof rubber plug. Enfields have recently modified them for just this reason. Hang on a minute and I'll go and get one." I got the modified plug aid fitted it in.

"Thanks, mate," he said. "You sure know what you're about." With this I put the new plug in and kicked up the engine. I then lightly retarded the mag and, on blipping the throttle, the knock had gone.

"That's great," he said. "How long will it last?"

"If I put half a pint of Redex in your oil, it will last for months, but it hasn't cured it, only stopped it getting worse." I poured the Redex into the oil tank. "When that gets round," I said, "it'll feed your engine instantly and that is just what hasn't been happening. Anyway, old son, all you owe us for is the plug and the Redex."

"That's great, and as soon as you say, I'll bring it in." Then, as he was about to kick his bike up, he said, "Do you think if I had a word with Frank, that he would let me get the engine out for you seeing as you're so busy? I'm not a bad amateur mechanic and I've had it out before."

"Possible, but you wouldn't be covered by insurance. It's worth a try."

"I'll go and ask him," he replied, and went back into the shop. Ten minutes later both Frank and the combo owner came down.

"This is Dennis Leeson," said Frank. "He's delighted by what you did for him and he wants a job here as a trainee mechanic. How do you feel about it? I told Dennis that it's all up to you."

"I'm very flattered," I replied. "I could certainly use some help."

"Right then, but you understand that George runs the garage? He's the man you'll be working under." Dennis was beaming. As we shook hands, he said,

"I won't let you down, George. I've always wanted to work on bikes."

"We'll get on fine," I told him. "When will you start?"

"A week on Monday," he said. "I have to give a week's notice, but I'll be here for sure a week on Monday."

Dennis arrived on time. In fact I was still unlocking the pumps and oil cabinets when he arrived.

"Morning, Den," I shouted. "How's the bike?"

"Very good," he said. "That Redex is good stuff. It's sure jipped my engine up and the big end hasn't knocked once." So I'd got a new helper, but not just a helper as Dennis turned out to be a very good friend. At this time, my old pal Dennis Jenkins had started courting my cousin, no, not Francis, Celia, the daughter of my Uncle Len, my dad's brother. I didn't know this at the time. It was little wonder we didn't see much of him. A week or so later, Dennis and I, working together, had moved a lot of work, so, on the following Friday, Dennis asked Frank if be could stop there on Saturday and take his engine out. Frank agreed and with my help we got it out and stripped, big ends refitted and the crankcase reassembled before 6.00 p.m. Frank lent Dennis an old push-bike to go home on, and by the following Monday night, at 5.00 p.m., Dennis kicked his bike up, and the job was done. While we were at it, I showed Dennis how to track up his combo. He was very pleased when he came to work on the Tuesday, he said that his wife Rita thought they were flying.

The next week I got a 197cc James Colonel to try out, from a member of the Antelope Club. It was a trials machine, and on the Sunday morning, I went with some of the lads from the Antelope Club, to 'ride the rough' as they called it. It was rough too, up and down slag heaps, some 120 feet high, and I soon got the hang of coming downhill in bottom gear with the compression lever pulled in. By and large I was soon riding in trials, but it meant practice twice a week and I knew that Ivy wasn't too keen, as I didn't get home before 7.00 p.m. as it was. So I promised I'd finish the season and then pack it in. I did a few trials after that, but it wasn't a regular thing, for really, I hadn't got the time. The climax came when I rode very fast into a river. I'd taken a wrong turn in a wood, and came tearing out of a bend far too fast, saw the river too late, then plunged straight in. I got out okay and was completely soaked. I got the help of a bargee to help me get the bike out with the help of a boating hook. To my amazement, the waterproofing held and after a bit of spluttering and back firing, the engine started with loud cheers and squirts of water from the exhaust pipe! It was the wettest ride home I'd ever had, and by the time I got home I'd covered 143 miles and was very cold.

I was getting a lot of fun and riding experience out of all this, and later on, I got up to Six Day Trial level, but all this was very time consuming, and, like any sport, practice is a must. This was keeping me away from home for too long. Ivy said that I was more like a lodger than the man of the house, so a few weeks later, I gave up trial riding, much to Ivy's delight.

The next day at work, a young chap came in on a 250cc Pride & Clarke Panther and asked if he could have a word with a bike mechanic. So I went out to him to hear what he had to say. Apparently, he'd bought the bike from Astons in Gosford Street and at first, all seemed well, until he went over a fifteen-mile run, then, he said, that the bike would get slower and slower, and finally stop altogether. The chaps at Astons had tried to sort it out, but hadn't been successful, so they told him to take it to us, and get a bill, and then they would consider a payment.

We had quite a busy week on, but I told him that if he came on Thursday night, I'd have a go at it on Friday. He was pleased about this, but asked if he might leave it now, as he didn't like riding it as it was, and never knew just how it was going to behave. So I took the bike in to be looked at on Friday. On the Friday I checked over the bike and checked the timing and tappets. Neither were far out, so, having started it up and reset the carburettor, which was far too rich, I put a drop of Redex in the oil tank and took the bike for a run. Sure enough, I'd only done eight miles when the engine started to tighten up. I stopped at once and shut off. On cranking over the engine by the kick-starter, I was pretty sure it was the piston that had tightened up. I took out the plug and, dipping a screwdriver into the oil tank, I let the oil drip into the cylinder. The engine eased off instantly and I was now pretty sure that the fault lay in the piston. Possibly someone hadn't gapped the rings correctly. However, I must get back and get the head and barrel off to see just what was wrong.

I rode it back slowly and got back without it tightening up. On removing the cylinder I had a shock. The piston was made of wood, it was a lovely piece of lathe turning and it had been made out of 'Ligman-Vita', one of the world's hardest of woods. The rings although correctly gapped, had embedded themselves into the wood, so as soon as the wooden piston got hot, it slowly seized up with expansion. The mystery was solved.

I got and fitted in a new piston and rings and the bike was fine. Little did I know that about three years later, I was to find how this came about. At the time, I would have liked to have kept the wooden piston as a memento, but of course, the owner needed it to show Astons, the firm he had bought the bike from, as it was a most unusual event in any repair. Incidentally, the bike owner was paid in full for the cost of our repairs by Astons, but of course, they kept the piston.

On the following Saturday, Dennis knocked off as usual at one o'clock for the weekend. As number one I did every Saturday afternoon on my own. About twenty minutes after Dennis had left, Frank came down to the garage where I was just fitting a new tyre and tube on a Rudge Ulster combo.

Frank said, "As soon as you've finished that, George, get the box out and go and tow Dennis in. He's stuck on the Brandon Road. He's somehow busted his crankcase, so take the plates and the tow rope."

"They are already in the box," I said. "And I should be finished here in about fifteen minutes." Sure enough, fifteen minutes later I was on my way to rescue my friend from his latest calamity. When I got there, Dennis was sitting in his own sidecar, but got out quickly on my approach.

"You're not going to believe this," he said, and I must admit, the trouble was far from normal. It appeared that a stone from the newly tarred and chipped road surface that we were on, had been thrown up and had gone along the top of the rear wheel chain run, and, on reaching the crankcase in front of the final drive sprocket, had gone round with the chain and pushed a lump out of the crankcase. The size of the hole was roughly three by two and a half inches, large enough to have half emptied the crankcase in less than half a mile.

"Cheer up, Den," I said. "It could have scrapped the crankcase. At least this can be repaired!" So I towed our pal back to base on his now 'fated bike', as he put it. Well, he spent the afternoon taking his engine out once more and by the time we were ready to close up shop, Dennis had got the engine out and stripped down to the crankcase. Before Dennis had come to work for us, he had been a signwriter and painter, so he said,

"I've got the right name for my outfit. I'm going to call it 'it's abugga'. I reckon that will suit it just fine." Sure enough, two weeks later, when it was all well again, the name, 'it's abugga' was neatly written on the nose of the sidecar and it certainly got a lot of smiles! After this, I'm pleased to say, Dennis had no more trouble with his outfit.

Also, by this time, Dennis had mastered the handling of the old box, which made it a lot easier now that there were two of us available to collect crashed bikes or whatever.

Chapter Eighteen

A Fabulous Ride

Although I enjoyed my trials riding, and reached a standard of riding that enabled me to reach the six day international trials, it was by now taking up too much time. I was practising three times a week, Monday night, Wednesday night and every Sunday morning. Also, when a trial came up, I would be away all Sunday, so that weekend I gave it up, for my real love was road racing. Both Ivy and I used to go to the meetings and I knew that if I had kept the Rudge I could have really had a go. But even so, it wasn't cheap and really, I hardly got a wage that would cover road racing. A few weeks later, I started to do the odd job at home, 'back yarders' was the term that was used. It all started when one of my neighbours had trouble with his car, and after I'd done it for him, he came to me on a regular basis and it wasn't long before others came too.

Back at work, Dennis Leeson had settled in fine, and he and I were now firm friends. He was a good motorcycle trainee and he soon learnt the jobs on the Enfield range, so for the first two years he was with us, it was mostly Enfields that he repaired. I still did all the big end repairs on all bikes, but now Dennis was confident on Enfields it meant that mostly, I did all the other makes and also a fair percentage of cars. I had to do this as there were too many for Bill to cope with after his mate, Harold, had left, but I didn't mind. It all helped to make me a real repairer and I could tackle anything, for I'd had wonderful experience in the Navy, both on marine petrol and high speed two-stroke diesels, both large and small.

One day, Frank came down and said, "Get the box out, George. There's a special bike to bring in. It's a Grand Prix 500cc HRD, and its owner has crashed on the ice and has been taken to hospital." The bike had crashed on the other side of town, and when I got there it was just inside the garden where it had demolished a wall. I took one look at the bike and it was a beauty, or rather, it had been before it crashed. I should have taken Dennis with me, for it was evident that Frank hadn't been told how badly it had been damaged. The front special forks and front wheel were folded back under the engine while the frame had arched along the top rail, ripping the bottom open on the fuel tank. You could see where the fuel had smothered the bike and pavement. This was going to be a struggle, as it was a big heavy bike, and it would have to be lifted. So, slinging all the loose bricks to one side, I made a pathway to pull the bike down. I was in luck this time, as the house owner came out, and he was a big strong chap, and, seeing me struggling, came and gave me a hand; between us we got the bike loaded up. Back at the garage I had to strip off for the insurance inspection, as it would be a complete rebuild, for the damage was heavy. Luckily, only the timing cover on the engine was damaged, it was as well, for I was told that about £400 had been spent on the engine at HRD's. In the meantime, my James Colonel, all cleaned up, stood outside in the yard with a big 'For Sale' notice on it, for I had owned it for the last twelve months. On the following Saturday, a chap came in and asked about the Colonel, as he'd seen me riding it in several trials, and was wondering why it was for sale. After I'd explained it all to him, he asked to hear it running, liked it very much and asked the price. He could nee that it was first class with no scars or bumps.

"I'll have it. How much tax is on it?" he asked.

"Eight months and it's in first-class condition." He must have been adamant about buying it, for he produced a roll of bank notes, counted out the ninety-five pounds I'd asked for it, and didn't even try to knock the price down.

'This will please Ivy,' I thought, as I kicked the bike up for him and handed it over, and that was that. Off he went; I'd never seen him before and I never saw him or the bike again – remarkable.

Now, also at this time, a young man had been in a couple of times after my Austin, so now I'd sold the Colonel, I had the money to buy a Morris 8HP two-seater tourer. So I rang up this chap and by the following week I'd sold the Austin and bought the Morris. Ivy was really smiling now, and so was I. After I'd gone right through it and decoked the engine and fitted a better silencer and wider tail pipe on it, the Morris 8HP turned out to be a first-class car. I taught Ivy to drive in it. I remember how proud she was the first time she drove it back from Malvern, our favourite place.

By this time, the HRD had been assessed for repairs and the new front wheel, mudguard, frame and forks had all arrived, so the next day, after I'd finished the Norton that I was working on, I was to strip out the fabulous HRD. It really was a super machine and I was really looking forward to doing it. It stripped very well, as you might guess. It had been very well looked after and three days later, when it was all but finished, the owner came in. He'd had a hard knock all right, he was limping, with a stick, and his right arm was in a sling. You could also see three deep scars on his face where the bricks had hit him.

"Hello there," he called out as he came in. "Good to see this again. I've just been talking to Frank and he tells me that you're only waiting for the tank."

"That's all," I replied. "Other than that, it's all finished, but while you're here, just tell me how you like your master brake adjustment, as I've fitted it up to suit myself." The HRD had coupled brakes like the Rudge standard models and I was a bit surprised to find it on a Grand Prix machine. This chap sat on the bike as I'd dropped the seat on for him.

"That's perfect," he said. "Frank told me you'd make a real job of it. It's great, and the insurance is paying the lot."

"Co-op insurance isn't it?" I asked.

"It is," he answered. "What do you think of them?"

"Very good indeed," I answered. "A very good company to deal with. We never get any trouble with them. I insure with the Co-op, house, car and bike."

Well, the tank came two days later, but the weather wasn't good and it was fatal to test a bike like this in the wet, so Frank said he'd let the owner know and I could test it as soon as it was fit to do so. Well, this was on the Thursday, but the weather didn't clear up until Monday afternoon, too late to test the bike, as works traffic would soon be on the road. So the bike had to wait until the Tuesday morning. On the Tuesday, just before I got the HRD out, Frank came into the garage and said,

"Don't take any risks. I know you've got to throw it around a bit, but do it progressively and mind how you go. You've got £2,500 worth of bike there," And at that time that was like testing a £10,000 bike today. The engine fired at the first kick as I'd had it running twice on the Monday, so I let it warm up for a few minutes and, blipping the throttle a bit, it sounded beautiful and had a crack like a whip. This truly was the best machine I'd ever sat on. I pulled in the clutch lever a couple of times and then, with the clutch right in, I blipped up the engine to clear the multi-plates in the clutch. At tickover, I slipped it gently into bottom gear and slowly took off, with Frank, Dennis, Bill and two customers all looking as I went.

Frank shouted, "Mind how you go and the best of luck!"

Well, I must try to describe the ride, as it was the very best ride I'd ever had. The Rudge was rough in comparison to this, for, to be fair, the Rudge was a solid frame 1930s design, while this was a 1952 model with a much more sophisticated engine which had been specially prepared for the Isle of Man. Right from the first roll, I knew that I was riding one hell of a bike. The smoothness for a single cylinder was unbelievable, the clutch was as sweet as a Velo clutch, but with a sharper bite, and I was so taken up with this bike that I'd got up to 90 m.p.h. without even noticing it. I slowed down, for my test was mainly for handling, so let's do it. I started to roll the bike around with my knees. It was as smooth and solid as a rock; increasing the speed I threw it around up to 90 m.p.h. and it was great. I loosened the fork damper off a bit, for the new fork would have to bed in, and I didn't want to 'step' the new ribbed Aven front tyre, for with a girder fork too tightly damped, that's what you get and it's got to be just right.

I pulled in and stopped for a good look round. It was all but perfect, the HRD girder hydraulic forks were a dream to ride, the spring frame too was very firm and gave a feeling of sheer stability. Having checked all round, including the oil, I started her up and took off a bit quicker. It was just as smooth on a fast take-off as it was on a slow one. The multi-clutch was not only lovely and light, but also highly effective. By this time I'd done about twenty miles, as a rebuild has to be put through its various tests for safety.

'Its time I started back,' I thought, and, charging along the straight, the big speedo showed 120 m.p.h. at around 6,500 r.p.m.. The very special feeling that I got whilst riding that bike was like nothing that I'd ever experienced before. This bike was a truly superior machine and it was very easy to imagine thundering around the Isle of Man course. The exhaust note at speed, was beautiful; it denoted the beautiful tune of the engine, the whole bike was as perfect as it was possible to get. A far cry from a standard production bike of any make. Truly a prince of bikes. I rode back for most of the way at around 90 m.p.h. and at this speed, the engine wasn't taxed and felt as if it would run like that all day.

When I got back, Dennis was filling up the box with fuel, as Frank thought I might be in trouble.

Frank came out and said, "Is everything all right, George? I've got its owner on the phone."

"Tell him that I've never ridden a finer machine and all I've got to do now is to recheck the mixture and have a general look round and then he can have it." Frank grinned and looked hard at me. I'd never been so impressed in my life and it showed. After this, my motorcycling was going to change. I knew that after this, I'd never be content on a production bike again. A week later, Frank and I had just towed in a car that had got stuck on Gulson Road hill; his clutch had gone and I was about to attempt to do it for him to collect later that evening. Normally in the week, this wouldn't have been a problem, but on Saturday, it was very busy and Dennis and I had been discussing the possibility of us having a petrol pump attendant, as sales, both on petrol and oil etc., had gone up considerably over the last six months, making it very difficult to do any work on a Saturday. I'd got the car over the ramp, when I heard the HRD come into our forecourt. I knew it was the HRD, so I went out to him.

"Howdy," said its owner. "How are you?"

"I'm fine," I replied. "But more to the point, how are you?" I asked him.

"A lot better now," he said. "And I've come to fill up and thank you for a lovely job. This bike has never run as good as this. You've got it spot on, and this is for you," And he pushed a five pound tip into my top overall pocket. I was very surprised, for a five pound tip was a very big one. Of course, I thanked him very much, but he said that it was more than worth it to have it running like this.

Dennis obliged by knocking off at 1.30 p.m. instead of 12.30 p.m. This gave me the chance to get on top of the clutch job, which I got finished for 6.00 p.m. At around 3.30 p.m. that same afternoon, a young man and woman came in pushing an International Norton with a Watsonian single seater sidecar on it. The bike had a flat rear tyre and both the man and woman looked about worn out.

"Hope you can help us, pal," said the man. "We've pushed it from Ryton and we've been told that Elliott's is our only hope."

"That's about right. I'll help if you don't mind waiting, as I'm here on my own so I'll have to keep leaving it, but I'll do my best for you." Well, I directed them to a café where they could get a cup of tea, and between serving I got his puncture repaired. He too, gave me a two pound tip, as I'd shortened his drive chain and reset the rear wheel and brake and relined up the chair so it was correct. To round the day off, the man with the Austin 10HP clutch job also gave me three pounds as I had removed his flywheel to reface it, so it wouldn't chew up the new clutch. The clutch of course was much better for it. So I'd got ten pounds in tips. One didn't mind missing one's dinner at this rate, but all the same, I was going to have a go at Frank to get someone to serve and look after the forecourt. As it was then, it must have been costing us money; if I put it like that, just maybe Frank would get us someone, for we sure needed it.

Chapter Nineteen
A Speed Slide and I Turn Salesman

One of the jobs I was doing at this time was the 'jipping up', as Frank put it, of a 125cc Royal Enfield. The bike belonged to the son of one of Elliott's oldest customers and although I knew that Frank didn't want to take it on, because of the time involved, be could hardly refuse without upsetting a good paying customer. So, because it was to be my project, I volunteered to take the bike's cylinder home and alter the porting to suit as it had to be spot on and I would be in a better position at home to do the job. After the work was done and the timing and carburation and exhaust altered to suit, it was a pleasure to test the finished project. The little bike sounded very well; the porting was altered, the compression raised slightly, the mag points had been strengthened to prevent bounce and the carburettor and exhaust system altered to requirements. So off I went to test ride this little bomb. It went very well indeed, but as I had pointed out to Frank, it's all right doing all this until one has to stop in a hurry, and just then I had this problem, as the bike was a good 18 m.p.h. faster and the front brake was far from adequate. After a good test run I knew that its owner was going to be very pleased with it, but I wondered if he would be safe on it. He'd had three incidents before, so what now?

On coming back on the Humber Road, as I took the left hander over the main line railway bridge there was a sharp bang, and the next moment the bike was sliding down the road on our side, as the rear tyre had burst on the nearside as I was cranked over at about 50 m.p.h.. We got away with it well. I got a slightly cut left hand, a bruised left shoulder and leg and the bike hardly got any damage at all. The handlebar was bent slightly, the nearside footrest was bent and that was all, but it shook me up a bit as my head was too close to the kerbstone for comfort. After this slide I had a crash hat supplied by Frank for all future tests.

Back at the garage I soon put the little bike back in shape and fitted a new rear tyre and tube. On examining the burst tyre it soon became apparent why it had burst, for all the way round the inner canvas walls of the tyre were the tell-tale marks of it having been run flat, a point its owner confirmed, for three weeks before, he'd had a puncture and ridden it flat to get it home; hence the damage to the inner canvas walls. What he should have done was to dismount, put the bike in bottom and let it pull itself home. That way he wouldn't have damaged the tyre and, what's more important, I wouldn't have taken a tumble at 50 m.p.h..

Frank of course was relieved that I wasn't hurt, for three reasons. One, out of genuine feeling, two, for insurance reasons; and three, because the following week, Frank and his wife were going on holiday for two weeks and I was to be left in charge, which meant I would spend most of my time in the shop, as I had strict instructions from Frank that I was to pay a lot of attention to the shop on account of the thousands of pounds worth of stock and, in any case, I was always a very good spares salesman. As a mechanic I was able to find spares quickly and give first-class advice on the best way of fitting them. So the next two weeks saw me as the 'gaffer' and believe me, it wasn't easy. I soon found out that one has no friends at the top. However, by and large we all did very well. There were no hiccups in the garage, the work went on very well and we gained two more satisfied customers. As for me in the shop, I sold three motorcycles. Two 350cc Enfield Bullets and a 125cc two-stroke. I also sold six cycles, one being a special order, so I suppose I was quite pleased with myself. They say that a change is as good as a rest and I must admit it did me good to meet more people and get involved in the selling side of the business.

Chapter Twenty
Velocette Love

When I tackled Frank about a petrol attendant-cum-general helper, to my surprise, he agreed it was the right thing to do as one of our customers, who bought a lot of custom to Elliott's, pointed out just how foolhardy it was for mechanics, sometimes in very awkward positions, to have to drop everything just to serve someone with oil or petrol. It wasn't fair on either the mechanic or the customer whose job was continually being put in jeopardy. As a mechanic, I realise only too well that on many jobs a mistake by the mechanic can cause disaster, so a serving person in a garage is, in my opinion, a very necessary asset. Frank too, had been worked very hard in the shop, and in many instances of late, I'd had to serve in the shop to help out, mainly dealing with motorcycles, for, although I say it myself, my knowledge of the bikes made me superior when dealing with spares, as I never had to look in the spares list, for I knew the lot. It was only the price that I had to look up.

Over the next two weeks, Frank must have interviewed at least forty people, and the result was a nice young lady petrol and yard attendant, and a smart chap a few years my senior in the shop. The girl, Pat, hadn't had any experience of this work at all, but then, the man for the shop had been dealing with car spares since he left school. I was to look after Pat, and of course, Frank would work with Ken in the shop, and both started on the same day. Pat was a very bright young lady and it didn't take her very long to become an invaluable asset to us. In fact, I soon started to take even more work on, as I was really gobbling it up and both our new friends were really making their presence felt. One Saturday afternoon, for now there were four of us there – Frank and Ken in the shop and George and Pat in the garage, a chap came in and asked Pat if he could see George, the bike man. When I met him, he told me that Bert Taylor had sent him to me, one of our customers with a Triumph Speed Twin, a bike I looked after for him. He asked me if I'd be interested in buying a Velocette motorcycle, and he went on to say that it was a 350cc MAC model, and that it wasn't a runner and he needed the cash as he'd got his girl in trouble, and in those days, people were much more responsible.

"Not really," I told him, but if he gave me the story and he didn't ask too much, I could be persuaded to have a look at it. Apparently, he'd bought it off his brother for sixty pounds and had taken over the payments, as his brother had got it new from Brandishs and was buying it on the hire-purchase scheme.

It was April time so I told him that I'd come down to see it on my way home, as his address was only a couple of roads away. There was still an hour of daylight left after work, so I could easily view his bike. I was very glad I did see it, for although it wasn't a runner, for it had stood five months, it was under two years old and had only done 12,072 miles. Although it was covered in dust, my trained eye told me that this was a very nice bike.

"What's wrong with it?" I asked.

"I don't know really. A pal of mine came to see it and he says the engine is in trouble."

"That's obvious. Let's have a look and see just what's wrong." After a good look round, it didn't take long to find out why it wouldn't run. The compression was non-existent. It was more than likely that the exhaust valve had gone and I was right. Its owner said that he must have a sale, as his girl was three months pregnant.

"Make me an offer," he said. "It's got to go." I felt sorry for him, but he'd got the girl in trouble, so he was going to have to bear the cost.

"I'll make you a deal," I told him. "My James is in excellent condition. I'll make you a level swap or I'll give you forty pounds and take a chance with the engine."

"I need the cash," he said. "I'll take the forty pounds and many thanks."

"One thing," I said. "Is it all paid for, and if so, can you show me a receipt?"

"It is paid for and yes, I have got the final receipt. I'll get it."

So, for forty pounds, I'd got a very nice Velo. Of course, I collected the bike in the old box, but this time I took it straight home.

When I checked it over that night, I was delighted to see that this machine had never been worked on or messed about with. A big asset when buying a second-hand bike. It cleaned up very well and it had been well-oiled and was in good mechanical condition, except of course for the exhaust valve. But it didn't take long to decoke and replace the valve, and, when done, it fired up on the second kick. Like all velos if right, the engine was mechanically quiet and I knew I'd done right in buying it. Besides, Pat knew a chap who, she said, would love my James to go to work on, so she said that she would see what she could do. This worked out well. The chap came to see it and bought it on the spot, so again I'd done a neat deal as I sold the James for sixty-five pounds. As I have already stated earlier on, I liked velos very much and because of the fabulous ride on HRD, I had made up mind to get myself a superior machine. How, I just didn't know, for the price of a 'Manx' Norton was four to five times more than the average bike.

However, now that I'd got the Velo and it was a lovely bike, here was the chance to do a spot of super tuning. For a start, I needn't strip the Velo out completely, for if I saw my two colleagues at Bernard & Alf Holland's, I could perhaps get a spare Velo cylinder head to tune up, and also a Grand Prix carburettor at the same time, and then, when all was ready, fit them on to the bike and retune as required. Doing it in this way wouldn't render the bike out of action for long periods. Besides, the gas flow and big inlet valve in the head, would take quite a lot of time to complete. It also had to be done very carefully as I'd seen many a cylinder head 'over done', rendering them useless. I must avoid that at all costs, so 'nice and easy does it, every time', as the song goes, and this is what I would do.

The swinging arm adjustable frame and the telescopic forks, made the MAC a very comfortable bike, and its general condition and low mileage made the bike an ideal tuning project. On visiting my two chums at Hearsal Lane, I got the cylinder head, spare cutaway slipper piston, a Grand Prix carburettor and a good megaphone that one could change the rear plates on to alter the back pressure by fitting another plate in its place with different sized holes in. When altering the carburation, in order to get it in tune, the exhaust must be 'rigged up', to suit, and this rule is a must in order to 'get it spot on'. I have known many cases whereby expensive carburettors have been fitted, only to collect other faults, usually 'flat spots', or even a worse performance. Let me make my own interpretation on this: it is as follows, and really, it's only common sense.

For a man and woman to live together as man and wife, both have to be 'tuned in' to the other for perfect harmony, likewise with a carburettor and the complete exhaust system. For perfect results, perfect harmony is required, but then again, common sense isn't so common! Three weeks later, I'd made quite a difference to the MAC. I'd got the head on and the big inlet valve did clear the piston, as all pistons on this model had cutaways for both valves. I'd got the Grand Prix carburettor on and got the mega on and altered the carb cutaways (carburettor throttle slide) and main jets to get it right. It was now that I discovered that the carb was picking up heat from the cylinder head, so it was then found that to stop this, a cooling block with a gasket 'fore and aft', had to be fitted. This again caused another minor problem, for when the cooling block was fitted, after making two longer studs to accommodate it, it was found that the carb wouldn't go on unless the oil tank was lowered, but just to try it, I fitted the carb on minus the air bell-mouth, but I had no intention of leaving it like this, only while I was experimenting with the carburation. To lower the oil tank meant making a different mounting bracket and shortening of both feed and return oil pipes from tank to crankcase into the oil pump. After fitting this of course, as I'd expected, it did alter the carburation, which in turn, sent me up to Alf Holland for a spare exhaust pipe to experiment with, but to be sure, I must first lower the oil tank. With any mechanical problem that requires experimentation, it is critical to deal with only one problem at a time, for to try to deal with two or more, one problem can easily mask another, so 'one problem at a time' is a must.

Well, after a week and a lot of work and many tests, I'd just about got the Velo 'on the mega', but I also now realised that a larger valve overlap was now wanted to complete the tune. To my delight, my mates at Alf Holland's had one. It was the Velo M17 Cam, used on the Thruxton. So, after fitting in the cam, five more tests and other slight alterations were made. The necessary alterations included the shortening or lengthening of the primary exhaust pipe, that is, the pipe from cylinder head to the mega. In this space of time, a small alteration by moving the mega in or out on the primary pipe can make all the difference on full throttle or pulling uphill. Of course, as you can imagine, the mega, or whatever silencer is used, has to be fitted with an adjustable bracket! On test it was very good, but my knowledge of engines told me that now, with this larger overlap, I would more than likely need to alter the ignition timing very slightly. The Velo was already fitted with a spring-loaded advance and retard automatic timing gear, so, by carefully setting up the timing on a timing disc fitted onto the main drive shaft to the clutch, I increased the timing by two degrees and this small adjustment made a big difference in as much as I was able to go back to a plate in the mega with $^3/_8$" holes, which, in turn, enabled me to again alter the cutaway. The result now was very good. The Velo was a real goer and it also sounded very different, so, that coming Sunday I intended, if it was fine, to get up early and take the bike on a good run through the Cotswolds: superb motorcycling country.

On the Friday prior to my Cotswolds run, a chap came in with his TDMG (TD being the model of the MG car), and asked Pat if he could speak with George the mechanic. So Pat fetched me out to him and he told me his problem. He said that two weeks ago his engine suddenly lost power and was also pinking under load. He'd been to two garages but they hadn't been able to solve his problem and a chap at work had recommended me to him.

"It isn't the timing," he said. "The timing was correct when it first started to lose power, then at the second garage, the mechanic there retarded the ignition by about four degrees to prevent pinking uphill. That did help to stop the pinking, but now the engine is running hotter and still lacks power."

"I can see his logic in retarding it," I said, "but if the timing was right in the first place, then the problem lies elsewhere." With that, I reset the timing to the timing marks on the crank pulley, and, turning the rotor arm in the distributor, I noticed that it only partly sprang back.

"Hold your breath," I said. "I think I've found the problem."

"I do hope so," he said.

"I think," I said, "that there is either a broken bob weight spring or that one has come off. Let's take a look," And, sure enough, on taking off the distributor base plate, there lay a broken spring.

"You're in luck," I said. "I think I can fix this right now."

"Will the shop have them?" he asked.

"You're not at Elliott's if we haven't," I answered. "We have the best stock in Coventry." He was all smiles as I came back from the shop with the Lucas packet with the two correct bob weight springs, and as I removed the old pair, I said, "This is going to make a difference as these two weren't the right springs anyway. They're too heavy for this engine."

"Are you sure? As far as I know, they've never been out."

"If Frank says these are right, then they're right," I said. "Besides," I added, "he looked the number up in the Lucas spares catalogue." Well, it only took a few minutes to fit the springs and start up the engine. The engine was now running too fast.

"Someone's been playing around with these carbs" I said. "I think I had better reset them up, as they appear to be a mile out."

"I wish you would," he said, "for it was I that altered the carbs and you're right; I didn't really know what to do." So I removed the air-box and loosened off the connecting throttle rod that linked the two SU carburettors together, having got both carbs drawing in an equal amount. I checked the mixture gland on each carb and both were a couple of flats too rich. Again the revs went up as the mixture evened out and I was able to close both throttle stop screws to the correct tickover of six hundred r.p.m. then, carefully locking up the connecting rod, I checked again to be sure that they were even. They were, so, replacing the air-box, the job was done.

"We'd better try it," I said. "You drive, then you'll feel the difference." We shot off quite quickly, and as soon as it got to top gear, he said, "Its just like another engine. I can hardly believe it. It's terrific!" And he took it up to about 80 m.p.h.. "It's never gone like this. It's bloody marvellous!"

"Only because it's right," I said. "As you can see I haven't got a magic wand."

"You've got a magic touch," he grinned. "And your garage has got another customer." He paid his bill with pleasure and, like the man on the HRD, stuffed a five pound note into my top overall pocket.

"That's for you," he said. "Don't mind me saying this, but you're wasted here. You should have your own place. I work at Jaguar's and there are blokes there that you could eat and they're on about twenty-five pounds a week. Get your own place. You'll never get rich here."

This really did make me think: twenty-five pounds a week – 'Streuth!' I thought, 'I'd be laughing on that sort of wage.' After this, this chap came in for everything, and in two months he'd spent a lot of money at Elliott's. New tyres, service, grease-up, new shocks, and he'd just decided to have two spotlights fitted, so Frank was very pleased with our new customer.

The last time he was in, when he left, he said very quietly to me, "Don't forget, George, you've never seen any rich garage mechanics, unless they're doing it for themselves." Of course, he was right. I was a fool not to have had a go on my own. Looking back, I couldn't have failed, and I should have done something about it. However, this chap was right. I'd have to do something. As it was I was doing 'back yarders' at home. I'd got a car at home at the time for cord oil control rings and a decoke, but it would be a bonus to get a better wage instead of 'living in the garage' as Ivy put it. Besides, two weeks ago, Ivy had given birth to our second son, hence the hard work, for children keep you poor, as only parents would know.

Going back to the Velo, my tuning and alterations had made a real bike of it. It was far better than any other MAC model and faster than the Velo 350cc by a good few m.p.h.. It made it a delightful bike to ride, and it was great to roar off and leave bigger machines behind. I gave Bernard at Alf Holland's a go on it and he was chuffed.

"Its great," he said. "It would take a racing bike to catch that." I valued Bernard's opinion, for both of them had raced bikes and both were first-class riders. The garage must have been doing very well, for that week Bill left us, and this again made me think. Bill had got a job at Rootes Group. His brother-in-law had got him in and he told me that he was going to get another seven pounds a week more and only a forty-hour week. The next week, Frank gave Dennis and I a one pound ten shillings rise, one pound fifty in today's money, but even so, the pay was low for what we did, as a good garage mechanic is really worth his salt.

Chapter Twenty-One

Making a Move to an Old Friend

To make me even more discontent, the shop and garage were both doing very well indeed, as our takings were increasing by the week and Frank's father Mr J W Elliott, had got over his illness and made a good recovery. The following week, Frank's father pulled up in a lovely Alvis saloon. No, it wasn't a new one, but it was a lovely car in grey and it had only had one owner, obviously quite an expensive car. Two weeks later, Frank came in, driving a brand new Phase II Standard Vanguard.

"When's your new car coming in then, George?" joked Dennis Leeson.

"When Nelson gets his eye back," I answered, and again I thought of Dick's words: 'You don't see any rich garage mechanics.' How right he was. I must do something besides back yarders, for I knew that Ivy wasn't happy about it. So, on my next Tuesday afternoon off, I went on my Velo on a tour of all the local car factories to see how the land lay as it were, and also to find out if there were any vacancies. I found out one thing for sure and that was that unless one was a Union member, and had been one for at least twelve months, the factories didn't want to know.

But I wasn't put off, so on my next Tuesday half day, I became a member of the ACU, Amalgamated Engineers' Union, a must, if I was ever to get into a car factory. I realised of course, that it would be at least twelve months before I could even apply, but as I was quite capable of providing adequate funds for my family, with help from my back yarders, as long as my health held up, I wasn't too worried. The next week I sold our Morris 8HP for now we needed a bigger car, at least a four seater, for now we had my father living with us. In the meantime I intended to keep my eyes open for a suitable car. I'd made a good profit on the sale of the Morris as it was in lovely condition everywhere. It was a good goer and because of my tuning did a good 45-50 m.p.g. and the engine used no oil. A few weeks later, about thirty minutes before I knocked off one night, Ivy rang to remind me to call in at the chemist's for a few things for the baby. I had the list with me, but as she said, if it had been parts for a motorcycle I wouldn't have needed reminding – need I say more!

In the chemist, after I'd got the baby's things, Mr Addy, the owner, came out from the back room. He now owned Elliott's old Armstrong.

"I thought it was you," he said. "You're just the man I wanted to see, as I'm in a spot of bother with the Armstrong."

"Not my old pal," I said.

"The very same," he said. "I've got gearbox trouble."

"That's most unusual, who's been mucking it up?" I'd hit the nail squarely on the head.

"You're dead right. It was slipping on take-off and I foolishly let a chap look at it for me. Now I daren't take it out, as he reckons the bands have burnt out."

"Okay, I'll come round on Tuesday afternoon and bring some tools with me. Privately that is. Not a garage job."

"That's what I was hoping you would say," said Mr Addy. "I did ring up Armstrong Service Depot and they told me that if the bands were gone I'd be looking at a £200 bill."

"Don't worry," I answered. "If they're gone, I'll take the box out and replace them. I would say about seventy pounds at the most, but let's check it out first. The bands run on six pints of oil, so if the oil is topped up, we just might be on a winner."

"That's very good to know. You see I couldn't sell it like that, and I've been offered a lovely Hillman Minx for two hundred and fifty pounds, but who wants a big old car like that anyway!"

"I would have it if the price was right," I said. Mr Addy stopped what he was doing and said,

"Do you know, I think that would suit me better? I'd rather have the Minx. It's smaller, more modern and a lot cheaper to run. Come and see what you can do, then we'll review it."

I think I told Ivy that I was going up to Alf Holland's when I left work on the Tuesday, but of course, with a load of tools in my rucksack, I went round to Mr Addy's to check out the Armstrong's gearbox. Well, it didn't take me very long to remove the front bench type seat and lift the six-ply thick floorboards out. Even the high-quality carpets were held down with big all-brass press studs. On taking off the gearbox lid, I had a good sniff, because if the bands had burnt, then I would have smelt the burning. The same smell occurs when a clutch burns out, but no smell was detectable and in any case, the oil level on the dipstick showed it to be more than half full, most unlikely, therefore, to find any burnt-out bands, for, with plenty of oil in the box, they would slip and not burn. It was then that I found that two of the band adjusting pins had their lock nuts loose. Just then, Mr Addy arrived.

"Sorry I had to leave you to it," he said. "There were a couple of prescriptions I had to make up. What's the verdict?"

"Good, I hope," I replied. "It looks as if its bottom and second have been slipping."

"So that's why it wouldn't drive out into the road. Does it need new bands?"

"I don't think so, but if you've got a torch I could borrow, I can make certain." He came back with a big powerful torch. "Just the job. I'll soon see with that." I could now see that they were all okay. All I had to do was to readjust all the bands and check the lock nuts. The action on the band pedal was consistent so I didn't expect any more trouble. When it was all back, I started it up and took it round the block to try all the gears and every one was just like it used to be. Mr Addy was delighted. "I now owe you for three jobs," he said.

"What about giving me fifty pounds and we'll call it quits and the Armstrong's yours?" I was flabbergasted, but he meant it and the fifty pounds would get him his Minx.

"You can't be serious," was the first thing I said.

"Its like this," he said. "I had a phone call today, asking me to let them know by tomorrow night if I want the Minx or not. You see, I've kept them on the hook for nearly two weeks and I know that there is someone else interested. By letting you have this, it means I can have the Minx for sure." Of course, I thanked him very much and told him I would collect it on Sunday morning. This suited him fine, for, like me, he was kept very busy on Saturdays.

When Sunday arrived, I told Ivy that I had a little job to do that morning, but it wouldn't take long.

"Not another one today," is all she said, but I knew that today, she was in for a nice surprise.

'Who knows?' I thought. 'Just maybe my luck is changing,' And although it took a little time to develop, it did definitely get better. I went on my cycle to collect the car, for it had a very tough thick rear body carrier, that let down at the rear. Suitcases etc., were slid under the back seat, but the lid or carrier was very strong as I'd had many a big load on it, including one or two motorcycle. It was no trouble to tie my cycle on it and I got some petrol on the way home, as it was now off ration and getting better in grading. I also blew up all the tyres at the same time, then drove the old car back home. As I went through the double gates in the drive, Ivy saw the Armstrong outside.

"What's that doing here?" she asked. "You're not working on that today, are you?"

"No way," I said. "It's ours. I'm going to take you all out in it after dinner, but first I must check all the oils." Ivy's face was a picture.

"Its ours!" she echoed.

"Ours," I said. "And it's all paid for." My family were delighted. I remember my father sitting in the rear seat and fully stretching out his legs, saying,

"This is something like a car. This is quality. I can see why old man Elliott hung on to this. You want to do the same." And indeed, after completing a few jobs on it, we all enjoyed it very much and the lads had enough room in it to sleep on a long journey, the dog as well.

Chapter Twenty-Two
All Because the Lady Had Nice Legs

The work at Elliott's was piling up. Dennis and I were both working flat out, but because Bill had gone, we just couldn't cope. I was doing as many cars as I was bikes, for it was only I who worked on cars – Dennis was solely a bike man. Frank mainly didn't worry us, for he knew he could trust both of us, but there were occasions when he'd taken on too much work to be done as promised, which caused him to try and get over it by putting both of us onto the same job in order to get it finished in time. Although this next incident doesn't deal with bikes, it is well worth a mention as far as garage work goes.

Frank could see that it was impossible to go on as we were. We now had a three-week waiting list for cars and a month's waiting list for bikes. Because of emergencies like punctures and minor breakdowns, the wait to get a big job done was increasing. I could talk to Frank, so I convinced him to get a good car mechanic as I told him that people would go elsewhere if our service didn't improve. Frank knew I was right, so two weeks later a new man started. I'll give him the fictitious name of 'Romeo' for reasons which will become obvious later. Romeo was a very good car man and he knew his job. Both Dennis and I got on very well with him and it wasn't too long after he started that we got ourselves sorted out into a steady working rhythm again. I was now doing more bikes than cars which suited me fine. Just prior to us getting sorted, a couple came in to have a sports sidecar fitted to their 600cc Panther motorcycle while they waited, as they didn't live in Coventry. We were very busy that day and all three of us had got jobs to go out to that evening, so Frank, not wishing to lose a good sale, doubled up Dennis and I to fit the sidecar. We soon got stuck in, but about halfway through, Frank came dashing down to say that one of our main customers was stuck with their delivery van. The van was driven by a woman, a married lady and, I might add, a very attractive one. Our new man had by now earned the name Romeo, as the week before he quickly left the car he was working on to serve an attractive female who had come in for paraffin. Normally Pat would have served her but she was busy serving petrol at the time. He knew one of us would have to serve her and asked for the privilege.

"My word," said Romeo, "we don't often get a beauty like you to deal with," and he slipped his arm round her waist.

"You don't waste any time," she remarked. "Why do they call you Romeo?" Dennis and I burst out laughing, then Romeo, to our surprise, said,

"You're so tasty I feel like giving you a kiss,"

"What are you waiting for?" said this attractive female, and the next moment a passionate embrace was taking place, just as Frank came into the garage! Romeo didn't see Frank as he had his back to him and he didn't hear him either as a noisy van was pulling out after filling up with petrol. Frank, seeing what was going on, stopped dead, spun round and went straight back. After the lady had gone, Dennis told Romeo that Frank had seen him.

"You'd better say you know her," I said. "I can't see Frank letting that go."

"He won't bother," said Romeo.

"I wouldn't bet on it," I replied, as Frank came back into the garage.

"What was the big love scene?" asked Frank.

"Oh that," replied Romeo. "I knew her from old. I used to go out with her," he lied.

"All right, but don't make a habit of. It will give us a bad name," said Frank.

Now, with the emergency, and Dennis and I tied up on the sidecar job, it was natural for Frank to get Romeo to go.

"Better take my car," said Frank. "And I'll give you a coil, a set of points, plugs and a condenser. Don't forget your tools. The driver said the van wouldn't start after a delivery, so I think it could be ignition." With that, off went Romeo, but not before Frank had told him to behave, as she was a married lady.

"Blimey, that's risky," said Dennis after Frank had gone up to the shop. "He can't take his eyes off her when she comes in."

"Don't worry about that," I replied.

"She won't stand for any hanky-panky. She'll belt him if he tries anything."

"I hope you're right," said Dennis. A short time later we had got the new chair fitted and all tracked up and Frank came down with the owners to see it. I gave him some instructions as to dos and don'ts, as he had only ridden a combo once before. They had only just left, when down came Frank again, but this time he was looking very angry.

"Get the box out," he said. "And both of you go and get them sorted out, as the driver has turned the van over and Romeo was a passenger. I bet the fool made a grab for her." He was dead right, for when we got there the van was on its side on a grassy slope and Romeo was waiting for us, but no driver.

"What's happened to the driver?" I asked.

"Oh, the police pulled up and they've given her a lift home. She's not hurt but very shook up."

"So's Frank," I said. "What happened?"

"Well," said Romeo, "I examined the van and found that the points were burnt so fitted the new ones and changed the condenser and it started a treat. I got the driver to take me to the island and back to be sure it was okay. On the way back I happened to remark what a lovely pair of legs she had and honestly, all I did was run my hand up the back of her leg and she panicked, hit the kerb, and over went the van."

"You'd better be honest and tell Frank the same," I said, "because you can bet your life that the driver will." When I looked inside the van a real mess met my eyes, as about eighty per cent of its load was ruined. There were all fancy cakes and eight wedding cakes in with them. The only ones that escaped were rock cakes and doughnuts, and we all got enough free cakes to supply our families for many days to come. But it proved fatal for Romeo, for a week later he had gone, after a very long discussion with Frank in private. After he'd left Frank told us that the lady van driver had also spoken up for the benefit of Pat, our petrol attendant, for, unknown to Dennis and I, he had mauled Pat on two occasions and she hadn't spoken out because she could have got him sacked.

"Bloody hell," said my pal Dennis, "and all because the lady had nice legs," And we both had a good laugh. We got the van repaired in record time and the boss of the firm who owned it came to thank us all and to say what good service we gave and how happy their two drivers were with us, as they had two vans of the same type. He also said that from now we would all get half a dozen different cakes free each week, a gesture which was very much appreciated by all.

Chapter Twenty-Three

I Meet the MOV

One day, Frank was studying my Velo at the top of the garage forecourt.

"Blimey, George," he remarked, "it would cost a bomb to have a job like that done. I bet it goes like hell. I can always tell when it's you coming up Gulson Road, it sounds beautiful."

"It is beautiful," I said. "I like it even better than the old Rudge, as this one is lovely to ride and very safe." Frank went back into the shop shaking his head, and I got the impression that he must be thinking that I was mad to go to all that trouble. But let me say this: if it's results you're after, or perfection, then time and trouble don't even come into it, and if you really know what you're doing, then you can save yourself pounds. Frank's main aim of course, was profit, whereas my main aim was perfection, so as I said, time and trouble don't even come into it. But on doing this job on my Velo it really got me thinking that if I was to get another bike, a 350 OHC Velo would be ideal, then I could strip it all out, frame and forks included, and tailor make myself a real road racer. I would have something to be proud of then, and the more I thought about it, the keener I got. So that was my next move. Look out for a suitable bike to do the job.

It was now winter again, but with a clothesline wrapped round my rear tyre and rim, being interlaced between the spokes and with only fourteen pounds in the front tyre and sixteen pounds in the rear and what with my trial-riding ability, I got by most cars in the snow and ice and made quite a few other bikers look as I went by them at sometimes three times their speed. I only had one accident and that was when I was going along a main road and on my left, about forty yards further down was a road at a ninety-degree angle to the road I was on. It had been snowing on and off for a week or more and the road had about a three or four inch depth of snow on it, hence my rear tyre pressure and the clothesline round my rear tyre and rim. As I approached this junction and as there was a 'halt' sign, the car at the front of the junction pulled out to try to turn right, but his tyres wouldn't grip and there he was with rear wheels spinning completely in my path, the same as the old Rover incident, when I was on my old Beezer. On the pavement coming up towards me and before the junction were two old ladies, so I couldn't go there and, coming up on the other side of the road were a number of cars close together, so I couldn't go there either. On my left was the road junction, but it would have been fatal to try to take that as the ice was too bad, and in any case, I was doing about thirty miles an hour, as I had no other traffic in front of me. The only option left was to try to stop, but it was all but impossible in the distance on ice and snow. I pumped the brakes like mad and got the speed down very well considering the conditions. At the last moment, to avoid a crash, I locked up my rear brake and brought the bike sideways on with the car, then, steering hard into the slide trials fashion, I stopped as my right foot hit his offside front door. I won't bore you with any details, I'll just say that at first, he was going to knock my block off, so I gave him the chance which he refused. Then he was going to sue me so I just said,

"Just get on with it the and the best of luck, but don't forget, it was you who came out on me."

"What about my door?" he yelled.

"It'll remind you not to be so stupid in future," I yelled back and pulled away, with snow shooting up from my rear tyre. We had of course exchanged names and addresses, but I didn't hear any more; after all, he came out on me.

The rush of work had cooled off during the winter, even so, we still had plenty coming in from our regular customers and breakdowns etc., and as usual, the bad weather had brought us in quite a few busted bikes, and if anything, even more than usual this year. As far as Dennis and I were concerned, the loss of Romeo was a bigger load for us but Frank seemed to think that because we had Pat, who was a very good serving girl, we should manage okay, but really, we were now back to square one. I told Dennis I'd have another go at Frank. After all, we didn't want a situation like last time, but this time, when I tackled Frank, he didn't seem too keen. He said he'd think about it and see what he could come up with. In the meantime work was coming in quite quickly and it merited another car mechanic. One week Pat was away with flu, so Den and I served in the yard on alternate days. That way we got a better chance to sort our work load out and leave the bigger jobs for the day we weren't serving. In a way this turned out just right for me; it happened like this. We were just about to lock up on the Friday night when Ted from Allen's Cash Stores, one of our regulars, came roaring in in his car.

"Glad I was in time," said Ted, as he saw the bunch of keys in my hand. "Fill it up please and will you get me a silencer and tailpipe for the car, it sounds like a lorry."

"Your wish is our pleasure," I answered. "Is your car a 1953?"

"It is," he answered and, coming up to me as I was filling his tank said, "Is that your Velo up there?" pointing to my bike.

When I told him that it was, he said, "I've got a Velo in my back garden. It belongs to my mate and it's just been standing there for nearly twelve months now. What I've done, I've used a lot of very thick cardboard from the shop and made a huge cardboard garage out of it. The roof consists of several sheets all taped up about four sheets thick. I've asked Frank to call and see it, but as usual, he's far too busy. Besides," and he dug me in the ribs with his elbow as he said it, "I'd rather you had it. Frank would only get you to do it up for him to sell. Come round and see it. It just might do you a good turn." After agreeing not to tell Frank, as he could sell it to him if I wasn't interested, and seeing as he only lived a couple of miles from the garage, I agreed to go and see it after work.

As it happened, Frank was in a hurry to close up that night as it was his wife's birthday and he was taking her out for a candlelit dinner.

"I'm always interested in the afters!" said Dennis.

Pat looked up at him and said, "Men!" and stormed off into the inner office for some change. When I got to Ted's house he'd left his two front gates open for me, and his wife was getting some crockery out of the boot of the car.

"That's a lovely bike," she said. "I'm afraid the one Ted has doesn't shine like that."

"Don't worry, neither did this one when I saw it. This was a derelict bike as well."

"That's hard to believe, looking at that," she said. "I hope you take this one, as Ted wants it out of the way. We want to have the garden landscaped this year."

"I'll go and have a look," I replied. Just then Ted appeared from round the back.

"Come round and have a look. I've just uncovered it and I don't think it's too bad." As soon as I saw it, I knew that it wasn't a 350 Cammy.

"Its a 250 MOV," I said. "But as you say, Ted, it doesn't look too bad." And indeed, it wasn't; taking into consideration that it hadn't been moved from this spot for eleven months, it was in a good state of preservation. The model MOV first came out in 1933 and it hadn't changed a lot over the years. This one was 1947 vintage and, like the model before it, had a solid frame and girder forks, and although the frame was only a single tube frame, the tubes were strong and under the crankcase was a sort of ridged triangular platform as a protection and strengthener for the crankcase. The rear wheel was a quick detachable type, with three heavy bolts fixing the actual wheel to the inside of the brake assembly. The wheel was easily removed by the removal of these three bolts and the steel bearing spindle that took the whole weight and went across the rear frame end with distance pieces at either and between inner frame and wheel for correct alignment. The rear end of the guard was hinged for easy access. The forks were the famous Velo girders, one of the best pairs of forks I ever rode, and many riders like myself swore by them and would much rather ride with them than with telescopic forks. I was one of them. You see, you could rig the fork to suit the rider. The robust 248cc high-cam overhead valve pushrod was without a doubt one of the finest 250 engines our island, or for that matter, anywhere else, had ever seen. The bore was exactly the same as the MAC. The extra ccs on the MAC were collected by a longer con-rod and bore to increase the cc to 350, the head and crankcase too were of course bigger on the 350, making it a taller engine. The timing chest was the same in principle, but more advanced on the MAC and both models had those lovely helical silent gears.

I dragged the bike out and rested it on its nearside propstand. I looked at it long and hard, noticing as I did so that it had only covered 2,002 miles from new. There was a GB plate on the rear guard and turning to Ted I said,

"It doesn't look as if it's done enough miles to have gone on the continent."

"He did a run to Le Mans in France," said Ted. "And when he got back it wasn't long after that he was forced to change his digs, only to be left with nowhere to put it, and that's how it ended up here. I hadn't got room in the garage, hence my cardboard 'garage'."

"And a jolly fine job it's done too," I replied.

"Thank you," said Ted. "It isn't too bad is it?" And indeed it wasn't, for even the tyres were both very good and were still half inflated. The battery, of course, was flat, but even so, there weren't any signs of corrosion from the positive terminal or on the casing.

"Just hang on, Ted, I'll get my tools. I want to take the plug out." So I got the tools I carried out from the tool box on my MAC. Taking out the plug, I noticed that the colour was light brown, just about perfect. Then I released the sprung loaded oil tank cap and looked into the oil tank. The oil was quite clean, so, slipping my screwdriver into the oil, I took it out and allowed the oil to run into the cylinder. I then turned the engine over briskly with the kick-starter and within thirty seconds or so, oil was pumping back into the oil tank. Putting back the plug and replacing the lead I turned to Ted and said,

"Ted, it's lovely. So if your mate doesn't ask too much I'll have it as I intend to make a special out of it."

"Leave it to me," replied Ted. "I want it out of the way and my mate has just bought a new Rover car, so I know he'll be pleased to let it go."

Putting the bike back I covered it as I'd found it, but at that moment I felt elated. Another low mileage Velo, what a stroke of luck! This machine was dead right for what I had in mind. Okay, it was only a 250, but it was low, sleek, and the MOV engine had done wonders on the racing circuit. A chap my own age had converted one into a racing special that shook 'em all. He called it the 'Ellbee Special' and his name was Les Diener, which gave me a boost of encouragement to do it for myself.

"I'll see my mate for you tomorrow," said Ted, "Then I can let you know."

"That could work about right, as I get Tuesday afternoon off, so it's possible that if we strike a deal I could come and collect it then."

"That would be fine and when can you do my exhaust pipe?" I arranged to do his exhaust the following afternoon. Ted was pleased about this. The following day I fitted his exhaust while he waited, also a set of plugs and two new wiper blades so that he was all set up.

As he went, Ted said, "I'll see my mate over the weekend and I'll either call round or ring you up on Monday." Monday came and almost went with no phone call or any sign of Ted. Then, again as I was locking up, Ted skidded to a halt just outside the forecourt.

"I've seen him," said Ted, and, putting his hand into his inside pocket, he brought out a sheet of paper with the address and phone number on. "He'll be in after 7.30 p.m." said Ted. "Ring him if you can't go," And with a wave he was off. When I went in and hung the keys up, Frank said,

"What was Ted doing here at this time? He isn't in any trouble is he?"

"No, his car's fine. He came to see me, as I hope that his mate will do me a good deal with the Velo he left in Ted's garden."

"Well I'll be damned!" remarked Frank. "I was thinking about buying that!" Dennis, who of course knew all that was going on said,

"I didn't know you were taking up motorcycling again, Frank. I should have thought you would have ridden an Enfield."

"Not to ride," said Frank scornfully. "For you two to do it up in your spare moments," answered Frank.

"Blimey!" remarked Dennis, "It would be a vintage in that case." Frank glared hard at Dennis, but Dennis was too poker-faced to give anything away. As for me, I was grinning to myself as I was now feeling sure of making a deal.

So, at 7.30 p.m., I nipped round to see this man on my flying Velo. As I got to his digs, for he lived in a large flat, the door opened and to my surprise the Velo's owner was a police sergeant.

"Come in, lad," he said. "That's a lovely Velo you've come on. Is it yours?" When I told him that it was, he said, "Well now, the reason I've never sold the bike is because as a policeman I just couldn't let any idiot have it, as it will have to be stripped. It's stood nearly twelve months and the tyres and the electrics would probably need replacing. In fact the whole machine needs a loving touch by someone like you."

"You are more than likely right, so if I have it, you can come and see it stripped."

"Good lad," said the sergeant. "Here are all the papers. If you would like it, how does twenty pounds strike you?" I was delighted. I'd expected to pay at least thirty pounds, but only twenty was a gift very well appreciated.

"That suits me fine," I said and handed over the cash. The sergeant wrote out a receipt and said he'd let Ted know that he could let me have it. On Tuesday morning Ted rang up to say that I could pick it up after 2.00 p.m. He wouldn't be there, but his wife would, so I could go and help myself.

Chapter Twenty-Four

The MOV Comes Home

The next day, Tuesday, my eldest son Brian had to go to the dentist in the afternoon, so I had my youngest son with me to fetch the MOV in the Armstrong. Bob was very excited about this, but his mum wasn't very happy about it at the time.

"Don't let him out of your sight," she said. "And please don't let him walk into the road."

"Don't worry, Ted has a bigger drive than we have. I can back the car in and there's plenty of room at the back to be able to load it up."

"Very well, but look after him," Ivy replied. Bob was only three and a half years old and he was thrilled to be able to go on a job with his dad, and in the car as well. We arrived at Ted's and Bob stayed in the car while I opened up the big double gates. The Armstrong was a big car, about the size of a two-litre Granada, certainly higher and perhaps a bit longer. Even so there was a good two feet of drive on either side of the car as it passed through the gates, as Ted had it extra wide to get his large van in. I knocked on the door to let Ted's wife know we were there, as she hadn't seen or heard the Armstrong come in. The old car still ran very quietly; having a silencer four and a half feet long had a lot to do with it, I suppose. Ted's wife was delighted to see young Bob and immediately went to get him a chocolate biscuit.

When we went round to the bike I was pleasantly surprised, for Ted had done us proud. He'd not only got the bike on the path for us, but had washed it in shampoo and blown up the tyres as well. The bike had come up very well and Ted's wife told me that on the last night, Ted had got carried away cleaning up the bike. He'd even used chrome cleaner on the exhaust and levers. I could hardly believe it.

"How ever are you taking it home in that?" she asked. "It's far too big to go inside!" I laughed and let down the very heavy luggage grid that also sealed up the boot.

"On that and a few bits on the sacks inside the car." I opened the rear door for her to see,

"Oh, it's lovely!" she cried. "Gosh, it's like a little room and how lovely and clean."

"Yes, it is nice," I said. "And Ivy, my wife, keeps the inside like she does the house. I'm responsible for the rest."

"What a lovely old car," she said, so I invited her to sit inside. She was amazed at the room and when I pulled out the two walnut tables that were folded up in the rear of the front seat, she looked really amazed and liked the old car very much.

"Right, our Bob," said I, "this is where we get cracking." Of course I was used to mauling big bikes around, so I didn't anticipate too much trouble with this one. Even so, I had to remove a few bits in order to get it on.

The front guard was a heavy valanced one, so that had to come off to even get the front end on the platform, so I took off all the bits it was necessary to. I even removed the front wheel and guard, then dropped back the wheel, the handlebars, silence offside footrest and offside tool box so as not to damage the car. To be sure, I fixed up two large sheets of the cardboard that had covered the Velo and fixed them across the back of the car with masking tape. The bike could now be lifted up. With young Bob watching my every move, I wheeled the bike up to the side of the platform and it didn't take a lot of effort to lift the front wheel on to the carrier. I'd tightened up the steering clamper for this very purpose. Then, with the steering straight ahead, it was an easy matter to lift up the rear of the bike and gently roll it on.

"There it is, no trouble at all," I said, but as I spoke, I could see that, like the bikes before that had been up there, the front wheel had to come out, as the length of the bike with both wheels in would make it too dangerous in traffic. I always kept two large wooden blocks in the boot, useful tools for any car, but in particular a car used for breakdowns etc., or, like this one, for carrying bikes. So it was no bother for young Bob to just push the block (with a screwdriver) under the crankcase frame cradle as I lifted up the front of the bike. With the front wheel out, I lifted up the bike by the forks and when Bob had removed the block, I lowered it onto a thick piece of cardboard that I'd cut for the job. All that remained now was to centralise the bike on the carrier and well and truly rope it tight.

The bike never moved on the way home and I'd been most careful in covering up the rear seat of the car to protect it from the parts that I'd placed there. Getting the Velo off was of course a reversed procedure which didn't take me long to get done. When Ivy arrived with Brian (minus two teeth), Bob and I were enjoying ourselves in the garage. Bob was sitting on the bike, while I was busy taking parts off it when Ivy came in. She hardly noticed the bike, she was more interested in the state our Bob was in.

"Look at your son, you disgusting man," she said. "He looks like a chimney sweep. Bob, go inside at once, you must have a bath." But Bob was enjoying himself and didn't want to go in, he loved all this. However, after I'd taken Bob in and told Brian how good he was, I got down to some serious stripping, but for now, I didn't intend to take the engine out, but I had it stripped as far as the crankcase for examination. It was, as the mileage showed, like brand new, so for now, and in order to check the bike over properly, I'd wash all the parts I'd taken off in paraffin, decoke it and get it on the road and use it for a bit and see what it was like. In any case, I wanted a word with my two chums in Hearsall Lane and see just what they had got that I could make use of. Back at work the next day, Ted rang to say that as I was a mechanic his mate had decided to leave me to it as he said that by the look and sound of my MAC he didn't need to bother. The battery, when topped up, charged with no problems and by Friday night, I was ready to put the cylinder head back on. Everything had cleaned up like new and there was no wear anywhere. The drop of stale fuel in the tank had, with my paraffin, helped to wash off all the parts. The valves only took minutes to grind in and the carbon, being dry, just flaked off. I'd blended in the induction while the head was stripped and even that took very little effort. Altogether it was in even better condition than the MAC was and sitting astride this lovely low machine, even now I could see that it was indeed an ideal bike to do a conversion on.

Using the bike at this stage would get me used to it; after all, I needed to know just what it was like in its standard form, and also make a few notes. This was essential on any project, for without notes, it isn't long before one is probing in the dark. Ivy was happy about the bike and what I'd paid for it. She also agreed that it would be better to use it as it was for a week or two, but her reason wasn't quite the same as mine. I'd got several jobs coming in over the next few weeks, and she didn't like me to get too tied up.

'So, I've got a few jobs coming in,' I thought. 'It won't be long now, and I'll have been in the AEU for twelve months.' I looked on my workbench for my notebook and flicked through the pages. In two months' time. The date was there but now I had a real reason to make a move. I loved the old garage and Frank was like a brother, but my latest reason was by far the one that would be sure to make me move, because Ivy was pregnant for the third and last time, so now I really must get organised and get everything sorted out.

I'd got a Tiger Cub with big end and mains to do at the weekend, a common fault on this bike if thick oil or the ignition were too far advanced, the high compression on this model didn't take long to do the damage. I also had a set of exhaust valves and a decoke on a Morris 10HP car. I was sure my back yarders would get us through, but Ivy was right: I shouldn't have to do this. My back yarders paid off, the motorcycle chap paid me three pounds more than I charged and the Morris owner was very pleased also, for I had to replace the timing chain too, making the engine much more lively. He too gave me five pounds over what I charged him, so at least I was holding my own.

The MOV, when I'd finished it, started up second kick and as I had expected, the engine sounded like a new one. The baffles in the silencer had gone, probably another reason why its last owner was reluctant to run it any longer. However, when Ivy heard it, she said,

"You'd better fix that before you use it, or you'll get pinched."

"I'll go and get one tomorrow," I said. The next day, Mr Addy came in for petrol, and while Pat was filling his tank, came in to see me.

"I'd be very pleased if you would drop in to see me after work," he said. "I've got a problem on the car and I'd like your advice."

"Will do," I said, "for I feel that I still owe you." At Mr Addy's he asked me if I could have a look at his engine as it wasn't pulling too well and when it was hot, it made a funny noise. On examining his engine it didn't take long for me to find the trouble. There was an exhaust valve gone, causing a loss of power, high fuel consumption and yes, it would make a funny noise when hot. Also, I told him, his engine would be running too hot.

"Oh dear," he said, "and in two weeks' time we are going to my mother-in-law's at Bournemouth. I hope we don't have to go by train."

"Don't worry," I told him. "I owe you as it is, so the least I can do is do the job for you, but I want to check something first." And, pulling out an old carpet from under his garage bench, I opened it out to lie on and look under the car.

"Ah, here's the real trouble. This looks to me like a Morris 8HP silencer and tailpipe. You've had back pressure, so the exhaust valves have been running too hot. This is the culprit," I said, tapping the silencer.

"What can you do about it?" he asked.

"All right, come up on Monday night, tomorrow I'll order you a silencer and tailpipe. You can pick it up in the car and come up to my house, then I will take you back home and I'll get your car done as soon as possible." After this lot had all been sorted out, Mr Addy had got a good motor that he was really pleased with, and I had just about got my back yarders all but finished. The MOV was a very nice bike and by now, I was quite used to it. It was a good goer and I felt sure with all the inquiries I'd made that my conversion would be well worthwhile. The following Tuesday I intended to go and find out how things stood at the factories. Bill, our old car mechanic, came in the week before, and he was very pleased he'd made the move and hardly got dirty like he did at the garage. I knew that I must go and see what I could find. On the Tuesday, Ivy knew I was a bit down in the mouth about it, for she said,

"I know you don't really want to leave the garage but it'll be for the best. You'll be working in far better conditions and getting a lot better pay. Think of this," she added, and patted her tummy.

"I'll do my level best," I said and shot away on the MAC.

I'd been to Armstrongs and Coventry Climax and both had taken my name and address, but there was nothing at the moment, then I remembered Standard Triumph. It was worth a try.

Chapter Twenty-Five
A Great Opportunity

On calling in at the labour office at the Standard Triumph Motor Company and being full of determination, I was hoping that the third time would be lucky. The gateman let me into the gatehouse and was at once attracted to my Velo.

"What a smashing bike. I like bikes and that one looks a cracker,"

"It is," I said, "and I'm hoping to find a cracking job to go with it."

"What job are you after?" he asked.

"Mechanic," I answered.

"They're after a mechanic right now, but I think they're after someone a bit special."

"That someone must be me," I answered.

"I'll go and see," he said.

'That's promising,' I thought, so into the labour office I went. The girl at the desk fetched the labour manager who in turn said that if I answered his questions satisfactorily, it was just possible I stood a chance.

"Fire away," I said. "I need a good job right now."

"I like your attitude," he replied. "So here goes." He then asked me how long I had been a mechanic, where I now worked, how long I had been there, why I wanted to leave, then finally, could I tune an engine with four carburettors?

"No problem at all," I answered.

"Right, young man, come with me," And he led me into a small office at the back and said, "If you are willing to answer all these questions, there's just a chance you could get a top job. It's for a competition mechanic with Ken Richardson and his 'gang'. Do you still want to have a go?"

"You bet I do! This is just the type of job I'd love to get. I'll answer any questions they ask."

"Well done, lad, and all the best," And he handed me a questionnaire and a dozen lined sheets of paper.

"Sit there," he said. "Now put your name and address on top and number each answer to the question and the best of luck," Then, looking at his watch said, "I'll see you at about 5.00 p.m., three hours from now."

I just ran my eye over the questions and then set about answering them in the order they were written. I'd completed the lot in two and a half hours, then, checking through again, I took them to the labour manager. He looked down the questions and he could see that I'd answered the lot, as I'd ticked them all off.

"That's very good," he said. "And a very good time, too. Quite a few blokes have had a go but I don't think any one has completed the lot. You could just get it. If you do, you'll be notified by post." I collected my bike at the gatehouse and the gateman was very keen to hear it run.

"I've not seen a Velo like this," he said. "Is it a special?"

"I suppose it is," I said. "I've done it myself, mind," And with that I kicked it up and he was keener than ever.

"That's a lovely bike. I bet you would get a good price for that." On the way home, I felt great as I knew I'd got the answers right, including two questions that had obviously been dropped in as red herrings. I was smiling to myself, as I'd answered the red herring questions in the same impossible way that the questions referred to. I chuckled to myself, for I was as wise as the one who set the questions, so I could only hope for the best.

Back home I shot up Balliol Road where I lived. I felt good so I rode good.

"Wherever have you been?" Ivy asked. "You've been gone five hours."

"I know I have," I said, "but it could just be worth it," And I told her my story.

"Oh, I do hope you get it!" Ivy said. "A competition mechanic is right up your street."

"Well, it's the only job with a written exam and I answered the lot, so now we can only wait and see." In the next two weeks, I stripped out the MOV, and I'd now got a plan of campaign. I'd do the engine first, for I knew that part best and also, I'd by now collected quite a few useful tuning bits. After two weeks, Ivy and I watched the post daily and by Wednesday of the third week, my hopes had sunk again.

"Don't worry, love. I'll have a go at Jags next week. I'll get something if I try every week." The next day, I got home late, for as I was locking up, a woman had a puncture right near the garage, so naturally came over for help. Well, we never refused to help anyone, so I whipped the wheel off, repaired the puncture and whipped the wheel back on again.

I even oiled the studs. The lady was very pleased and gave me a 2/6d tip. I came roaring up our road as usual, and, as I got to our house, Ivy opened the double gates to let me in, which was most unusual. As I shut the engine off, Ivy, with a big grin and her eyes really shining, stood in front of me and said,

"Darling, you've done it, you've got the job!" I'd got the job. It made me feel really queer; I'd got the job. "You are to report at the Allesley Works on the 13th June at 8.00 a.m. with all your tools. I'm sorry I opened it," she said, "but I couldn't wait," And she brought from behind her back the letter from the Competition Department, Standard Triumph. I read the letter for myself and it was as Ivy had said, and it went on to say that a forty-hour week would bring in a drawn wage of just over twenty pounds. Overtime, of which there would be plenty, was paid at time and a third, Sundays, when required, earned you double time, and all Continental work paid time and a half plus expenses. The average wage on Competition over the last twelve months was twenty-five pounds plus, the letter was signed 'Ken Richardson, Competition Manager'. I read it all again, and I tell you, I was almost in tears.

"Streuth," I said, "I've got it. Frank will do his nut."

"Darling, I don't care what he does, you're dead right for this job and I want you to take it. Don't work tonight. Have a rest and watch TV a bit, then you can tell Frank in the morning and I should take this letter with you." So I stopped in and watched telly, not half as interesting as tuning or working on a bike, I thought, so at about 11.00 p.m. I said to Ivy,

"I haven't got over the shock yet. I've still left the Velo out," And believe me, my mind was still in a whirl.

The next morning, I opened up the garage as usual and, like any other morning, both the garage and the shop were functioning before Frank, Pat or Ken arrived, for since Dennis had got the job sorted out, I used to put the float into both cash registers and open up the shop, for I knew it almost as well as Frank did. Of course, by now, I'd told my pal Dennis all about it and showed him the letter. When he read it, he said,

"Blimey! Frank is going to throw a fit! This place won't be the same without you. I just can't imagine it."

"We'll soon see," I said. "Here comes Frank. Wish me luck, I'm going to tell him as soon as he's settled."

"I don't envy you," said Dennis. "I'm going to get stuck into this." He had a 500cc Enfield Bullet with a big end gone, another crankcase job for me, for Frank hadn't let Dennis have the time to do a few flywheel assemblies. He was going to regret this now.

"You get stuck in," I said. "You might be in for a rise in a few weeks' time." I hung back from telling Frank until Ken and Pat had arrived. Ken was late, for he had missed his bus, but at last, the time was right for my bombshell. So, I told Frank my news and showed him my letter. I felt really sorry for Frank at that moment. He went very pale and sat down.

"George, lad. I've only got myself to blame for this. Stan and Marty have been on to me for months now for you to become a partner." Stan and Marty who Frank had referred to, were Frank's sister and her husband who were themselves partners, although Stan was a boss at Rootes Car Company. Frank handed me back my letter.

"I'll call a board meeting tonight and see what can be done, as I know that the garage won't be the same without you."

"Frank," I answered, "I've loved it here, but this job is just right for me. I've got to move on and this job has good potential and very good pay. I must take it, Frank, as it's a rare job. A golden opportunity." The next fortnight was a very awkward one for me for as the word got round about me leaving. I kept having customers wishing me well and also telling me how very sorry they were to lose me. In fact, quite a few told me that they doubted if the garage would survive. On the Friday, Frank called me into his office and put an envelope on his desk. "There's £200 there, tax free. Pick it up and, starting from Monday you'll be on two and a half per cent of all profits from the shop and garage. You'll be in complete charge of the garage and I won't interfere. Pick it up." I felt just terrible, and my face must have showed it. Frank looked at me and said, "I know how you must be feeling. Pick it up and say no more."

"Frank," I replied. "If you had offered this twelve months ago I'd have been over the moon, but it's too late. I've got to go. I really am truly sorry. I've loved it here. Like you, it's been my life." I felt my voice cracking with emotion, for what I had just said was very true. I couldn't say any more. I just had to get out of the office before I changed my mind. For despite my low wage I loved the old place and I'd been very happy there, right from a kid. It was really hurting me now, as Frank was like a brother. Then I thought of my darling Ivy, what a great wife she was, and then I remembered what she had said. I must not weaken. I must go through with it. When my last day came, on the next Friday, I cleared up all the jobs and also found time to show Dennis how to do flywheels.

"Frank had better get someone right away," said Dennis. "I'd hate to end up working on cars."

On my last afternoon Frank said, "George, I know you're going and I understand, but if that job doesn't work out, please come back. There's always a job for you here."

"I really appreciate that, Frank. I'll never forget this place. It's been part of my life and I've loved it. Please give my regards to all, especially Marty and Stan. Tell them I won't forget them."

So, I finally did it. I'd left Elliott's Garage to start a very exciting life in the Standard Triumph Competition Department, a job that was about to change my life so much so, that just maybe, I might write another book about it all, for it would cover three Le Mans, many rallies, crashes most spectacular with myself included, races, record breaking and all about the famous TR3, one of Britain's greatest sports cars, and, last but not least, the Competition Department itself and all the work and tricks that took place under Ken Richardson, the man from BRM, who was head of the team.

1939, war is declared and I
acquire my first bike at the age
of seventeen-a 248cc BSA,
with a top speed of 58mph.
Note: the cowl on the head
lamp.

Dennis Jenkins repairs his 'Blue Star' 500cc OHV BSA Combo.

Myself astride an Army Norton 500cc SV, Singapore, 1945.

'Road tested and approved', myself trying out my 1934 498cc Scott Yowler with its customised exhaust system.

Ivy Hylands *(left)* and Edith Keene *(Werner's mother)*, the Austrian lady who saved my life with Austrian herbs when I had leukaemia.

'King of the Cotswolds': the famous MOV Velocette.

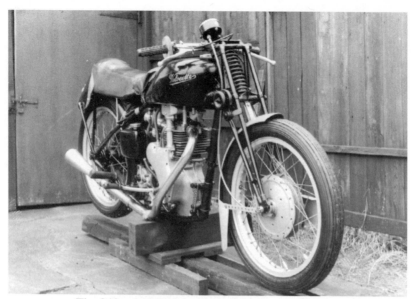

The 248cc MOV Velo. *Note:* the lowered oil tank.

The 248cc Velo semi-desmodromic with a grand prix all-alloy engine.
Note: the large air scoop on the front brake.

A 1929 348cc Mark I OHC-the bike is undamaged and in
possession of all original features.

The ex-army 248cc can-amm Bombardier. Its features include:
five-speed gearbox, multi-plate clutch, ES2 and 16h wheels and
a rotax two-stroke disc-valve engine.

The two restored Bombardiers. Werner's Bike *(foreground)* retains its front mudgaurd in its original army position. *Note:* the high mounting of the exhaust system designed for the crossing of streams.

The author
George Hylands.

Chapter Twenty-Six
The MOV is Reborn

On the first day at my new job, I went to work in the old Armstrong, in order to carry my tools. After the first day, however, I used both the MOV and the MAC as transport to and from work. At Allesley Depot, where I worked, there was a good motorcycle shed to put any bike in and when I first arrived there on one of my bikes, I was the only one at the time to use a motorcycle as transport. Apart from the auto electrician on the team, I was then the oldest mechanic. I was thirty-six years old and the fact that I was the only motorcyclist among them, I guess got me a lot of attention. I soon settled down as it was first class work. In fact, I hardly got dirty and I soon found out that my garage experience soon paid. Apart from Tom McCulloch, who became one of my best mates and had also been to the same school as myself, I was the only 'outsider'. The rest were nearly all Standard Triumph ex-apprentices. I'd only been there about a fortnight, when I was given the job of collecting and returning Ken Richardson's secretary to and from her home, as she was without transport for about two weeks. It was then that I found out why I'd got the job. For a start, I got ninety-eight per cent on the exam paper. The second point was for being at my last place of employment for over fifteen years and lastly, I rode and tuned motorcycles and that is just what Ken Richardson had done before he joined BRM.

After six months at this job, my financial position had improved a lot. We had a lovely baby daughter now, who I adored, so at last I could get down to the conversion of the MOV. By now, I'd collected a lot of gen and I'd also been in almost weekly contact with my two good motorcyclist friends Bernard and Geoff Holland. The result of all this was that I'd got all the oiling mods worked out, and many parts and mods to get on with the job. I had a Velo modified timing chest, a three-start oiling worm to speed up the oil pump, pumping the oil through the engine approximately thirty per cent faster, the idea being to thrape the oil and not the motor. I'd now got the MOV completely stripped out; to set about the job, I'd polished the flywheels but not skimmed. I'd fitted in an Alfa racing extra large big end assembly and got them all balanced up with the thick alloy con-rod and special cutaway slipper piston. The con-rod was drilled at the top, so that at over half revs, oil would be squirted up under the piston crown for cooling. Now I was in this super job that I loved, I was really going to town on my 'dream machine'.

One day at work, one of our lads, who had very much regretted selling his Ariel 350cc Hunter, was very interested in listening to my various stories about bikes, especially the Squariel story. He thought it was a cracker, anyway be asked me to let him have a little ride on my MAC one day. As we only got thirty minutes at lunchtime I lent him my helmet which fitted him perfectly, warmed up the engine on the MAC and let him try it. He had been gone about fifteen minutes and for the first time since I had owned it I heard my own bike coming back. It sounded lovely and he changed down beautifully and I was very pleased to hear it, for it sounded like a TT bike, with a really healthy crackle. The smile on his face said it all.

"Terrific," he said. "I could hardly believe it – it goes like a rocket, and I tell you this, George. If you ever sell this bike without first telling me, we shall fall out. I'd love it. It's something really special." Well, the word soon got round that my MAC was all I had said it was and more. He just couldn't stop talking about it. Although I was the oldest mechanic in the team I was by far the fittest, so, prior to our first Le Mans in 1959, I had the lads out in the car park for physical exercise, as a team is only as good as its weakest member, just like a chain is as good as its weakest link. All this made me a popular chap and it was a lovely arrangement, under my suggestion, that in future, if any of us had a problem with our own vehicles, we should as a team, work as a team on our cars and, I added, if anyone has a motorcycle or a cycle I'll do it for them with pleasure. This scheme went down very well and as time went on, every member of the team was benefited by it. One chap had his car almost rebuilt and all it cost him was the parts at cost price.

Tom McCulloch and I were always working together. He had owned motorcycles in the past, so right from the start, Tom and I were good mates. I fitted into this job very well and my wages were very good, averaging about twenty-seven pounds a week, a very well-paid job in those days. Although I'd loved the work at the garage, this job was far superior in every way. Coming back to my MOV, the cylinder head was modified with a larger inlet valve and seating, and the induction was widened to suit it as the metal in this area was strong and thick. I then progressively gas flowed it and finally, especially on the induction side, highly polished it. The head, when I'd finished it, would have been an asset to any racing stable and when I passed it round at work, the lads were very impressed. It caused a lot of interest, especially with regard to their own cars. But it was as I told them, the cylinder head was a must. It also had to be spot on and it was a job of love, so if anyone had any ideas about attempting it, then my advice was to get a spare head and do it on that. Not only does it take a lot of time, also, why risk scrapping your present one! Well, now that one of the bigger jobs was done, I could carry on with the rest. At this stage the frame had to be tackled as it all had to be altered to fit me in a racing position. Admittedly, the engine position wouldn't change, but I had already found out on the MAC, that to fit up a Grand Prix carb and induction cooling block, it was necessary to lower the oil tank and shorten the pipes, so again, this all had to be worked out with the engine in its place. I intended to make new stainless-steel engine plates, so now was as good a time as any, for the engine must be in the frame before I could make any alterations.

With this done, the almost new carb and the oil tank lowered and the pipes altered, I could now fit the cylinder and piston on to the crankcase and place it in. I say place it in, for at this stage, I would most likely fit it, or rather place it in many times before I finally got the whole thing sorted. As I've already mentioned, the MAC and MOV had the same bore size, and likewise, the pistons could be swapped as well, but the MOV, having the shorter stroke, gave it a huge advantage over its MAC counterpart. In theory, the cylinder design of the MAC was rather out of date, whereas the cylinder design of the MOV was much more in keeping with the times and yet, this is a little strange. The MOV first came out in 1933 with the same bore and stroke, whereby the MAC came out later, having a larger stroke. At this time, the newly designed shorter-stroked Manx Norton was proving to be a success with the higher revs and the improved acceleration which would obviously give scope to different gear ratios, a very important point, particularly at the Isle of Man. At this stage I felt rather confident that my MOV, if done right, should be faster than my MAC, even as it was at its present state in time. At this stage I was glad that I had tuned the MAC, for not only had I done myself a favour, I'd also got a very nice bike to boot. With the mods I was going to do, it was going to be a very interesting project, bearing in mind that the MAC was already superior to the standard MACs, also, it was faster than the 350 Cammy, so I'd taken on a real challenge.

The footrest would have to be repositioned further back by about ten inches and if the gear change lever was positioned to point back instead of, as it was now, facing forward, then that could work as well as the distance, for the footrests would come about right. The gear change would then become reversed, one down, three up, but then again, the 350 Cammys were like that anyway. It didn't take an expert to see that once this had been done, it would alter almost everything on the bike. There was a lot of work to do before this project took shape, and there would be a lot more snags that would show up before it was completed. Before I could alter the frame it all had to be measured and worked out. Even the seat would have to be made, as I'd borrowed three different seats from my pals in Hearsall Lane, but to no avail. After about a month or so, I'd got most of the frame sorted out and the footrest tubes and other alterations brazed up into place. The kickstart was done away with completely, for it wasn't possible to reverse the gear change round by one hundred and eighty degrees with a kickstart on, so it would be like the Rudge, run and bump it! It was now time to get the seat sorted out, for now I had to be 'fitted on' as it were, in order to get the rest of it done, which of course meant also altering the handlebars and controls.

The frame for the seat I made from half-inch diameter tubing, measured and shaped to fit the frame in the right position. I had to use a mock-up in order to get the brackets right, but once done, and all brazed up, the seat frame was ready for the trimmers, who did me a very nice job, with a slightly raised rear end. The handlebars for a start, I cut out the middle section of a pair of Velo bars and clamped the remaining outer pieces to the top of the legs on the girder forks. This done, I could now sit down across the machine, after dropping in both wheels, and get the footrests made up to suit. Having done this, I then found that I would have to make up and fit on two steering lug stops, otherwise, the bars would hit the fuel tank on full lock. Here again, several alterations were needed in order to get it right and when

I'd finished it, I found out that the MOV steering was on a par with that of the old Rudge. In other words, very limited. However, taking the snags in hand as they came up and not rushing any part, the project was coming along very nicely. Already, on looking at it, one was looking at a road racer, even at this stage. That point was very much apparent. The engine output, when done, would obviously be knocking out more BHP and it would more likely be wise to fit a twenty-toothed engine sprocket to replace the standard nineteen-toothed one, in order to keep the revs down. However, this was jumping the gun a bit, but an important point nevertheless. After another three weeks or so, all the alterations on the frame were completed, so now, everything, including the forks, had to be taken off, for by now the frame was awash with brazing and brackets with no paint on. The frame and forks were now all ready to be 'cooked' in enamel as this is much harder than cellulose paint. Once I'd got the frame back I was now able to start building up a racing bike. It was taking shape and looking good and I took great care in order to get the two wheels absolutely spot on in a straight line. They were near enough for ordinary use, but not for a racer. By altering either with washers or by filing down the width of the locking nuts, I got the two wheels bolted up in a dead straight line. It was now just as important to do the same with the engine, clutch and gearbox, for perfect alignment here meant a very smooth drive and a few thousand here and there made all the difference. Having got this lot all sorted out, I realised what a pity it was that it wasn't a six-speed gearbox that I was bolting in. A six speeder would make such a difference, but the price of one was far too costly for what I was doing. After all, my family had to come first, and in any case, I wasn't building it up for the lightweight TT. All the same, I'd keep my eyes open just in case I got lucky. After months of hard work and heartaches I finally got to the stage where I could start it up. No, it wasn't finished, there was still a fair bit of work to do, but it could be started. So now, taking every precaution, like priming up the rockers and timing gears, I put the bike in second gear and pushed the machine up and down our drive with the spark plug out in order to complete the oil circulation prior to starting. Now the moment was here. Would it start and what would the result be like?

Chapter Twenty-Seven

MOV Music

To start it was the same drill as starting the Rudge, but of course, the Velo was a lot lighter, so I wheeled my latest project into the road, which, apart from four or five parked cars, was amply good, I thought. Just right for the job, as it was about 3.00 p.m. on a Saturday afternoon, so let's have a go.

I switched on the fuel and after a few moments, to allow time for the fuel to run through, I carried out the starting drill. Taking a mighty run, I dropped in the clutch, dropped sideways onto my new racing seat, the engine turned over beautifully and it was mechanically quiet. After about four or five turnovers, the engine fired into life. The lovely exhaust note was music to my ears. It sounded better than the MAC, most probably because the mega on the MOV had been made of stainless steel to my specifications by one of the best tinsmiths at Standard Triumph. I'd done my very best to get the volume right on the mega, the discrepancy would be compensated for by various cones made up with three different sized holes drilled in them. When the cone was found that gave the best result, then one could find out whether slightly smaller or larger holes would be the right way to go. I pulled up at once in order to make sure that the oil was circulating properly. It was belting round and the engine felt very good. I'd only got a slight throttle on and the engine was eight-stroking on a rich mixture, but after a minute or so, the eight-stroking stopped and the true feel and sound of the engine became apparent. The oil I was using was Shell, with a little Redex added to aid running in.

One or two of my neighbours had come out to see what I'd got this time and quite a few of them were interested, for they all knew where to come with their cars if they were in trouble. Well, I needed to go up and down the road a couple of times, so here goes – let's do it.

Dropping it in bottom gear, I pulled away. It was lovely and smooth, a really big improvement, and it wasn't the same bike. The gear change was right and my new riding position was comfortable on the very nice seat. I'd got it right, it fitted me perfectly. Opening it up a little in second gear, the bike was sharp and sweet and I knew this was a very big improvement in every way. On my third run, I got third gear at about 40 m.p.h. and it was lovely and smooth. I was very, very happy. I'd not just got another very good Velo, I'd got a Velo GJH. Special, my own concoction. Ivy and Bob came out to see it. Bob had got his hands over his ears. I came up to where they stood at our gates and Ivy shouted,

"That sounds very powerful. I hope you haven't overdone it." I hadn't overdone it, as Ivy put it, and actually, it wasn't far out, so, with the engine still running, I blipped up the throttle a couple of times and it cracked like a whip at shutdown; it was almost uncanny, the dead slow throb proving without a doubt that carburation, balance and exhaust must be almost in full harmony, for, with the engine in this form, there was no way one could get it to run as slow as this if it wasn't for the cam I'd got in it; it was designed to go. I gave it one more rev up, then stopped the engine and, on taking the plug out, I was delighted to see that the mixture was almost spot on, just a little on the rich side, which at this stage was just about right. Far better to be running on the rich side than the lean side, for a lean mixture runs hot and will burn exhaust valves if run too long too fast. Also, a lean mixture requires a very advanced ignition to do any good over half throttle. On the other hand, a mixture leaning to the richer side runs cool, doesn't burn valves or plugs, and the bearings also got the benefit of a slightly retarded ignition setting for the same results. Today's emissions leave a lot to be desired and we all know why. One of my neighbours, after his carburettor had been adjusted at the MOT Station, used to sit with his engine running for a good five minutes before his engine would even pull his car along, completely defeating the object. I could go on about this, but as it is a complex subject, I'll just wet your appetite. The modern cars are fitted with a catalytic exhaust convertor, but did you know that before a 'cat' becomes effective enough to burn the emissions, it would have to do about thirty to forty miles in order to be hot enough to work! The cats knock the tuning of the engine so badly that they are now producing four-valve heads. What a waste. Sad too, is all this electronic diagnosis rubbish, for in many instances, I repeat, many instances, what is done and what is charged for it is a very touchy subject.

Checking over my engine in my garage, I was very happy with the results up to date. Not only had it run well, but the whole bike was so different. I could hardly wait to get it finished, but I knew it had to be done right and that meant taking my time as a risk isn't even worth considering. It had just got to be right. On a more careful examination of the spark plug, which was a KLG FE70, it looked as if either a larger cutaway (throttle and slide) was needed, or a slightly smaller jet on it, but in any case, it would be fine for now. As it was running now, I wasn't likely, if I was careful, to run into any trouble on the carburation side. The thing to concentrate on now was the completion for its new MOT, for, prior to this conversion, there was only a week of tax and MOT left which meant that now it would have to be rechecked in it's present form. 'This will cause a stir,' I thought.

The apprentice I had with me at work had bought himself a 250 Enfield Clipper which he was using for work. One morning he arrived at work all hot and bothered, as his bike had packed up and he'd pushed it for a distance of around three miles. After lunch that day, he and I went out to examine his bike and found the engine to be seized up. Well, he hadn't got much cash and it was obvious that it was too much for him to tackle, so I got permission for us to repair it at work, but in our time. After work that day, my apprentice and I went into the bike shed and in roughly twenty minutes we'd got his engine out. That night I took him home on my MAC and he said he would catch the bus until his bike was finished. The piston had seized due to an oil pump failure. The spindle drive worm had broken, so no oil had been getting through. Fortunately it had happened at low speed, for only the piston had seized. The big end and main bearings were not damaged, so we didn't have to strip out the crankcase. The only new parts required were the piston rings, oil pump drive spindle and the crankshaft drive gear which I got for him with a discount. The bore cleaned up very well. It didn't take long to get it all built up and it ran very well. The following morning there was a large banner that red, 'Velocettes and Enfields Fully Reconditioned'. The lads never missed a trick, but for all that, they knew I would have helped any one of them and my apprentice of course, was a very helpful lad and thought be was with the best chap in the shop. My head was getting bigger every day!

Chapter Twenty-Eight
MOV Testing – A Surprise From the Past

Over the next two weeks I got stuck in to get the MOV all finished. I'd got a larger throttle cutaway, but I needed a smaller size jet, and in any case, there was no way that I was going to refit the big heavy front mudguard back as an unbalanced weight on the steering could spell disaster on a real 'earhole' type of bend. At Alf Holland's hopefully I'd pick up a nice light alloy front guard, and at Alf's one could get alloy strips and tubes to make stays and braces out of. The only place in Coventry that stocked them, but that wasn't surprising, for at Alf's one was dealing with true motorcyclists. After work on the Monday night, I went up to my old chums to see what I could get, for calling at Alf's was never a wasted trip; besides, they were good friends.

"Hello, our George," said Geoff as I entered. "How's that project of yours coming on? Is it a runner yet?" So, for the next five minutes, I told him the latest news and he was very pleased and interested.

"What about Elliott's Garage?" remarked Geoff. I looked at him, and by my look, he must have realised that I didn't know what he was on about for he continued,

"Frank was in here last week. He bought one clutch cable for an AJS and said that he'd just about had enough, as he'd had five blokes since you left and now he's doing no more repairs. He's had enough and the garage is closing at the end of the month."

"Streuth, I knew he wasn't having it easy. Dennis Leeson told me the last time I saw him, but he didn't mention this," I replied.

"He didn't know then," said Geoff. "Frank made up his mind last week. Apparently he got Dennis on cars and it all got too much for him. He left too."

"Hell," I said in a daze. "Frank didn't deserve this."

"Don't blame yourself," said Geoff. "Everybody could see it, but Frank. He just had to find out the hard way."

"And the shop?" I asked.

"Ken and himself will run the shop. Your old petrol attendant, Pat, leaves this week. I think that for now Frank will serve petrol and oil but no repairs, and the Enfield agency will go as well." I was speechless. I could hardly believe this. It just seemed impossible. I felt ill at this moment. I felt like dashing round and taking over again, but in my heart, I also knew that it wasn't possible any more as I was too much involved at work, as I was a valuable member of the team.

I was still in a daze when I got home with my bits and pieces and when I told Ivy she replied,

"I'm not surprised. Like you, I've known all along who kept that garage going and now, so does Frank."

"I'd like to go and see him," I said, "but it would only make things worse."

"That would be a crazy thing to do," said Ivy. "Frank lost his chance two years ago. There is nothing anyone can do, so don't be stupid. He's still got the shop." And of course, she was perfectly correct. It was the end of an era. Well, I'd got a very good job. Everyone in my family was happy, I was happy, the firm I worked for was happy, so I'd get on with my MOV and get it finished.

The new alloy guard fitted very well and I'd fitted it very close to the tyre. It looked very smart. The only electrical unit on the bike was the mag and I'd gone over that and reskimmed it and repacked the two bolt-races, cleaned the cam and replaced the pick-up brush. The electric horn I'd replaced with a bulb horn which I'd fitted just under the seat and I could easily reach down with my left hand if it was needed. One of my last jobs prior to the MOT was to rig up a space under the seat for tools and spare plugs. I'd even made up two very short twin platinum point plugs, adapted from a Spitfire's Merlin engine. All was now ready for the MOT on Saturday. At 10.00 a.m. on the Saturday, I took the MOV to the Ace Garage for its MOT. Wilmot Evans ran the Ace Garage and I knew he'd be very interested in this, as he was an old TT rider himself, having done it on a

Triumph. I was right too. It did cause a stir at the garage and yes, Wilmot was very interested and what's more, he gave me full marks for what he called a nice piece of balanced engineering. Of course, I had no problems getting the MOT.

Apart from just looking the bike over I didn't touch it during the week, but Ivy taxed it for me, so, by Sunday, everything had been done. The weather was fine so at 5.00 a.m. Sunday morning, I was all set for a nice steady run through the Cotswolds. It's not a bit of good trying to test in traffic, hence my very early start. Besides, I wanted to be on my own. I wanted to suck in the Cotswolds air and throb away with my new love. So that I didn't disturb my neighbours I side-saddled the bike with a dead engine until I was just yards from the Ansty Road. Here I fired her up and with a light throttle, eased the bike away from Coventry.

On the London Road, past Elliott's Garage, the engine sounded very good, but of course, I was taking things very easy, for I didn't know for sure just what I might find. One thing I had already found, and that was how easily my new riding position took the bike through the bends.

I had already noticed that although my footrest positions were correct, I must cock up the actual footrests by about twelve degrees, for when going right over on a bend, I bottomed out very slightly, but the new position I loved. You could really get down to it, yet you felt very safe and in control. I was cruising along at about 50 m.p.h. and I'd left the nineteen-toothed engine sprocket on as it had to be proved or otherwise. By now I was on the edge of the Cotswolds (superb motorcycling country), so as soon as I came to a lay-by, I stopped to have a good look round. I had got just fifty-two miles on my new project. I was well pleased with my first check as there were no oil leaks or petrol leaks at the carb. The clutch was spot on and it only took a couple of minutes to adjust the front brake up a bit. The plug reading was a bit on the rich side, but then again, I hadn't yet been over half throttle, but it did appear to be cutaway problems rather than jet, as the throttle would affect the mixture at lower speeds, whereas the jet would only show up above three-quarter throttle. The main drive chain was okay, as I'd given it a good oiling with SAE 90 Gear Oil the night before, but I could see that for fast long runs, some sort of oiling would have to be rigged up to prevent any chance of the chain running dry. The only other alteration that I made, was to loosen off the side damper on the girder forks that controlled the up and down movement of the fork, for with the extra weight being taken off by the replacing of a lightweight front guard, it had obviously tightened up the fork movement. Apart from that all was very good.

Away again and the engine fired first drop, a very good sign, indicating that the carburation was as near as 'damn it' is to swearing, so now I settled down to a faster run. After a few miles the road started to lengthen out quite a bit, so I slowly opened up. The response was very good, one could definitely feel the benefit of the large inlet valve and carburation, and it didn't take many seconds before the speedometer was reading 70 m.p.h.. At this speed it was very hard to believe that I was riding a 248cc, for the engine was very smooth and the exhaust was sharp and very healthy. I kept 70 m.p.h. up long enough to get a plug reading and at the next stop I shut off the engine at 70 m.p.h. in order to see the true reading. The plug at this speed was only slightly too rich, so if I changed the cutaway and retuned the mixture screw, it wouldn't be far out. The engine otherwise was running well so this job could be done back home. Slamming the throttle shut as I shot away at around 70 m.p.h. over the brow of a hill, megaphonics went 'wow-wow-wowing' back in the morning air, but opening the throttle slightly soon brought this racket under control. The bigger valve overlap was coming into effect at around 68 m.p.h. so if I wished to bring it in earlier, then I would have to shorten the exhaust pipe or replace the baffle with slightly smaller holes or fit a cone. Obviously, until it was sorted, the baffle plate was very much the easiest move. I didn't go above 75 m.p.h. at any time on this run, but the whole machine felt very good, road holding had definitely been improved and I felt that when I'd cranked up the footrests, fast cornering wouldn't be a problem. As for the tyres, well they'd do for now as there were stacks of miles left in them, but fast cornering, well I wouldn't like to chance it on the front tyre and really the back tyre would be better if a wrap around tyre was fitted as they were just coming out then. I was pleased about all this and I intended to leave the nineteen-toothed sprocket on until I'd got the carburation spot on, one rectification at a time being the golden rule on which to make positive progress. Keeping the speed around 65-70 m.p.h. I enjoyed a very good run and many heads turned on my way back when the megaphonics were heard on the change down prior to a slower bend. The bike had run great, a very good start, and another two hundred and fifteen miles was added on to the speedo. I was back well in time for a big breakfast, which I thoroughly enjoyed.

Chapter Twenty-Nine

The MOV Samples the Cotswolds

Monday morning was nice and fine so I thought I'd let my mates see my handiwork, for it didn't get dark until 7.00 p.m. so even if I worked over for an hour, I would be all right. The bike when seen caused quite a stir, for during our half-hour lunch break there must have been all our Competition Section there and two-thirds of the Service mechanics as well. Of course they all wanted to hear it run, so in the car park, and with only a short run, for by now, I'd got the starting all weighed up, I started it up. The two hundred and ten miles that I did on the Sunday morning had settled the engine down so I had been able to check the head studs, tappets and have a general look-see and nut and bolt check. I hadn't as yet done the combustion, but the lads at work were very impressed and all agreed that it was no doubt a very different bike. Later that afternoon one of our lads came over to me and said,

"Don't be surprised if Ken Richardson comes up to you, because he and Marshal Dors, the under manager, have been looking at your bike for over ten minutes." Nothing was said that day, but about ten days later, after he'd been going over a job with us, Ken, turned to me and said,

"And while I'm here, tell me, just what have you done to that bike of yours? It sounds beautiful." Ken knew his job and I could tell that he was like me. He never let a job beat him and he loved the story of the MOV and asked if I liked working for them. All I could say was, I loved it. I doubt if it could have been better.

One evening the following week, I changed the cutaway, and sure enough, it cured the eight-stroking on shut-off and the plug colour was almost perfect. The acceleration had also improved so I was now looking forward to my next run in the Cotswolds. I was again back on the MAC for work. For one thing, the MOV wasn't designed for use in traffic any more, and besides, the MAC was equipped with lights and two large canvas panniers, a far safer bike in the rain and in traffic. Now that the carburation was all but right, I changed the engine sprocket to the twenty tooth and reset both primary and main chain tensions, so, with the new sprocket on, I'd made a few notes on speeds in the gears, so now I could get a comparison. It rained on the Saturday but stopped on Saturday night, while Sunday came up fresh and fine. I started out as before and at the same time as last time. I'd seen very few cars last time and I was hoping that this run would be the same. The engine fired up instantly, for the previous run had settled it down beautifully. I could feel the power, it wanted to go. It's surprising the effect that razor edge tuning can bring, but I rode it at a very steady forty to fifty until warm up had taken place, a distance of around ten miles. Even at this lower speed I could feel the difference with this bigger sprocket. The acceleration wasn't as sharp, but higher up, and now the carburation was about right the engine at 70 m.p.h. was very smooth and running easily. I was paying too much attention to the running of the engine and not enough to the road, with the result that I took a bridge too fast. The bike was airborne for a few seconds and because the road turned to the left, I had to throw it over to get it round. It did it and proved the handling, but it was a good job I'd cranked up the footrests by twelve degrees or it could easily have been a very different story.

A few miles further on I stopped for my usual check over. This time I could find no faults, even the plug was almost spot on. So, satisfying myself that all was well, I decided to open up a bit more, for the difference with this sprocket gave me the confidence to do it, for it was very unlikely that I would over-rev it. At 75 m.p.h. it was as smooth as it was at seventy, so, approaching a long straight, I crouched down and slowly opened up. I was very well rewarded, for almost before I knew it, the bike was over 93 m.p.h. so I slammed the throttle shut, for I'd got cold feet. No, not for myself, for the bike, with the wow-wow-wowing following me down the road. I was glad at this moment that I was well clear of the houses, but I can still remember my feeling of sheer delight, knowing that 100 m.p.h. was within my reach and it was only a 248cc. Now that I'd achieved this, I knew I could run the bike near the seventies and it didn't take me long to clock up two hundred miles and be back before 9.00 a.m. for a big breakfast, a very contented man. This extra fast run had proved something else, that at seventy and over there was a fatal delay before I got a result from the front brake. The reason was simple, it wasn't big enough. After all, it wasn't really designed for it. No, I'd have to get it changed and quickly, for now the bike was such a goer, it was up to me to rig it up with a nice big stopper, for to start something you can't stop is fatal. My best bet would be a Velo twin leading shoes racing Cammy front wheel, so Velos would be the best place to start looking. After all, they knew me well.

Chapter Thirty
A Rider's Nightmare

The MOV was now running great, so that coming Sunday I'd decided to do one of my longer runs in reverse. For one thing I wouldn't know the bends so well and for another, it would make it more interesting. During the week leading up to the Sunday, I'd had two dicey moments on my MAC. One was when a car pulled out from the kerb and obviously hadn't looked in his mirror, for he came out quite quickly, almost pushing me over the centre line where a coach was coming, and he in turn was almost on the centre line himself as I was passing a car on his left, which was parked at the kerb. But thanks to my good brakes and the stability of the MAC in an emergency, I was able to brake and pull back behind him, and fortunately no harm was done. But it was very close and I didn't intend him to just drive off, so I dropped down a cog and in seconds I was alongside him, and pulled him in, and asked if he knew what he had just done. His offside mirror was non-existent, but the easy manner in which I caught him had shaken him,. However, he said be hadn't seen me and in turn I pointed to his mirror and told him to get it fixed before he killed someone. Incident number two happened a little later on the same journey, as I overtook a lorry, and the nearside rear dropped into a deep drain near the kerbstones. The shock wave loosened a large thick plank that was lying loosely on top of his load of building materials. I was forced to swerve violently to avoid the plank which hit the road with a crash and a car behind narrowly missed it. The lorry stopped and, looking back, I could see that the car driver had also stopped, so I carried on and left that one to him.

Two incidents in one day should have made me give the Sunday morning a miss, as it was drizzly rain, but I thought a wet run would let me see how my new riding position was in the rain. The road-holding was great, so because of this, I foolishly decided to go. The run in reverse meant that I entered the Cotswolds through Banbury. I was very pleased with the road-holding of the MOV. Out just past Banbury I was in for a shock, for as I negotiated the island on the Oxford side of Banbury I ran into trouble before I knew it. The very next moment I found myself face down in the road, sliding at great velocity, for the large, high kerbstones on the other side of the road. I hit them hard with both my head and my shoulder. There is no doubt at all, that it was only my crash hat that saved me from a very serious injury, or maybe even death. The blow knocked me out for a few seconds, for the last thing I remember is lying face down in the road with a very strong smell of diesel oil in the air. Also, I could hear the Velo ticking over, but where it was, I hadn't a clue.

I got up feeling terrible, then immediately went down again, but this time just on the pavement, for to me, everything seemed to be spinning round. Just then I felt a dog sniffing my face and heard a female say,

"Are you all right?" I looked up and saw a lady with the dog's lead in her hand, with the dog on the other end of it.

"I don't know," I answered in a daze. "I feel very queer and my bike's gone."

"Your bike went through that hedge," said this lady, as she pointed across the road. "You were flung off. I saw it happen. There is oil on the road. You were flung off when your bike spun round and then shot over there, through the hedge." I was more confused than ever over where the bike was. I don't think I was thinking clearly. What had happened hadn't really sunk in yet. Apparently, just prior to me arriving at the island, there had been quite a few gallons of diesel oil spilt. From what I didn't know, but with rain and a very smooth, tarred surface, the road round the island was as dangerous as sheet ice. I got up again and this lady caught hold of my arm to steady me.

"If you can walk, I'll show you where your bike went." Just as she said this, a large white Ford van appeared, coming from the Banbury side like I did. The next moment he too came across very close to us in a series of spins. He stopped about five feet from us. The driver got out looking deathly white.

"What the devil's happened here?" he asked. He hadn't hit anything, but he was badly shaken. The lady with me told him what had happened, she also said that her house was just down the road, so she would phone the police.

On approaching the hedge I could hear the lovely throb of my engine, and looking over the four-foot hedge, I saw the bike leaning on a grassy bank as if someone had parked it there. I could also see where it had gone through the hedge, and the hedge must have knocked it out of gear, for here it was, still running. At this moment, I felt very queer again and switched the petrol taps off. The next thing I knew, water was being splashed on my face, my crash hat was off, and a man was bending over me.

"Don't try to get up," he said. "It looks as if you've been concussed, so just lie where you are. You'll feel better in a little while." This man was the husband of the lady who had seen it happen, so I did as I was told and lay on the grassy bank to recover. After a time, I got up, and when this chap could see that I had no broken bones, he asked me if I'd be all right.

"Yes, and thank you very much. I'll go and sort my bike out." Still feeling terrible, I went over to the bike and I could see that it was damaged. There was about a one inch dent in the exhaust pipe, a small dent on the nearside of the fuel tank, which I guess is still there to this day. The nearside footrest was bent and the alloy clutch lever was minus about two inches, which had been broken off. The nearside dummy handlebar rubber was missing, which I found in the hedge, split from top to bottom, and a branch from the hedge, still with all its leaves on, was jammed between the frame and the gearbox. But worst of all was me, for I felt terrible and the whole earth started spinning again, so I sat down fast.

I lay back on the grassy bank where my Velo was, and rested for a good twenty minutes. By this time, a police car had arrived and the two policemen were throwing sand all over the road. As I was on the other side of the road, and the other side of the hedge, they didn't even know I was there. I must have been there for a good hour by now, as my watch, which hadn't got damaged, said it was nearly 7.00 a.m. Feeling a bit better, I found a long piece of wood about two inches by two inches and about three feet long, which, by anchoring one end into the wet ground, I was able to use as a lever to straighten out the bent footrest. At least, I got it good enough to ride it back home. Well, I must have been concussed as I never even thought of swapping the brake and clutch levers over, as this would have made the ride home very much easier. As it was, it was a struggle. After checking all round, it was an easy matter to get the Velo back on the road, for the hedge ended about twenty yards further down, so, still feeling very weak, I pushed the bike back to the road. The wet grass by now had washed any remaining diesel off the tyres. The rain had all but stopped and the part of the road which I had pushed my Velo back onto was on a slope, just what I needed for an easy push. Getting the gears sorted, I selected second gear and went through the drill. The engine fired at once and I let it gently take me down the road, as I still felt terrible. About two miles down this road, there was a signpost on my left, pointing to Banbury, so I took it, for all I wanted was to get back home. I got through to the road from Banbury to Coventry and opened up a bit, but I'd only done about three miles when the road appeared to be rolling from side to side. I stopped immediately and, getting off the bike, I pushed the prop-stand down and let the bike lean on it. As I did so, I lost my balance and rolled down a grassy bank into the stream at the bottom. I came round with my legs and one thigh in the stream and I was now feeling very cold. It was the cold I think, that had brought me round. I sat up and looked at my watch, it read 7.50 am.

'Streuth,' I thought. 'I must have lain here for at least thirty minutes.' So, removing my crash hat, I gave my face a good swill in the stream, which was nice and fresh. I felt a bit better after this, so I carried on with my journey.

The bike fired at first drop, but I wasn't out of trouble yet, for I had three more stops before I got home, and although I felt queer, I didn't black out again. It was a big relief to get home as the broken clutch lever had made the clutch very heavy and the fingers on my left hand felt as if they were dropping off. Had I been thinking straight it wouldn't have taken many minutes to change the clutch and front brake levers over. It would of course have made the journey easier, the clutch being used more often than the front brake, but after my bump my mind just wasn't up to it.

I'd decided on my way back that I didn't intend to tell Ivy anything about it, but when I got home, about my usual time, 9.00 a.m., Ivy took one look at me and said,

"You look terrible. Have you come off?" There was no way I could fool Ivy, so of course, I told her the full story. I didn't eat my usual big breakfast, but I did have a couple of pieces of toast with marmalade, and I felt a lot better for it. The rest of the day I just lazed about and I was groggy on and off all day, but at about 8.00 p.m. I was a lot better and the colour had come back into my face. There was no doubt that I'd taken a hard knock, as my left shoulder and arm were badly bruised and my left leg was also stiff and swollen. I was now limping and I'd also felt sick a few times, but managed not to be, and by Monday morning, I felt well enough to go to work. As for the MOV, I had a new exhaust pipe made and chromed and my pals at Alf Holland's fixed me up with a new alloy clutch lever and a dummy rubber for the nearside handlebar, so after completely resetting the nearside footrest, the Velo was back to square one and thanks to my crash hat I was still here to enjoy it, but a new helmet was now needed which I got from Alf Holland's.

Chapter Thirty-One

A Vintage Cammy, Clutch
Problems, and a Grand Prix Engine

On the Tuesday night of the following week, Ivy said to me, "I'm either a fool to tell you, or I'm a very good wife to you. Listen to this, 'KTT 350 Velo, all there, but needs attention'," She had just read me an advert in the *Coventry Evening Telegraph*.

"Blimey," I said. "Where's the address?"

I pulled up on my MAC at the address Ivy had given me in Binley Road. On arrival I was very disappointed to see two long-haired youths pushing the 350 Cammy away. The chap who had just sold it looked up when be heard my Velo.

"I wish you had come earlier," he said, "for by the look of that, it would have gone to the right chap," And he was pointing at my Velo.

"I'm very sorry, too," I answered, "but you can't win 'em all."

"Never mind," said this man. "I have something more interesting that I wouldn't let people like those two even know I had." And with that, I followed him into his lovely workshop.

"What do you think about that?" and as he spoke he pulled a dust cover off a lovely Mark I Cammy Velo.

"Oh boy, that is beautiful," I remarked. "1929 KN I see," said I.

"You know your Velos," he replied. "I knew it as soon I saw yours. Yes, this was my father's machine and I promised my mother that I'd find a good owner for it. I think I've found him."

"It's very nice of you to say so," I answered. The bike was a beauty, and it was in beautiful condition, all in shiny black and gold, with all chrome fittings, as chromium plating became available in 1929.

"This is the last one left," he said. "We had five, two 350 Cammys, one MOV, one 500cc MSS and this one, the one that started it all."

"What are you asking for it?" I asked. "The man who has it is to me, more important than the price. Tell me, what's your job?"

"Competition mechanic for Standard Triumph and before that motorcycle mechanic at Elliott's Garage for over fifteen years."

"Now I know I've got the right man," he replied.

It was indeed a very nice machine, and because of its low mileage of 7,502 miles, the cylinder head had never been off. It stood off the floor on a wooden stand and even the tyres were original and were polished with boot polish, and the Dunlop letters and the tyre sizes were painted in gold so they matched the bike perfectly.

"It was purchased new by my father from Brandish & Sons and he only rode it for pleasure. The reason we have sold up is because we are moving to Scotland."

"And the price?" I reminded him.

"Well, if it had been a runner, I would be asking fifty pounds, but as it has stood and never run for twenty years and the head will more than likely have to come off, what about thirty-five pounds, for as I said, I'm sure you're the right man for it."

"That's more than fair," I said, and we shook hands on it and I put a ten pound note down as a deposit.

"There are one or two bits that go with it all wrapped up in oil soaked rags by my father. I have a 10cwt van and I'll bring it up about 7-7.30 p.m. on Friday. By the way, I can find you a battery for it, too." I'd done it again, thanks to Ivy. She should be pleased about that, and that, I think, called for a box of Cadbury's Milk Tray.

I knew right away that I'd got a real bargain. In fact it was almost a gift. I think the chap who sold it to me was more interested in who got it, as opposed to how much they got for it. I was the lucky one. It was Coventry registered, the number was KV 7130 and the model was a KNTT. The extras included a foot change mechanism to fit on the gearbox, for in its standard form, it was a four-speed hand-change, a short sporting front wheel guard, a shorter and lower handlebar and two different sizes of engine sprockets, all as brand new, as they had never been fitted on. The high quality of Velocette Motorcycles was very much apparent on this machine. It was black ebony, a real vintage show piece. At ten past seven on Friday night it was delivered to me, and the man who sold it to me, was the one who delivered it, but when he saw my Velos, and especially the MOV, he was with me for almost an hour as he reckoned that he hadn't seen any better. When he had gone, I took out the big 18 m/m/KLG plug and poured out about a tablespoonful of Redex into the cylinder. I also poured about half a pint into the oil tank, then, with the bike on its wheels, and the tyres having been blown up, I cranked the engine over for two or three minutes with the kickstart until the oil had circulated and was returning back into the oil tank.

One could tell that it felt a lot easier, and the Redex would soon sort out any carbon or potential dry spots. Redex is a very high quality oil and no carbon can live in Redex. It is the only safe oil additive that I would use, but only in mineral oils. The bike had been very well stored as there was thin oil in the fuel tank to prevent rusting, so after draining this out, I took out a gallon of fuel from the old Armstrong and poured it into the Velo's ebony black tank. The needle in the carb was stuck, but a tap with a screwdriver handle stopped it leaking. Just then, Ivy came into the garage; the chap had come back, as he had forgotten to give me the battery and the dust sheet. I then checked the spark. It was excellent so I cleaned the plug and checked the spark at the plug; that too was a deep blue crack. After half a dozen kicks it started up, and smoked like hell for a minute or so, but soon settled down to a lovely steady beat of a long-stroke vintage. It was like a new bike, mechanically very quiet, and the powerful throb set the whole bike gently rocking up and down to the rhythm of the engine. The silencer gave it a nice healthy note, no, it wasn't a Velos can, it was a 'Brooklands Can', as Velos hadn't made their own silencer then, but when they did it was very much in keeping with the 'Brooklands Can', the Brooklands being half as big again and all but covering the rear wheel.

I was filled with pleasure, this was one classy bike, probably a far better buy than the one I had missed. The lights and horn all worked, it was charging at a steady five amps, and the whole machine was in first-class condition. I let it get warmed up properly, and when I lightly revved it, it sounded great. I stopped the engine on the valve lifter and felt the compression. It had gone up considerably, in fact, there was no need at all to remove the head as the Redex had sorted it out. I'd got Velo number three and it was a lovely specimen in first-class condition. I ran the engine up again for I loved the sound of it, and this time it felt like kicking up a 500cc; the compression had increased so much that I felt sure it wouldn't need a decoke, as had first been thought. Stopping this lovely old engine, I pushed it over on the kickstart on to compression so that both valves were closed, and this is how the engine had been left, with both valves closed, most probably by its original owner. So, giving my latest find a good oiling and a wipe over, I put it next to my MOV and covered it over with its oily dust sheet. When I told our gang at work, some thought that I was joking, but when I told them that anyone could come up and see it for themselves, they knew it was true.

My next move was to get a twin leading shoe front brake for the MOV. I didn't care whether it was just a hub or a complete front wheel, as long as it was large enough. I didn't mind. So, on the Saturday morning, I went to Velos on my MOV to see if I was in luck, but here was where my luck ran out. The dealers had taken them all by what the spares manager said. They sold them as soon as they got them and he said that there were only about thirty of them anyway, so I still was no nearer. But the MOV got a lot of attention, so I showed it to some of the engine builders who came to look at it. They were very impressed and reckoned it was a little cracker.

One night, a knock came at our door. It was a chap on his 498cc MSS Velo; one of our coachmen at work had sent him, as he was his next door neighbour and he was in trouble with his bike. He'd got clutch trouble and although he'd had a new clutch fitted at a Birmingham dealer's about six months ago, he was now in trouble again. When I spoke to him, I could see that he wasn't happy about it at all, as it cost him forty-two pounds last time, and here he was again.

"Bring it in," I said. "Let's find out why." In my garage, I checked through the clutch drill, only to find that the main problem was too much play in the gearbox main shaft. The bike's owner was with me while I did this and he was very pleased that I'd taken it on.

"I'll do my best to get it done for the weekend," I told him and gave him my phone number, as we had had the phone installed so that I could be contacted from work, for only the mechanic that built the car was allowed to work on it. By Saturday afternoon I'd got his bike out of trouble. The gear shaft was solid and I'd fitted in new clutch plates and reset up the clutch in the Velo clutch drill. I tried the bike round the block and it was fine, but although it was a 500cc, I couldn't help but notice how sluggish it was compared to my two Velos; it made me see how well mine went. At 5.00 p.m. he rang up to see how his bike was, and he was delighted to know that it was ready and when he came round and found that I'd done it for twenty pounds he was very happy and after he'd paid me, he said that he'd be forever grateful if I would do all his repairs for him. Looking at my three Velos, as I'd uncovered the vintage for him to see, he said,

"Stanley Woods' relations live near me, and they used to have the engine of the 248cc Velo that won the 1951 New Zealand Grand Prix. I've heard that they blew it up, but still have it. It might pay you to go and see them," And he wrote down their address for me.

After my Sunday morning run on the MOV, I called round to the address I'd been given, but the chap who owned what was left of the bike's engine was out. His dad was in, and when he knew why I'd called, and he could see that I'd come on a Velo, and I had the Velo transfer across my white crash hat, he asked me in.

"I'll take you through to the shed and show you what it's like, what's left of it." In the shed, he pulled a wooden box out from under the little bench.

"That's all there is," he said. Looking into the box I saw a Velo crankcase with a three inch diameter hole through it, but the Alfin alloy cylinder that was bolted across it was a big one. Also in the box was a big finned alloy cylinder head with an open valve mechanism; the timing chest was missing and the only part of the gear train that was left was the crankshaft driving gear, but there was an oil pump in it.

"Sorry," he said. "I told you it was scrap."

"Is this all there is?" I asked.

"Not quite," he replied and pulled out another wooden box at least twice the size of the other one. This one was full of Velo bits.

"What's happened to this?" I asked, pointing to the busted engine.

"Oh, the idiot used it on the grass and it's seized solid. It's scrap, and now he's engaged to be married, he's sold his bike. I reckon he ought to get rid of this lot."

"Tell him if he's interested and if he isn't expecting too much, I might buy them off him as a job lot, so I'll give you my name and address." About 7.00 p.m. the same night, the phone rang. It was the son to say he'd be interested in selling, so I arranged to go from work to his home, as he knocked off before me, as this week, we were all working over. I went to work in the Armstrong the next day, just in case, and it paid off. At his home, he didn't hum or ha over the spares, he simply said,

"You can take the lot for twenty pounds, and I've got one or two new bits under my bed. I'll drop them in as well."

"A pleasure," I answered and slapped twenty pounds on the table. "Give me a receipt and I'll take them all now. I've got the car outside." So I was in and out in less then ten minutes. The new parts he dropped in were themselves worth more than twenty pounds, for there was a new oil pump, which was the same in all the big bike ranges, two sets of valves for an MAC, one $^5/_8$" drive chain, a complete clutch also for an MAC, and a clutch cable. When I got back home, I left the car in the drive so I could tip out the bits to see what I'd got. I'd just done this, when Ivy came in and said,

"Dinner in ten minutes and what's all this junk?"

"This junk, my love, is Velo gold dust," I answered.

"If you say so," she said, tossing her head.

Well, on searching through all this 'junk', as Ivy called it, I was really chuffed at what there was; it was a real bargain. There were about eight pushrods, five used valves, ten valve guides, two cylinder heads, one MOV, one MAC, five slipper pistons, four main bearings, twenty-seven inner and twenty-five outer valves springs, three cylinders, two MAC one MOV, one oil tank MAC and, best of all, five Grand Prix carburettors, three complete and two incomplete, and last but not least, one MOV silencer and three exhaust pipes, one MOV two MAC. It was indeed a real bargain basement of parts. Looking at the old engine I could see that it had seized badly. The rusty bore was solid, so after I'd eaten, I decided to strip it out. I had to warm up the bore and piston with a blow lamp before I could get any paraffin or Redex down past the piston, but once I'd got it to move, I was able to belt the cylinder off with a wooden block without damaging the finning. The large alloy con-rod was all right and the flywheel assembly did turn in the crankcase. But on taking out the oil pump after again heating up the casing, I found out why it had seized. The oil pump drive had sheared, so even the oil pump could be salvaged. When I took the crankcase apart, I found that the flywheel assembly had been skimmed and highly polished, obviously done for maximum acceleration, so all this lot, when done, would be worth pounds, and not only that, I'd got a historic engine that I knew I could repair.

The cylinder head was interesting for a start, the valve gear was exposed and had no oiling to it, only a grease nipple to lubricate the inlet valve. The hemispherical head had a very large inlet valve about $^1/_8$" in diameter, larger than the one I'd got in the MOV. The exhaust valve stem was thick, as it was sodium filled for cooling, the valve springs were extra strong for high revs, and the hemispherical combustion chamber was a higher compression than mine. This engine had been built to do a job and it was going to take a lot of work to convert it to be a fully-rigged oil-fed engine for the road. As it was now, it was only a skeleton engine for a short fast run only, but even so, I'd already got a plan to make it work. My pals at work thought that all I ever done was Velos. They weren't right, but then again, I was known as 'George, the Velo Fellow' and I did get quite a few jobs sent along via the grapevine as it were, from Velos when they were extra busy. So, in the next week or so, I started to make notes on what was to be done in order to convert this engine. The biggest job as far as I could see, would be to convert the cylinder head to a super fully-oiled enclosed racing head. It was certainly beautifully made and if I could get it working, I would without doubt, have an engine and that would make my MOV very special indeed. I meant to see this through, for if I succeeded, I would then have a one-off bike, which would of course, make it much more valuable and of course, a real joy to own as well as to ride.

Chapter Thirty-Two
Lucky Bites 'Iva-Clue'

As I was working away on these problems, the garage door opened and in came Ivy.

"Just to remind you that you'll be going to work in the Armstrong tomorrow and taking Lucky. I'll get his food and water all ready, so perhaps you had better put it in the car boot now, so you won't forget." Lucky was the name of our Cardigan Corgi dog, and because he was a biter, I was to take him out of the way for the day, as we were having a new electric cooker installed.

Now Lucky loved the car. He'd stay in it all day. Well, he was going to do just that. I would of course go and let him out at morning break time, also at lunchtime and again in the afternoon tea break, so although he would have to stay in the car for the main part, he would be well looked after.

The next morning after breakfast, I looked at Lucky and said,

"Lucky, how about coming to work with your dad?" He got my meaning immediately and jumped up to come with me. As I said before, Lucky was a very good traveller and he loved the car, so when I got to work and parked up the car, there was no real problem in leaving him in the car. In fact, he would, I knew, lie on the floor and no one need know that he was there. There was plenty of room in the car, so with both rear windows open about two inches I left him in charge of the car. Lucky was an excellent guard, but little did I know just how well he would demonstrate his guarding ability.

I'd been out to Lucky at break time and gave him a walk round the car park and his water and a handful of his favourite biscuits, so he was just about fine. Around ten thirty that morning, we noticed that 'Iva-Clue', the name we gave to the works detective, was in the workshop; this usually meant trouble. A little later we heard that something valuable had gone missing. But, unknown to us, at this moment, 'Iva-Clue' had decided to check over the cars in the car park. He was of course, only doing his job, but he should have got the owners' permission before opening car doors. He was okay until he got to KV 5830, my Armstrong. On opening up my rear car door, he was immediately set upon by its guardian. Lucky got hold of his right arm and wouldn't let go. One of our lads dashed in to fetch me out. Of course I dashed out and got Lucky off, but it was too late for 'Iva-Clue'. His arm had been badly mauled and he was suffering from shock.

Ten minutes later, when 'Iva-Clue' had been taken to hospital by car, yours truly was summoned into the workshop superintendent's office for an explanation.

"Well," I told Mr J Male, our superintendent, just why Lucky was in my car. I also pointed out that 'Iva-Clue' had no right to open up employees' cars without permission, as Lucky was only guarding his property. I got away with it on this reasoning, but I was told that if for any reason my dog was to be brought in the car again, I was to lock him in.

Later in the afternoon, 'Iva-Clue', with his arm in a sling, came back into the workshop. One of our lads, whose name was Benny Benjer started to sing, *How Much Is That Doggy In the Window*, a popular tune, and half of the workforce took up the rest singing, "The one with the waggily tail!" It was a very red-faced detective that stormed out of the workshop, and to the lads, Lucky was a hero, for he'd certainly made their day, and of course, completely ruined the day for 'Iva-Clue'.

Chapter Thirty-Three

Repairs, Strip-outs, and a Front Brake Conversion

Coming back to the work that I'd done to the MOV, I'd decided that I would convert the cylinder head on the old Velo racing engine. For one thing it was a one-off engine, and secondly, with the size of the inlet valve, and, if I got it done right, such an engine would give me the edge, so now I intended to do all that was necessary to complete it.

Over the next month or two I'd had a new standard size sleeve fitted and bored into the alloy finned cylinder. The cylinder, like the head, had polished up until it shone, for they had been highly polished at Velos. The flywheel assembly was likewise, and had also been skimmed but not a lot, as they were not much lighter in weight than the ones now in the MOV. Velos were too experienced to overskim flywheels, as it was done for a reason, and that reason had to be acceleration. The flywheels were in very good order, but even so, thinking of the high-compression cylinder heads, it would be a favourite to fit a large 'Alfa' big-end crankpin to stand the extra power. After all, the engine, when finished, was to be used on long runs, and as such, it had to be altered accordingly. It would mean more work and more cost, but that isn't considered when you are after perfection, and again, that means great attention to detail. When I attempted it, the flywheels needed very little drilling to get them right and I can remember having to get my two knife edges resharpened to make sure of it. I must have spent around sixteen hours or so in making sure of their balance and trueness of running. The large alloy con-rod was drilled with about an $^1/_8$" hole all the way up to feed the little end. Also an $^1/_8$" groove was apparent in the alloy round the outer side of the phosphorus little end bearing, and through a hole in the top of the con-rod to cool the piston. The hole in the con-rod also fed the phosphorus bronze sleeve of the little end bearing. By now it was August, and in a month's time, I'd be laying up the MOV for winter, for it was far too risky for a semi-racer to be out on slippery roads; it would be suicide. And while I'm on the subject of slippery roads, I'd had three rear wheel slides on the MOV on my last two rides and not through braking, for I hardly used them on my runs. It was the tyres. They were fine for ordinary use on a standard road bike, but not for the angle of lean I was doing, so come Spring, I was planning to fit a 300 x 19 rim and ribbed tyre with a security bolt on the front, with probably an Avon Speedmaster, and on the rear, I hoped to fit a Dunlop Racing, that's a semi-cling rubber wrap around tyre, quite expensive, but very well worth it.

At present the front rim was a 3.25", so by replacing it with a 3.00" rim and tyre it would give less gyroscopic pull on the front wheel when taking fast bends. I'd already got two large alloy control levers on the clutch and front brake, the clutch lever making the clutch lovely and light. The brake lever too had an improved pull, but it wasn't a substitute for the loss of braking area, so for the next season, and in particular if I succeeded in this other engine, then a twin leading shoe big front brake would have be found, before the new rim was fitted. During the next month I tried hard to find the right hub or complete wheel but just couldn't locate one, then one day, I'd just pulled up on my MAC at Alf Holland's when a chap on a 250 Honda Sports pulled up also. I let him go in before me, as I hung back to have a good look at his front wheel. It was a beauty, all alloy with a nice big twin leading shoe front brake, and by the look of it, it wasn't far out from what I wanted. So, nipping into Alf's, I borrowed his tape rule.

"Be back in three minutes," I yelled, and went outside to measure the width of the Honda's front hub. It was only about $^3/_8$" wider, no problem; I must have a real brake for Spring. I didn't of course really want to use a Jap brake in the Velo, but until I got the right one, then why not? It would be safer than to run out of road!

After getting what I had come for, I asked Geoff where my best place would be to get a good used 1250 Honda front wheel or just a hub. He knew right away.

"Leicester," he replied. "There's a Jap bike breaker there. I'll give him a ring if you like."

"Please do," I said. "Either a wheel or a hub, I don't mind which." So, within two minutes, Geoff had located one for me and not only that, he was going over there tomorrow.

"Call tomorrow night and I'll have it for you." I called next evening after work and sure enough, it was there, complete with tyre and tube and the anchor strip. "That is great. How much do I owe you, Geoff?"

"I gave eighteen pounds, give me twenty pounds being as you're nearly one of us." Well, I was more than pleased as it had hardly been used, hardly any wear as it had been taken from a machine with a busted rear end. I smiled to myself over this for I'd just paid twenty pounds for the front wheel, which is what I paid for the bike, but when you compare the price of a new front wheel of eighty-six pounds, less tyre and tube, Geoff had done me a very good turn. Taking the wheel to Len Booth's, Coventry's wheel builder, I saw his son, as Len was no longer with us, and writing down just what was required, I left the wheel with him. It was a centre build-up, so even type spoke could be used on both sides. I was also having the rim drilled for a security bolt which the wheel builder would supply. Two days later I collected my new wheel and indeed, it looked brand new, as the builder had done a very nice job. The 300 x 19 rim was a chrome one and had been drilled for a security bolt, six spokes in the rear of the valve hole. The spokes were rustproof and double butted to stand up to heavy braking. Also, they were beautifully laced, a first-class job. Of course, the tyre and tube were now spares, for they were too wide for the new rim. At home I offered my new wheel into the Velo forks. I had measured it correctly, for it required $^3/_{16}$" to be turned off the width of both spindle lock nuts, also, I found that the spindle would also have to be slotted, as the diameter of the spindle too was roughly $^3/_{16}$" too wide to fit into the fork lugs. So, after these two alterations had been done and the wheel was fitted up with a new Avon Speedmaster tyre, tube, rim band and security bolt, I was able to get the new wheel into the fork lugs. It now fitted perfectly, a light blow on the tyre being all that was required to tap the flats on the spindle into the fork lugs. After fitting it all up, I marked the spindle to be drilled for a $^1/_8$" split pin so then, with a castle nut fitted, the wheel could never work loose, and the same method was used on the anchor strip, which was also done in heavy chrome.

This done, I could now make up a heavy brake operating cable to fit it perfectly which I did, and I must say, it felt very strong and firm, a big improvement. To complete the job I decided that I'd go all the way and mark and drill the rear of the brake drum, then in turn, drill holes in the brake plate, (the opposite side of the brake drum), and then make and fit on an air-scoop to ram air in for cooling. Of course, the wheel had to come out again and the brake plate be removed in order to do this. So, for the next night, I was to be found very carefully measuring and marking brake plate and brake drum for air ramming the brake. The actual air-scoop I made out of $^1/_8$" thick aluminium sheeting, again from my pals in Hearsal Lane. I got the shape right, by the use of a formed piece of steel at the right angle, known as a former. When completed, in order to ensure that all the air going in the wider end of the air ram all passed into the brake drum, I made a thick gasket and, sealing it with Welseal, fitted it between scoop and brake plate. The scoop I bolted on with four 2BA chromed bolts, and for complete safety riveted the bolt ends over the inside nut, as a loose nut in a brake drum could prove fatal. When fitted all up again, it looked and worked a treat and within half a dozen applications of the front brake, I could tell that now I'd got myself a real front stopper, which would make the bike much safer at speed.

Chapter Thirty-Four

The Alloy Engine Build-Up and its Problems

Having now got the MOV back on its wheels, work could begin on the very careful line up of the new engine. I had already placed it in with just three bolts holding it, for I could see that it was of different dimensions than my cast iron one, and I wanted to find out if, with this big finning, a rocker box could be fitted on under the top rail of the frame. It was close, but yes, it could be done.

The main problem would be adapting a rocker box for full oiling, as the springs on the valves in the alloy head were air pin springs, but I had got in the spare two sets of coil springs that I felt sure would fit the alloy head. So, having found this out, I could now fit the crankcase into place, with the barrel and piston on it. The alignment of the engine was very important, so that meant that the clutch and gearbox would have to be fitted up as well to prevent any alterations later. Having got this done, my next problem would be to sort out and alter a rocker box to fit on the cylinder head, for it would be tragic to go to all the trouble of rigging up a rocker box with all the oiling mods etc., only to find that it wouldn't then fit onto the head, so of course, the rocker box to head was now my number one problem.

I had at this stage, got five spare rocker boxes in standard form, and two cutaway for open valve gear, as on grass track engines. I must admit that , through being too eager, I scrapped my first attempt, as I hadn't measured the height of the bolt holes in relation to the height of the finning; there was only a thou in it, but it was enough to put a hairline crack on the base of the rocker box when it was bolted down. But I made certain on the next one, for I took off $^{1}/_{8}$" off the top of the fins under the rocker box, also, I made four steel collars to mount it on, which, if I hadn't been in such a hurry, I should have done in the first place. This time it was on level and tight; now for the rockers and the oiling. This had to be spot on, for a trip up here would be fatal, also, the length of the pushrods had all got to be accounted for. After many attempts and alterations I finally got the rockers all rigged up and working and there was also room to fit hardened valve caps on top of the valve stems. This would help to prevent hammering at speed, also I was able to fit in the side thrust springs, as standard on the iron head. Now I'd got this right, I would polish the rockers, then check to see if it would be feasible to drill the rockers in order to reduce the loads generated at high revs, as it is this loading that causes valve bounce. A pipe was made up to feed the rockers, and holes drilled to make a complete circuit for oil to reach all moving parts; also, I milled grooves along the runners in the rocker box roof as further oiling. Carefully checking over all this I felt sure that I had covered every possible way to make sure that oil was supplied under pressure to all parts. However, I'd overlooked one thing; it wasn't serious, so I'll let it develop here as it did at the time on the bike.

Now at last it was sorted out, hopefully, I could now get it all built up. This was going to be a one-off engine, all Velo, yes, but different to any other Velo engine. It was going to be a very interesting test when I'd finally completed it all. It was all but new, so it would all have to be run in. Like the iron barrel, the alloy barrel and its steel sleeve had been drilled on the thrust side for oil to be pumped up on to the piston. The piston I took out of the busted engine was a cutaway lightened slipper piston with no oil control ring. The piston that I had fitted back and of course very carefully balanced up, was also a slipper piston, not all cutaway and with an oil control ring. The timing chest too was altered for maximum lubrication, the timing gears and M17 cam I would use from the iron engine, except the magneto driving gear. This I replaced with an automatic advance and retard gear as fitted on the MAC. The oiling system would all be pressure fed, leaving nothing to chance, so with the oil circulating thirty per cent faster than normal, it should easily stand the extra revs.

The cylinder head was of a higher compression that the iron head, not just for more power, but to make more heat, as Velos had had problems with alloy heads running too cool. But the problem only related to short circuit racing. The job I was building it for was long fast runs, so really, I didn't expect any trouble in this area, but it would have paid me to pay more attention to this, as I knew it was a critical area, but I hadn't got a Burdet to measure the volume and made an assumption on what it had been like before, but it was a mistake, as you will see. Again, because of this I was pretty sure I'd have to reset the ignition timing, as on the MAC, and most likely too, the carburation would be too rich. Both proved to be correct when this little lot was put to the test. I felt now at this stage, that I was really getting down to it. It was at last taking shape.

Chapter Thirty-Five

Don't Knock the Rockers

It had taken all winter to complete all this, in fact, through one snag and then another, I didn't get the job finished until mid April, so if all proved well I could get it taxed for the first of May. I could have really used a private road or circuit right now, for it all needed to be run in before its MOT, but I was already a month late in getting it taxed, so I'd just have to wait and see if I had done the job right or not. As yet, I hadn't even had it running, but the next day was Saturday and the whole of our gang had got the weekend off. Saturday came up fine and dry and from 8.30 a.m. till 10.00 a.m. I was busy making my final checks. I'd deliberately waited until 10.00 a.m. as I didn't want to wake any late sleepers, because if this fired, the whole road would hear it. I'd put half a pint of Redex in with the oil, and at this stage, I would like to bring to your attention the brilliance of Redex in the oil for running in any engine using mineral oils, so with the engine lubricating system all primed up, I attempted my first start up. The engine fired at once, only to splutter out with a wet plug, so, fitting in a new, softer plug, I tried again. It fired again as soon as it turned, but this time it kept running. It smoked well for about twenty seconds or so, and I could see in the oil tank that the oil was flying round.

The engine had certainly got a healthy throb all right. One was easily aware of a high compression engine, but mechanically, it was lovely and quiet. It was, of course, nearly all new, and had to be run in, but this moment was a special one, and I felt really good about it. I pushed the bike back into our drive and allowed it to gently warm up while I checked for oil leaks. It was as dry as a bone, fuel-wise as well, and there were no signs of distress. I couldn't be certain at this stage that there wouldn't be any oil leaks at all, for any engine, and especially an all-alloy one, would have to be fully warmed up or even given a fair old run before one could be sure, but an all alloy special like this one, well, one would just have to wait and see. The way that this engine had started was in itself a very good sign. It was just trying to eight stroke, but I was happy about this, as it was what I had expected.

While the engine was warming up, I ran and got a spanner to loosen off the oil feed pipe up to the rockers. Oil just spurted out, the feed was perfect, so, having satisfied myself that all was well, I gently blipped the throttle. The response was instant so I had to be careful. The thing was alive and ready to run. After a few more minutes, and when I could no longer place my hand on the cylinder head because of the heat, I gently opened up the throttle and revved it up and down. As I was doing this, I heard a very faint metallic knocking, but only when it was revved. Of course, I was really on metal now, so with my ear all but in the engine I listened very carefully to trace its origin, and it was now getting louder, as the engine warmed up. I now listened very carefully and, keeping the revs high enough to produce the knock, it suddenly clicked as to what it was, so I stopped the engine immediately and removed the spark plug. My theory was this: the extra large inlet valve was kissing the piston, and I was right. Shining my pen torch into the cylinder head through the plughole, I slowly turned the engine over in second gear, and after lifting the bike onto its wooden block stand, both wheels were now clear of the ground by about six inches. As I turned the engine over, I saw the piston coming up as the exhaust closed and the inlet opened, and yes, as the piston got to the top of its stroke, I felt the slight judder, as well as seeing the inlet valve touch the piston. The piston was a Velo cutaway high compression racing piston, so it was obvious that the compression was at a critical 'too high'. What had happened was very easily explained. When the engine first started up, it was dead cold, but alloy soon warms up, so with the very high compression and the rapid expansion of the alloy piston, contact between valve and piston took place.

Snag number one had made itself known; no MOT this week, for it meant that the engine had to be taken down as far as the crankcase in order to fit a brass shim plate under the cylinder, thus raising up the cylinder by whatever thickness the plate was. In this case I was to fit a 030" thick plate in, and so, lowering the compression, and providing the working clearance at the same time, the safest way out. Other than that, the rest of it appeared to be very good, but again, nothing can be assumed until a test run, and as I have already stated, a private track would have been a blessing at this point. I had a couple of brass plates, one was the right thickness but too small, while the other was big enough but not thick enough, so off up to Alf's I shot to get the right one. I did this, in fact I got four pieces, two at 030", one at 025" and one at 020". As I left the shop, Geoff yelled, "And don't forget the drill hole for the oil feed!" A great one was Geoff.

Back home, it didn't take me long to take the engine down as far as the crankcase, for now I was able to strip it in block and not in bits, thus making it an easy strip and build. By 4.00 p.m. I'd just about got the job done, too late for an MOT as they didn't take any on after 12.00 noon, but at least, it would give me a bit of time to run the engine up a bit and look for any other snags. Before I started it up again, I changed the cutaway for the next size up, as it did try to eight stroke a little, so it would allow me the chance to check this out as well. The engine fired up in the length of our drive, as I'd put the car outside for a change, so I could run the bike in the garage. It ran lovely and smooth and sounded great, and the brass plate had sorted it out, for with the engine thoroughly warmed up, the knocking had gone and it was very mechanically quiet. Even Ivy remarked how good it sounded, for after being with me all these years, Ivy had a good ear for an engine. The eight stroking had gone, I'd put the correct plug back; as far as I could tell, the mixture was near enough right, and there wasn't an oil leak in sight, what more could I want? No more could be done without a run, and that wouldn't be until after the MOT next Saturday. Anyway, I could pack up three different baffle plates for the mega, two or three spare plugs and a few tools. I would get everything ready for a run on Saturday, and if possible, early Sunday morning, as by now, I was longing to try it, for only a run would prove it or otherwise. I was really looking forward to the test, this was the life.

Chapter Thirty-Six
Cotswold Calamity and Chicken Wire

Saturday came round at last; like everything else, when you're waiting for something good to come up, it always seems to be a long wait. The bike fired up first drop, and after a little warm up, I took off for the MOT. The bike felt great, it was a lovely engine and even though it was tight, it had a potent solid feel to it and I knew I was going to really enjoy the running in. I intended to get about seven hundred and fifty miles on the engine before I started to even speed up, for the running in of an engine, can make or mar it for life. At the MOT station it caused a stir, and quite a crowd gathered round the bike. In fact I was dying to get going, but found it a bit awkward to do so, but at last, I got away, for I'd intended to take off the seven hundred and fifty miles just round about Coventry just in case I did have any problems. It wouldn't be so far to push home, should I have to do it, and just for the record, when the front brake was tested, it pulled the tester out of the wall, bricks as well!

Throughout the week the bike had run beautifully, and by Friday I'd got 872 miles on the clock and the engine was raring to go. So, on the Sunday, I took off as planned into the Cotswolds, having first checked over the whole machine. Up until now I hadn't exceeded 50 m.p.h. and the engine was running like a watch. I'd checked the tappet clearances three times and they hadn't moved; that was a good sign, as it showed that the engine was settling very well. During my running in around Coventry and districts, I'd swapped a $^3/_8$" holed baffle for a $^5/_{16}$" holed baffle and the carburation felt nice and sharp and the plug colour, a light brown, just the job. Through the Wolds the bike was simply gliding along and it was full of power, so after I'd covered about 100 Cotswold miles I took it just in a burst up to 60-65 m.p.h.. It sounded marvellous, I was really chuffed. But it was to be short-lived. Two miles further on was a long hill, and about two-thirds of the way up, I heard a sound that I didn't think was possible, for it was the sound of a cylinder head gasket going, and looking down at the engine, blue smoke was coming out between the head and the barrel. I pulled in at once to find the cause, and it didn't take more than a minute to find it. The high compression of this engine was just too much for the front studs holding down the front of the barrel to the crankcase, for it had literally ripped the two studs out of the crankcase.

The reason for my surprise, was the fact that a Velocette cylinder head has a spigotted lip and is ground onto the cylinder top, then a thin all-copper gasket is fitted in between, hence my utter surprise when I heard the sound.

'Hell,' I thought, and I'd kept away from the Wolds, just in case. Now what, for I realised that I was then about 90 miles from home. To further explain this calamity, the thrust of the piston was on the rear of the cylinder, putting more load on the two front studs.

Well, I was quite high up in the Wolds, as I'd been up several long hills before coming up this one. It had certainly taken the Cotswolds to sort it out. About forty miles from where I was, at Shipton-on-Stow was Arthur Taylor's garage, a big noise at Velos, and it was Arthur who had built the record-breaking 500cc Velo that had run over 100 m.p.h. for over twenty-four hours, a remarkable feat in those days. Now, if I could get there! I'd try, it was my only hope. My plan at this moment was to limp on and get to Arthur's where I could safely leave the Velo and go back home on the bus, for I knew that just past Arthur's garage on the other side of the road was a Midland Red bus stop, then at home, I would have to get either Geoff or Bernard Holland to pick it up for me in their box combo.

So, having this thought in mind, I pushed the bike to the hilltop, got my breath back and started it up on the long slope on the other side. The engine fired at once, and once on to level ground, and of course, on a very light throttle, it was going along very steadily at about 38 m.p.h..

On coming to my next hill, I changed down early to ease the load and quickly realised that third gear was the gear it ran most easy on. As I was going along, I thought about my number two snag, for this was a nasty one, and of course it meant the engine would have to be taken out and stripped, splitting the crankcase, but then what? Well, it needed added strength. I had, of course, my other crankcase from my original engine, but with this power output, it would most likely do it all over again, so the answer was to have large steel inserts either screwed and pegged, or brazed and ground, for in this way, the studs would then be threaded into steel, and not alloy. I felt a little better after thinking this, and then I had another inspiration; truly necessity is the mother of invention. If my idea worked, I hoped I could get back home still riding the bike. Well, my brains seemed to be working on full bore, even if my engine wasn't, so let's have a go. The idea was a very simple one, most good ideas are, that's why they usually work. The idea I had in mind was to find a length of chicken wire and run a tourniquet in between the finning of the cylinder head, say two fins in on either side, under the rocker box, and right under the crankcase. The wire could then be tightened sufficiently by fixing another smaller tourniquet across from side to side, so pulling the wires inwards to effect a tighter pull. Now to find some suitable wire, for of course, no one was open. There was one garage open for petrol and oil only, the workshop was all locked up, so that was out. It must have been about halfway between where it blew to Arthur Taylor's before I found some wire. It was hanging from a fence, but it was worth a try.

The wire was long enough, but a bit on the thick side. However, I got hold of a suitable length and cut it with the side cutters on my large pair of pliers and about ten minutes or so later, I'd got it fixed, and I coiled up a spare length and put it in my rucksack, just in case. The engine fired straight away and I was very pleased at the result, for the next hill I ran up easily, in top at about 50 m.p.h. and no blow. I'd done 962 miles since the engine rebuild, so as long as I rode steady, I had no problems with a tight engine. In fact, the engine kept wanting to go. Going up a big hill around ten miles from where I'd done my emergency repairs, I heard my first faint blow, so I slowed down, changed down, and over the hill, I pulled in and made use of my third tourniquet, this time behind the engine, but it worked fine, and ten miles further on, I had arrived at Shipton-on-Stow still under power.

Arthur, on hearing my bike, came out and we shook hands, as it must have been two years since we last met. He couldn't take his eyes off the bike, and he loved the engine, so I told him and his two sons, who had joined us, my story.

"You poor old devil," he said. "Bring it in and we'll fix it up good and tight." So in went the Velo and up onto the motorcycle bench, lifted by the four of us.

"This old bench has had many a TT winner on it," said Arthur. "I built my record-breaker on this."

"I'm very honoured to be attended to by such famous people."

"Think nothing of it, lad," replied Arthur. "Any one who can build an engine like this makes them one of us, and this one is a beauty." I felt very flattered, for praise by an expert such as Arthur Taylor, to me, was like receiving an honour from the Queen. Just then a very nice-looking young lady came in and handed me a cup of coffee.

"Hello, I hope you take sugar," she said, then she saw what was being done to the Velo. "Chicken wire," she said. "I knew this place was going downhill, the best of luck," And she went back into the house. I think the young lady could have been Arthur's daughter, for she seemed to me to have Arthur's dry humour. However, the coffee was real coffee, and it was very welcome.

Arthur's two sons made a cracking job of wiring it all up and there were no less than eight lengths of wire passing over the head, four left and four right, then tightened crossways both back and front.

"If that doesn't get you home, then my name isn't Arthur Taylor," said Arthur.

"That's terrific," I said. "By the look of that, I could tackle the island." By this remark, they knew that I meant the Isle of Man.

"What do you intend to do about the crankcase?" asked Arthur.

"I think I've got that worked out. I'm going to take them to Velo's and get them inserted and pegged, then the studs won't be screwing into alloy and I'll get all four done. In that way, the thrust load will be distributed right across the top of the crankcase."

"You cunning old fox!" replied Arthur. "That's clever. I like that. Do you know, you could become a good mechanic one day!"

So, after many, many thanks, as Arthur wouldn't take a penny, I got going again, and, but for the wire showing, there was no way one could tell what had happened and I was able to ride home at a steady 55-60 m.p.h. without stopping as the wire held up beautifully and I'd kept my record of always getting back on the bike.

Chapter Thirty-Seven

The Last Snag but One

The next week found me stripping down my MOV engine in big chunks, for at least I didn't need to strip the flywheels. So on the Saturday morning at 8.30 a.m. I was off to Velo's to tell them my problem and my answer to it. At the Velo service counter, they were very surprised to hear and see my problem. The service man fetched the workshop foreman who listened very carefully and also took notes on what I said.

"I've never known this problem to happen," he said, "but this engine is a real special and it is obviously developing more power than the crankcase was designed to take, hence the steel inserts. Right, young man, come at this time next week and it will all be ready for you." Thanking him I went back home where I surprised Ivy and the two lads by saying,

"Hands up all those who want to go out in the car tomorrow, as we can spend all day in the country." So the family benefited by it and a lovely weekend was had by all. 'I must do this more often,' I thought, so once the Velo was right, I intended to take the family out more, as I was getting too carried away on these bike projects.

Next Saturday found me at Velo's on my MAC dead on time. The job had been done just as I had explained it, and it was a first-class job in every way. There was even a set of strengthened studs and cylinder head nuts and washers to go with them, and a note tied to the studs for the head torque to be pulled down eight pounds stronger.

"How's that?" said the foreman who had come in to see me.

"Absolutely beautiful," I replied. "A first-class job in every way. It looks as if you've really got down to the problem."

"Yes, I think you could safely say that," he replied. "And that is also why we've supplied these studs which are much stronger, and we would like you to torque them down in three stages eight pounds more than normal, and that should do it."

"A cracking job," I replied. "How much do I owe you?"

"The management said no charge, as they reckon that it shouldn't have happened."

"I can hardly believe it!" I said. "This is fabulous! I've never known such service."

"Well, we've got to look after you racers," he said. "After all, chaps like you get this firm a lot of orders."

"That's wonderful, but I insist on giving the man who did this a drink," and I put a five pound note on the counter. It was wonderful personal service that made the firm of Velocette unique, for they made no distinction between little men like me, or a firm like themselves. Truly, Velocettes were a wonderful firm; I cannot praise them enough.

As I was getting on my MAC a chap came out and ran up to me. He was the chap who repaired and modified my crankcase.

"Many thanks," said this chap. "That was a very good tip and all the very best with your bike. We'd all like to see it when it's done."

"Thank you. I'll come on it in a week or two, than you can all see it." We shook hands on it, and I went off feeling over the moon about it all. What a super job, by jingo! I'd have a bike now and it didn't take me long to get back home.

Throughout the next week, I'd got it all together again with the new studs, nuts and washers. All I had to do now was to get it warmed up properly and pull the whole lot down in three stages to the final torque poundage. On assembly, I'd noticed how well the piston and bore had bedded in. That was because, prior to first assembly, I had taken the time to 'lap in' by hand the piston in the cylinder, by so doing removing any high spots that cause piston pick up; in other words, I'd 'honed it in', attention to detail. I also checked the valves and valve seats. They were all in excellent order and now that the motor was all but run in, I could hopefully look forward to some interesting runs. The front brake was lovely and it felt very strong and safe. I could also feel the grip of the two new tyres which were also now run in, so after the bedding of the head and studs, and again checking the tappets, she was all ready to go. Sunday arrived nice and dry, a bit dull, but good enough for a test run, so I took off at

5.00 a.m. with great hopes for a trouble-free run, as I intended to do this run in three stages, just in case.

The whole machine felt like a new one, the engine was raring to go, but I held it in check for the first fifteen miles, for I had to be very sure this time. So I pulled in and checked it all over. It looked perfect, bone dry everywhere and the carburation was crisp and hard. I was sure that I'd got it right. The plug reading was as before, just a light brown, there was no eight stroking on shut off, and the acceleration, as far as I had tried, was very good. During last week, I'd made a chain oiler out of a Redex can, one could buy them in those days. It was a simple affair, having an oil tap silver soldered in the base and in the tap. I'd soldered in an 'amal' 90 jet, letting one drop of 'SAE 90 Gear Oil' onto the inside bottom chain run every two and a half minutes, just keeping the chain nice and wet, and so eliminating chair wear. This too was working very well, so, being satisfied, off we went again. I hadn't exactly planned a run, and I decided on about two hundred miles, calling at Arthur's on my way back and telling him what Velo's had done for me. He'd like that. I'd done about a hundred miles from leaving home and up to now I hadn't been over 65 m.p.h., so, coming out onto a nice tarmac road with a series of fast bends in it, I opened up a bit. The engine really responded. This was great. This is what it was all about and at 75 m.p.h. the exhaust note was fabulous. I increased to 80 m.p.h. and it was so smooth that I increased just a bit more, and for half a mile only, I easily reached 95 m.p.h. on the clock. The engine felt wonderful, absolutely full of power, so, with just two long bends left to take, I kept it on song at 95 m.p.h.

When I got clear of the bends I looked back. I don't know why I did, and it was then that I saw it, blue smoke, pouring from the exhaust pipe like a petrol-oiled two-stroke. I slammed the throttle shut, and the smoke all but stopped and I pulled in at once and shut off. Then, for a split second, I thought that I'd burnt a hole in the piston. 'Impossible,' I thought, for the mixture was perfect, so what the devil would cause engine oil to be burnt in the combustion chamber? I took out the spark plug and, turning the bike so that the sunlight shone into the cylinder, I got my first clue, for I could see that the inlet valve was awash with oil. It appeared to me that this had only happened at speed, so if I was right, all that was needed to cure it was a small modification to this already modified oiling system. For, in my theory, what had happened was this. The oil in this engine was being pumped round at least thirty per cent faster than in a standard engine, so oil pressure would be up, and supply at speed very rapid, and this was the cause of the problem. So the only way for the oil to get back to crankcase from the rockers was down the pushrod tube, the same as my MAC. I'd put the extra oil feed in but had overlooked the extra amount to drain out. So, if I drill the rocker boxes at a distance just below the level of the top of the valve guides, presto! The extra escape would be made, for as I saw it, the oil at speed, had built up faster than the drain off would allow, so once the oil level built up to the height of the valve guides, the suction from the inlet would be enormous and oil would be sucked under extreme pressure down the inlet valve guide and into the combustion chamber. That's the only way that the inlet valve could become saturated in oil! If my theory proved right, then it wouldn't take a major job to effect a cure. So, in order to check this out, I waited for five minutes to allow time for the oil in the overfilled rocker box to drain back into the crankcase. If this theory was right, then, when I started, blue smoke would appear just for a moment, for the piston expansion would have shrunk a little, so for a minute or two, too much oil would be in the crankcase waiting to be pumped back. Let's try it. I looked into the oil tank and the oil level had hardly dropped, a further proof that this theory was correct. Refitting the plug I took off and sure enough, a slight blue haze followed me along the road but had cleared in less than one minute. I kept the speed at around 75 m.p.h. and at this speed, no smoke at all was emitted from the exhaust, so it looked as if my theory had proved to be correct. I slackened off now to around 60 m.p.h., then when I'd done about another twenty miles or so, I pulled in and stopped the engine and took out the plug. The inlet valve was bone dry, and so was the combustion chamber, so, finally checking the oil tank level, and finding that it hadn't moved, I was now convinced over what I had to do in order to put it right. Calling in at Arthur's at Shipton-on-Stow, I told them the full story. I don't know which intrigued Arthur the most – the crankcase repair or the oiling-problem, for whichever it was, Arthur said,

"This is a wonderful story. Do get it all down on paper. It will thrill the younger generation, for you and I are a dying generation and a true story like this needs to be told." Well, I hope he was right, for if you are enjoying it, he was, but as for me, well I did it, and it is giving me a real bonus to live again the fantastic rides I had on my beloved Velo. After all, it was my 'dream machine' come true and praised by one of the best, Arthur Taylor of Shipton-on-Stow.

Chapter Thirty-Eight
King of the Cotswolds

Two weeks later saw the MOV in its very latest form. I'd made a better chain oiler out of a brass drip feed off a milling machine and with a tapered needle, cut down from an SU carburettor it was fully adjustable to suit all conditions. Besides, it now looked like it was in keeping with the rest of the bike. From the base of the rocker box, there were two brass drain-off tubes and attached to these, were two thin plastic pipes running down to the top of the timing chest, where two more brass pipes were fitted, and the other ends of the plastic tubes were fitted on them; these were my oiling drain-off modification. The two brass pipes or adapters in the base of the rocker box, reached up to within $^3/_{16}$" of the top of the valve guide, leaving enough oil in the valve area. Also, I had sewn up in our trim shop at work, a nice-sized sorbo rubber pad, wrapped in thin black leather with two leather straps underneath; this was strapped on the bike between fuel tank and seat as a protection in the event of a crash or a violent stop. The bike was then about complete.

That coming Sunday, I'd decided to take a completely different route, as I had to be careful, for I was now getting quite a batt on, but even so, I always eased off and ran the bike very gently through the villages. The run I'd planned would take me through the Wolds, then back through Chipping Norton, Broadway, Chipping Campden and then Stow-in-the-Wold. It would work out about 230 miles but I wanted a long run, for I reckoned that I'd got it right, so this run would be a big test for it as I didn't intend to hang about. I'd changed and bled the oil system and added just a drop of Redex, so all was ready. The fuel I always used in the Velo was Cleveland Discol, a fuel with a small percentage of alcohol added. It wasn't a lot, but an ideal fuel for a high compression racing engine such as mine, for alcohol is the cleanest burning fuel of all and also, much higher compressions could be used if this fuel was used. I had recently heard that Cleveland Discol was being phased out, a bitter blow, but Geoff-Holland had urged me to try Jet, as he reckoned it just might do it, as for now, I'd got a tank full of Discol. I set off at 5.00 a.m. and the bike was running very well, it was a fine day, a bit breezy, but fine and after the first ten miles, and after I'd stopped for a final look at the engine, I started to move. The engine was all run-in now, so I could concentrate more on my riding and less on the running of the bike but of course, I wouldn't ignore it, for only a fool would do that, but having the bike running right made all the difference to one's riding.

Well, I'd done about ninety miles going very well at speeds between 60-80 m.p.h. and there was no sign of any blue smoke, but I knew that to try it, I should have to go above 90 m.p.h., so, coming up to where the blue smoke had appeared before, I hammered on at about 75 m.p.h.. Taking the next right-hander, quite fast, brought me right behind two big bikes. One was a Triumph Thunderbird 650 twin and the other was an Ariel EN 500 single. Too late to slow down, so I increased speed just as I approached the 'blue smoke bends', as I called them. It was then as I overtook these two bikes, doing about 87 m.p.h.. I wasn't bothered about the bikes, I had a fast test to do and do it I did; at around 95-98 m.p.h. 'on the clock', I shot a glance behind, no bikes and no smoke. My mod had paid off, and easing off the speed, I dropped steadily back to 70 m.p.h., where I pulled into a lay-by. As I got off the bike and leaned it on its prop stand, I could see the new oil pouring down the drain-off pipes and I knew I'd won. Looking over the engine I was delighted, for there wasn't a leak on it. I had every reason to feel pleased, it was a very satisfying feeling after months of hard work, at last I'd got myself a racing special of my own concoction.

I'd just finished looking all over the bike when the two riders I'd passed pulled in and stopped.

"What in the world of wonder is that?" asked the Ariel rider. "Velocette 250 special," I answered. "Come and see for yourself." The two riders came over to inspect the bike.

"What a beauty!" said the Ariel rider. "I've never seen one like that. Is it a works bike?"

"No, it's my own concoction and I am just giving it a final test after a few hiccups, and now it's just about right."

"Wish I'd got my camera with me, this one really is a special," said the other chap. And I must have spent a good fifteen minutes, telling them about the Velo and answering their many questions.

This test was really the final one, for now I'd really got it right and over the next couple of months I met quite a few riders who tried to catch the Velo, and most of these machines were either 350 or 500, but the road holding of my tailor-made machine plus its very special engine, proved just that bit better. Only a TT bike would ever be able to hold the Velo. On one of these runs, a chap on a lovely 350 Cammy Velo lay in wait for me, and as I came thundering along, he came out into the road and waved me down. I pulled in and stopped my engine and this chap came over, grinning all over his face.

"Got you at last! I've been looking out for you for the last three weeks and I just want to see the bike they are calling, 'the King of the Cotswolds'. By the way, my name is Dick," he said, and he held out his hand to be shook.

"Very pleased to meet you, Dick, my name is George." And I got off my bike and put it on its stand.

"Bloody glory," said Dick. "What is it? It's beautiful, just beautiful." I felt about six feet tall. This was praise indeed, and Dick was by now almost inside my engine.

"What did you mean, Dick, by 'King of the Cotswolds?"

"Well," said Dick, "you must have been aware of several bikes having a go at you over the last few weeks. I've had two tries to catch you and so have several of my mates. One of them has a Thruxton and he couldn't catch you either, so they've named you 'King of the Cotswolds."

"Thank you," I replied. "I'm very flattered."

"Just what is this?" asked Dick. "Is it a 350?"

"Two hundred and fifty. The frame," I said, "isn't tall enough to hold a 350. Besides, if you look, you'll see MOV on the nearside crankcase." Dick went round to the nearside of the bike and saw the MOV stamp and engine number on the crankcase.

"I can hardly believe it," he replied. "Tell me, this must be a works special engine then!" I laughed, and in the next ten minutes or so, I'd told him my story.

"That's a lovely story, George," said Dick. "Have you been back to Arthur's or Velo's since you've got it right?"

I told him that I intended to do just that over the next two weeks. We got well acquainted over the next twenty minutes or so, and we sat on each other's bikes. The KTT was a beauty and Dick, too, had spent quite a bit of cash and a lot of time on it. Sitting astride my MOV, Dick said, "This is a super riding position. It fits me a treat and I haven't seen a neater front wheel and brake. It's a cracker." And indeed, Dick and I were about the same size and weight and I could see that he had fallen in love with it, as he just couldn't take his eyes off it. Looking at Dick's bike, I said,

"You're using Castrol R, then?"

"Yes, but how did you know?"

I pointed to the knurled boss on the top end of the camshaft drive tube, where a drop of tell-tale oil had appeared.

"Leather and tallow fat," I replied.

"What do you mean?" asked Dick.

"I mean if you carefully cut a strip of leather, about $^3/_{16}$" thick and wrap it around the cam drive tube and cut the joint accurately at a 45° angle and smother it in tallow fat, then it will fit in and stop your oil leak without you taking the head off."

"Thanks a lot, George," replied Dick. "You know your engines." So, by now, we were both very friendly.

"My mates won't believe me when I tell them that this is a 250," said Dick, looking at my bike, then he said, "I don't suppose I could just go up the road and back on it, could I?"

"Why not?" I answered. "I'll have a ride on yours."

"That's great," said Dick, so I started up my bike and Dick was fascinated by the way the bike was rocking to the throb of the engine. He then kicked up his bike and said,

"Don't worry, George. I'll be very careful and I won't do anything daft."

"Lead on, Dick," I yelled. "I'll be right behind you." Both gear shifts were the same and it would be very interesting to get a comparison with a 350 Cammy.

Dick took off quite sharply on the MOV, for of course, he hadn't got the feel of it yet. I, on the other hand, was easily at home on the Cammy, for I had ridden these machines many times before. Dick, once we were in top gear, shouted, "This is brilliant. How far shall we go?"

"Fish Hill," I yelled back. "It's about twelve miles away." Dick was grinning all over his face and I could tell this had made his day. We were only doing 50 m.p.h. as Dick was showing respect for my bike, so I shot by him and called him on, and at 70 m.p.h., Dick's eyes were shining behind his goggles. I increased to 80 m.p.h. and Dick held me, still grinning, then at the top of Fish Hill that goes down into Broadway, we pulled in and stopped.

"Terrific," smiled Dick. "You'd never believe it was a 250. It's got more poke than mine. You've only got to look at it and it's away. And thanks for the ride. You've made my day." We spent another ten minutes or so before we parted company, during which time Dick had offered to swap bikes with me and throw in a spare engine and all his spares. It was a very good offer, but I'd designed this myself, it was my baby as it were, and besides, I could never replace it, so, thanking Dick, we agreed to meet in this spot two weeks from now, or any Sunday at the same time when it was fine. Over the next five weeks or so, we met up again and Dick brought several of his mates to meet as he put it, 'the King of the Cotswolds'. At one point, there were nine of us, all about twenty yards apart, roaring along at about 80 m.p.h.. It sounded like a lot of aircraft, but I could hear the high note of my Velo just an octave above the rest. I'd done the job right and my 248cc special had made its mark, for every one of these lads was a true motorcyclist; their bikes were their lives.

Chapter Thirty-Nine
A Brush with the Law

Meeting different riders and their machines was good and a nice time was had by us all, particularly when big bike discussions were indulged in. I remember one Sunday, around five or six riders and myself were all looking at a drawing that I'd done on the road in chalk, when a police car drew up to see what was going on. It turned out great; for one of the policemen was a keen motorcyclist himself and in two minutes flat, two more pupils were added to the class, and ten minutes later, two cars had pulled in as well, all wondering what was going on. The police, of course, then called the meeting off for road safety. This friendly meeting with the police was to save me from a nasty, or rather, what could have been a nasty encounter five weeks later.

I always tried to vary my speed routes, so as to distribute the flying Velo over the Wolds, but meeting at the top of Fish Hill caused rather a problem, as you will see. By now, I was well known throughout the Wolds, and by various riders and, as I said, I really enjoyed meeting all these lads on their different bikes, and that was the problem. So, on the following Sunday, I let my pals know that I was having a go next week, and I wouldn't be going slow or stopping, for I must get the final test all done as I had promised to go and report back to Arthur.

The next Sunday was a lovely day and on the Saturday before I'd changed the oil and done a very thorough check on the bike, including fork shackles, mag points and even a geometry check for perfect line up, as I didn't intend to hang about. So at 5.00 a.m. I was away. The tank was full and after my usual ten-mile warm up, I started to go. Near Halford I had gone by a Morgan 4.4 uphill and he obviously didn't like it, for, like all the other speedsters, he followed me up. A few miles further on, I was at 90 m.p.h. and the Morgan wasn't very far behind, but once we reached the bends, he was soon left far behind. On reaching one of my landmarks, I looked at my watch and my mileage and I'd just done thirty-eight miles in thirty minutes, that's exactly 76 m.p.h. for a 248cc. The run was a good one and only two riders took up the challenge, one on a 350 Ariel red Hunter, and, to my surprise, the other on an Ariel Square Four; both shot away after me. I was grinning. This was the life. The Square Four was a 1,000cc and the adrenaline was running now. I was in my element, and yes, I was really shifting. The road holding was excellent and I was gong through bends like a rocket. I tell you, I knew as soon as I saw the two Ariels that I wouldn't see them again. Big-headed! Yes, it was, but I'd got the Velo and I knew that this bike was in the class of a racing machine. It would only be a racer that could hold me through the bends and he'd have to be a very good rider at that. Coming into Broadway, I'd got the bit in my teeth, and I shot up Fish Hill as if I was going up Snaefell on the Isle Of Man mountain circuit. There are six bends in Fish Hill and I broke the law at every one of them, for with the hill clear of traffic, I cut straight across those bends using the racing line, that is, 'the nearest distance between two point is a straight line', and I took it. I'd never before gone up any hill like this, and I was halfway up before I changed down. I changed down again just before the top and then, with my front wheel trying to lift in second gear, I literally shot over the top, screamed away in second, and, charging away to around 60-65 m.p.h. in third, I was about to change up into top, when I saw it. Oh yes, there was no way out.

For, parked on the grass verge, about a hundred yards down the road was a large motorway police car, and it was facing the same way that I was travelling; I'd had it. Slamming the throttle shut, the noise was almost as loud in volume as the take-off of a Vulcan bomber. The full volume of the complete valve overlap was echoed in the megaphonics that came on shutdown. To be fair and honest, I was asking for it, for really, the noise was disgusting, 'bloody awful', if you like, and of course, I had to slow down fast in order to stop in time; changing down to second sent the volume of sound even worse than the first one and a load of crows went squawking into the air adding to the clatter.

I'd stopped about ten yards to the rear of the police car and the police sergeant who had been standing in my path with his hand up, came slowly over to where I had come to rest. Just then, the police car doors opened and two policemen got out, one of whom I had been explaining desmodromic valve gear to, with my drawing on the road. The sergeant didn't speak for quite a time, for he couldn't take his eyes off the Velo, so I took off my crash hat so they could see that I wasn't just a long-haired yobbo. Still the sergeant didn't speak, until held gone right round the bike again. When he did speak, he said,

"That is one of the finest pieces of machinery I've ever seen, so, because I can see how immaculate it is, and for what it is, I'm letting you go. But," And then he paused, to give emphasis to his next words, "if I ever catch you again, using Broadway as a test bed, you and your bike will be barred forever, because Sir Gerald Nabarro, the Worcester MP, has had me and my two men up at 4.00 a.m., looking for the madman who is waking up the whole of Broadway," And he raised his voice in anger. "4.00 am! Because you can't sleep, but you'd better think about sleeping, because if you don't, I'm going to make certain that you'll get plenty of time to do just that. Now, get going and don't come back!"

"Thank you, sergeant, I'll give you no more trouble," I said, and, fixing on my helmet and pulling the bike back in second gear, I took off. I didn't look back until I'd reached a long straight. No police car was in sight, but it meant for sure I'd better keep well clear of Broadway in future. It was of course, quite possible that I was known to be the rider who had committed this offence, for the police constable had more than likely told the sergeant about the drawing and of course about me and the Velo. After all, he too was a motorcyclist.

I didn't go out for the next two weeks. At least, that is, not on the bike, for I took the family out for two weeks running and a happy time was had by all.

Chapter Forty

Velo Semi-Desmodromic and the Man Who Invented It

It had come to me via the grapevine that at one time, Arthur Taylor had been involved with some sort of desmodromic conversion at Velocettes. As I realised what a big advantage all this was, I got more and more determined to look into it.

So, on the next Sunday I went to Shipton-on-Stow to see Arthur Taylor once more. When I explained what I was after, he said,

"Oh, now you're moving into the realms of blistering headaches and big bank accounts, because believe me, lad, I know. I've been there. But all is not lost. Come with me." I followed Arthur into the rear of his garage and right at the back was a small office with a cabinet with about eight drawers in it. Pulling out one of the drawers Arthur said, "Here it is. This can really help if it's done right and the cost to you is nothing, for I'd like to make you a present. You're the right man to have them. Here they are," and he brought out two very queer-looking springs. "Let me explain," said Arthur. "As you more than likely know, to fully desmo an engine would mean a very complicated cylinder head and all that goes with it in order to pull valves off to stop loading."

I nodded my approval.

"So, with these," said Arthur, holding up two of the four springs he had taken out, "you can ease off almost the complete loading of the rockers and pushrods, but to work, it has to be done right. These springs I had made to do just that. As you see, they are long and narrow. That is because they are pushed right through the hollow rockers. This large end hooks up under the rocker arm over the valve, the smaller end, after a one-turn twist, is anchored onto the base in the rocker box, so the load of the rockers and the pushrods are countered by the spring pressure, thus elevating the load onto the valves."

"Now I know why Arthur Taylor is one of the best," I said.

He laughed and slapped me on the back. "You can get a good safe 500 to 600 r.p.m. extra with these, and it will give you the edge."

"Arthur," I said, "this is terrific. I don't know how to thank you."

"No need," said Arthur. "Just go and fit them and all I ask is a visit to let me know how you got on."

"Splendid, Arthur," I answered. "You are indeed a gentleman."

Arthur grinned and said, "How do you think the record breaker kept running at over 100 m.p.h.?" He tapped the side of his head. "They're still working, but I give them a rest these days." So, dear old Arthur, bless him, carefully wrapped up two sets of his very special springs. Very few people knew about them at the time, as wise old Arthur didn't exactly broadcast it, but, by gum, he was right. It would give me the edge for sure, and now I felt sure that 100 m.p.h. was going to be achieved on my own modified 'one-off' engine, and it was only a 248cc.

On my way back home, it was very obvious to me that Arthur had accepted me as one of the breed, for he would never have given me two pairs of his special springs if he hadn't. I felt very proud of the fact, for I also knew that only a person worthy of them would even be told about it, but here I was. I'd had two pairs given me. The cost of the springs wouldn't be a lot, but the idea was all Arthur's, and Arthur had given it to me. I tell you, I was choked up with pride. Two days later found me with the MOV rocker box all stripped out on my bench. I had fitted the springs through the hollow rockers and under the rocker arms. Now the problem was to get the correct place for the anchor, as its friction-free movement depended on it. What I found out was that with no tension on, the anchor spot was different to when the tension was on, so it rather seemed to me that if I made the anchor point slightly adjustable, then when they were fitted with the tension on, the friction-free spot to be anchored would be found. So, after various ideas, I finally came up with the idea of drilling the bottom of the rocker box which was quite thick, tapping the holes, and making two off-set adjusting anchor pins, being adjusted from right to left, and up and down in the threaded adjusting pins which I intended to make for the job. My work on the rocker box was a huge success, for in the process of doing this, I'd found another method to alter the tension, but I intended to keep this to myself, with the exception of Arthur, of course, for I knew that he would be very interested in what I'd done. After I'd finished this job, of course, I was longing to try it, for I had every confidence now that I wouldn't be risking valve bounce.

It was fine on the Sunday, so I could now try for the 'magic ton'. I wasn't going out for a long run, for I had in mind just where I intended to go to do it. The bike was running very well and I was very sure that every part was working well. Also, I was pleased that I'd fitted hardened 'top-hats' onto the top of the valve stems, of course an extra .002" clearance had been allowed for the extra expansion of the head, but it was as Arthur had mentioned in our conversation, that with hardened caps fitted, and the semi-desmo springs, I could now safely reduce the clearance by the .002" as the desmo effect would help it considerably, so this had now been done; also, to play it safe, I'd put some Redex in with the petrol, a thing that I didn't normally do, but here again, this would hardly be a normal run. By this time I'd found out that it wasn't necessary to fit a larger oil tank, for at no time had the oil temperature been any higher than normal. It was just fifty-two miles from home to where I was now, the place I'd intended to do the run. The weather was perfect and there was no traffic, so without even a stop, I got down to it. The engine at 70 m.p.h. really was running easy, so I slowly increased to a steady 85 m.p.h. and the exhaust note was beautiful. I was now approaching the three bends, then a straight bit, taking all three bends between 70-85 m.p.h.. I came out, increasing the speed as I did so; there was an open-top MG just in front, I guess he was doing about 50 m.p.h.. I must have been doing about 90 m.p.h. when I went by, and I bet he enjoyed my exhaust note as I passed him. Anyway, this was it, the bike was really moving now and as I crouched low, I saw the needle creep up to 109 m.p.h. and I wasn't on the full-out throttle stop. I shut off, no doubt about it now, here was a king of bikes. Over 100 m.p.h. on a home-brewed 250. Arthur was going to love this, so back to 70 m.p.h., I made my way to Shipton-on-Stow. I'd got my camera with me and I was hoping someone would be kind enough to take the picture of Arthur and I as both stood behind the bike, for I doubt very much if the engine would have reached this speed without Arthur's 'desmo springs', or, would I have had the guts to try, knowing that it could have just all blown up? I shall never know.

On I rode, destination Shipton-on-Stow, and at this moment of triumph, I got the same feeling that I'd had a few years ago on the HRD, and it was a feeling of poetry in motion. Arriving at Arthur's I noticed that the garage was all shut up, so, knocking on the private door, I was full on enthusiasm for what I had just done, but I was about to receive a shock. The door opened and a white-faced young lady looked out at me, the same young lady who, a few months before had joked about 'chicken wire'. I sensed that something was terribly wrong, I could see it in her face. I hesitated.

"Arthur," is all I said. The young lady shook her head and said,

"Arthur died in his sleep." Her eyes filled with tears and she slowly closed the door. I was stunned, and for a full minute, I stood looking at the door, then it hit me, and I found myself trembling, with tears just pouring down my face. Arthur had gone. One of the greatest names ever to deal in Velocettes and I was most probably the last Velo rider he ever helped. I was so upset that I don't remember starting my bike up. The next recollection that came to me, was that I was about ten miles from Shipton-on-Stow and going in the wrong direction. I turned the bike for home at the next road junction, but I was too upset to ride it properly. I just let it take me back home at a very moderate 50 m.p.h.. I phoned Velocettes the next day and no wonder the young lady who opened the door to me could hardly speak, for I'd called one day after the funeral and, I might add, I was very upset for many weeks to come. In fact, I didn't ride my MOV for one month, in the way of a memory and respect for a great man, and a very good friend; one of the greatest motorcyclists and tuners that ever was.

Chapter Forty-One
A Very Sick Bike Made Good

I should have loved to have been able to race the Velo, but my job took me all over the Continent, so I could hardly expect my family to give me up altogether, for that is what the outcome would have been, had I attempted to race it, and of course, the cost was another problem, even if I'd had the time, so officially, I never raced it, except for one short event, which I'll relate later.

When I was the bike mechanic at Elliott's Garage, it was a habit of mine to go round the local bike dealers to see what was going, but with all the time that I'd spent on my MOV, I hadn't visited them for twelve months or more. So, during my rest of not using the MOV for a month, I went for a browse round one Saturday afternoon, and at Gray's second hand motorcycle dealers, I noticed tucked away in a corner a 500 Enfield Twin. I lifted a couple of bikes to one side so that I could get through to it for a better look, where I could see that someone had put the engine together with Stag jointing cement, made for the sealing of joints on a steam engine, and by the look of it, the whole engine had been sealed with it. On attempting to feel the compression, I found that the engine had seized. Obviously this was the reason it had been stuck in the corner out of the way. The salesman had been watching me, for he knew who I was, and he didn't intend to tangle with me, as he'd tried it before only to be left floundering. However, I went up to him and asked him the price of the Enfield.

"Seventy-five guineas, sir," he replied. By the way, Gray's always dealt in guineas, obviously they made more that way. I laughed and said that it would cost that to repair it.

"I'll give you thirty pounds for it and take it seized up as it is. No one is going to pay your price for a scrap bike."

After a big display of how much they had paid for it and what the last owner had spent on it, he finally, when he knew that I knew it was seized, went in for a word with his manager. When he came out of the office he said,

"We knew it was seized, sir, so because it's you, the manager says that you can have it for fifty pounds cash."

"I'll see you in a couple of weeks time, for no one in their right mind would give fifty pounds cash for that," And as I got to the door I said, "If you haven't sold it by the end of the month, I'll give you thirty pounds for it, but only till the end of the month," For he was about to find out he wasn't the only smarty-pants when it came to motorcycles; I'd tackle anyone.

Two weeks to the day I went back and the bike was still there.

"No sale yet then?" I asked the salesman, for I knew that Gray's always placed a big 'Sold' notice on any bike they sold.

"No, not yet," answered the salesman.

"See you next month," I replied, and quickly shut the door behind me before he could answer. Two weeks later, as I promised, I was back again and this time, the salesman, on seeing me come in, came over with a big smile on his face.

"Hello, sir," he said. "The manager says that as no one has shown any interest in the Enfield, you can have it for thirty pounds."

"He's too late. The end of the month was my last offer, as I don't need it now. I've got a far better offer and it isn't seized." The smile vanished at once. "But a deal's a deal. I'll still take it for twenty-seven pounds delivered." He was speechless. I find that these kind of people just hate a customer who can get the better of them.

"I don't think he'd take that, sir, but I'll go and ask him." As he went into the manager's officer I played my last card by walking out of the showroom, slowly going across to my MAC and sitting across it. A minute later the salesman came running out.

"Hang on, sir, hang on. The manager would like a word with you please."

'Got him,' I thought. 'Just be adamant now and it's mine.' So I got off my bike and when I saw the manager he said,

"Come, come, sir. Thirty pounds is less than we gave for it and now you're only offering twenty-seven pounds and delivered as well, so why not thirty pounds now?"

"Because I offered the thirty pounds until the end of last month. Now I don't need it as I have a better offer," I replied.

"But we gave more than that for it, sir," he pleaded.

"I don't doubt it," I answered. "But you would put up the price on the bike you sold him, as Gray's don't buy in bikes only as an exchange and that is why Gray's don't lose and you are the manager." He was taken aback, so before he could think of a suitable reply I said, "My offer still stands; twenty-seven pounds and delivered."

"You're a hard man, sir," he said. "You had better come in the office." I went in and took a seat and put seven pounds on his desk. "Give me a receipt for seven pounds and my wife will give you the other twenty on delivery, any Tuesday or Thursday after 2.30 p.m." Without a word he wrote out a receipt for my seven pounds.

"Oh, and while I'm here I'd better have all the paperwork. We don't want to forget that now, do we?"

The manager was shaking his head but he handed over the necessary papers and said, "Tell me, sir, do you want it for spares?"

"No, I shall strip it and save its life. Who knows, Gray's might be interested in it when I've finished it !"

"Best of luck, sir. I'll get it delivered next week."

When I got home after work on Thursday night the Enfield was leaning on the side of our house in the driveway and I had to laugh, for when Ivy heard the Velo, she came out and said,

"Whatever have you got this heap for? Someone must have thought they were working on a steam engine. It's all stuck together with Stag joining cement."

I gave her a big kiss and said,

"Lovely baby, you would say that." Ivy took a bit of fooling as well when it came to bikes. When I'd pushed both bikes through our double centre gates and we went inside, Ivy said,

"Two very nice young chaps brought the Enfield in a big box combination and they wished you all the best and said how much they enjoyed the way you handled Shylock, the manager."

I laughed myself, then told her the story.

"You should have been on your own years ago," answered Ivy, and I knew in my heart that she was right.

The next week I took the engine out of the Enfield and stripped it all out. I'd never seen anything quite like it before. The Stag joining cement hadn't just been put on, it had been poured on. It was in all the oil passages and even in the oil pumps. The engine must have seized cold, for the piston seizure was only light, for I freed them both with a drop of Redex and a light tap with the end of a hammer shaft. After that I was able to turn the engine but it was all but dry; but for all this, I'd got a very good bargain. The big end shells were new, the mains were new, there were new valves and valve springs in the cylinder heads and it been hardly run after a decoke, as both heads were clean. The carburettor was new, all three chains were new, i.e., timing chain, primary chain, and drive chain. The mag chain was original but very good. The clutch was new and assembled wrongly. The forks had been changed not too long ago and the ribbed Dunlop front tyre and tube weren't very old either. The dual seat was nearly new, the rear and stop lamps were new, the rear number plate wasn't very old, the rear Dunlop tyre was half-worn but quite good, and in any case, I'd got two nearly new ones on my garage wall, and last but not least, both oil pumps and driving worm spindle were new and the oil pumps hadn't been lapped into their beds. What a bargain! I fetched Ivy down to see it.

"Good for you," she said. "No wonder those two lads were having a laugh."'

Well, just ten days from the day it was delivered, I'd got a very nice cheap Enfield 500 Twin; now to get it started, for although it was such a mess when I got it, now it was a very nice bike and it had cleaned up very well. Someone had spent a lot on that bike; they obviously hadn't got the know-how and had traded it in to Gray's at a loss. I felt sorry for the chap who had spent the cash, but not a bit sorry for Gray's. I'd done okay on this deal. The bike had got to be worth £250, I knew I'd bought a bargain. So, having a last look round the bike I satisfied myself that all was ready so, priming up the carburettor, I kicked the engine over, and on the third kick it fired up and I was rewarded by a very quiet running engine. It was very nice and sounded very healthy and smooth. After I had tuned the carburettor and got the timing spot on, it ticked over lovely and slow and was very smooth. Ivy heard it running and came into the garage.

"That sounds nice and quiet," she said, and to my surprise, sat on the bike and blipped the throttle. "I'd love this," said Ivy.

"Its yours if you want it," I said.

"If I could manage it I would," replied Ivy. "I'm fed up waiting for buses." And that remark made me think. It wouldn't be very long before her birthday, and *that* year, I'd made up my mind that Ivy was going to get the best present I'd ever bought her, and now that she had shown such a keen interest in the Enfield, it had really made me think.

Chapter Forty-Two

The Velo is Challenged

Two days after I'd got the Enfield running I'd got it through the MOT and Ivy had taxed it for me, so the next day, on Friday, I went to work on it and a very smooth ride it was too. Everybody assumed that it was mine even though I'd only told my pal Tom McCullock about it and I knew he hadn't talked. It somehow had my touch, as one of our lads kindly put it, and in just one week, I'd had two offers for it. But it was a nice bike and, with winter only two months away, I'd got thoughts about putting a sports chair on it. One reason was for safety on the ice, and the other reason was that my youngest son Bob had just come top of his class and won a place at Bablake, the best, or I'd better say, one of the best top schools in Coventry at that time. So, with a chair on the Enfield, I could pick up Bob many times when I didn't work over, and we didn't do too much overtime in the winter. Bob of course didn't know about my plan, so until it materialised, I wasn't going to say anything. My workmates all liked the Enfield and I let two of them have a go on it and it got full marks from both. The following morning at our breakfast table, one of our lads came over, and in a scornful manner said,

"I suppose it's all Enfields now? I was about to give you a challenge, that's if you're interested." He smirked, as this one chap had never liked me ever since I had corrected him about a bike he was on about; now he was having another go.

"Yes," he said, "we all hear about your marvellous Velo and I can see that it's a very nice bike, but nobody has seen it really go, so I've got a proposition for you. It's this. I've got two mates, who for a bet, are willing to take you on. What about it?"

All eyes were turned on me.

"Any time, any place. I'm at your service, my dear fellow," I replied. "They know where I ride. I'll take 'em on any time."

A big cheer went up when I said this. These lads were Competition lads; they all loved a challenge.

"That's just it" said this chap. "You know the Wolds so good you've got the edge. This has got to be done where all can see, not miles from anywhere!"

"What have you got in mind?" I asked.

"I don't know," was the answer. "You're the bike bloke here. I thought that you could think of something."

I looked hard at him and said,

"If you're really serious about this, I'll hire Honiley Airport for a Sunday morning."

He was speechless, his mouth twisted, and his face went very red as he replied, putting himself deeper in the mire, "And I suppose you'll organise seconds with stopwatches as well!"

"I wouldn't have it any other way, for there are plenty of stopwatches in the office and I know my mates will all volunteer without asking."

A mighty cheer went up, and it wasn't long before the whole workshop and the office knew about it.

Back in the workshop after breakfast, one of my pals came over to the car I was working on and said,

"It was great in the canteen this morning, but tell me, were you really serious about hiring Honiley Airport?"

"Absolutely," I said. "But before I do, I want his challenge in writing, just in case he thinks that he and his mates needn't show up, for I've got permission from Warwick Council and if they don't show, he pays." My pal looked at me and a big grin spread across his face.

"You're a brama," he said (a real old Coventry saying). "This is going to make him think," And off he went to let everyone know the terms. At breakfast next morning I laid down my terms.

"Just put it all in writing and get any two people to witness it and I'll ride on to hell and back,"

Another mighty cheer went up; he'd done it now and he knew it. My pal Tony Stringer said,

"He doesn't know what he's done. He's just woken up a sleeping tiger." And in a way, he was right, for there was no way that I wouldn't take up a challenge like that, all the way. The next morning, this chap came over.

"I want everybody to witness this," he said, and reading out the agreement and of course bringing in Honiley Airport, he slapped it down on the table.

"Come on, Mr Velo Fellow. Get your signature on that and I'll get it witnessed while we are all here."

Another mighty cheer followed as I put my signature on it and waved it in the air.

"It's on, it's on! And everyone everywhere is invited."

The cheering and noise fetched the foreman in to see what all the row was about, and about fifty voices, all started to sing, *For He's A Jolly Good Fellow.*

"One last thing," I said. "How much did you wish to bet?"

You could now hear a pin drop.

"Twenty pounds," he said.

"Not very sure are we?" I replied. "If I had the bet it would have been a hundred pounds,"

And a terrific cheer followed, and I could see one of our lads explaining to the foreman what had caused all this racket, and by the way, the foreman was laughing. I think he was enjoying it too. Now that this challenge had been sorted out, that evening I wrote to Warwick Council and asked permission for the use of Honiley Airport for two hours to be used for racing motorcycles, and stating that I would be responsible to get it clear at the given time. This was on the Friday night and by Wednesday when I arrived home from work, the permit was there, giving me two hours between 10 a.m. and 12.00 a.m. on the following Sunday morning.

On Thursday morning my challenger was feeling a bit cheeky again, for, looking over at me, he used one of my own expressions when he smirkingly asked,

"When are we getting Honiley Airport then, when Nelson gets his eye back?"

"You'll need both of your eyes to road this," I said, and, going over to where he sat, I put down my permit. "Perhaps Nelson would like to read it out?" I remarked. His face was a picture and I suddenly realised, that all along, he had been thinking that the hiring of the airport was all a bluff; I could sense it by the look on his face. He went white, and then, when the truth hit him, he went very red; then one of my pals shouted,

"What's up, Nelson? Lost your tongue as well?"

Well, he read it out, but his voice gave his true feelings away, as a mighty cheer echoed down from the canteen into the workshop. In the tea break that afternoon, my challenger looked across and asked,

"By the way, don't you want to know what you've taken on?"

"As long as it isn't Geoff Duke on his Gilera or John Serters, I'm not too worried," I replied. Another big cheer, the lads were loving this.

"Well," he said. "One is a 500 International Norton and the other is a 350 racing Matchless; they'll both eat your Velo." The canteen was alive with excitement; someone shouted,

"What about making a book on it? I'll risk five pounds on our George!" That was it – the whole place went wild. My pal Tom turned to me and said,

"Since you've been here there's never a dull moment. I wouldn't have missed this for anything. It's got them all going. Look at 'em!" And believe me, arguments were rampant all over the canteen; it was a treat to come to work.

That same afternoon, Mike Smith, who was known as the bookie, came and asked me how I felt about it.

"No worries," I said. "I might have been pushed on the road, but a circuit!" And I laughed. "I don't think they stand a chance!" Mick went away rubbing his hands together, then, looking back, he said,

"Best of luck; that's all I wanted to know."

Tony Stringer agreed to use his car to carry my gear, for I was taking fuel, two more sprockets and tools and, we had agreed to be there for 9.30 a.m. to clear any rubbish off the circuit and to mark all the corners, also to pick a good vantage point for all to see. On the Friday before we knocked off, as there was no work on Saturday this week, the lads got another big laugh, because at tea break, my challenger suddenly shouted,

"How about if it's raining?"

I yelled back, "It's covered. Tony Stringer and Tom McCullock are making umbrella holders for the bikes!" One of our apprentices was drinking his tea at the time and he lost control at my remark and blew tea over his mates sitting opposite him. It was a very happy canteen.

Sunday found myself and quite a few of my mates at Honiley. The weather was dull but dry and there was plenty of branches and rubbish to be moved and everyone lent a hand. Also, all piled together were about fifteen or so forty-gallon black painted oil drums with yellow bands at one end, just the job for markers on the corners, so Tony and I set about doing just that. We could roll them along on the two raised bands on them, so in about twenty minutes or so we had got it nearly ready. Tony looked at his watch.

"They're leaving it late," he remarked, meaning the challengers. "Its five to ten."

"Don't worry," I told him. If they didn't show I would still get paid and I'd give them a demonstration on my Velo. Just then, the sound of bikes came from the road, my challengers had turned up. As they rode up to where we were, I noticed that the Norton with two up was pumping out blue smoke and the Matchless sounded like a bag of nails.

"No contest," I said to Tony. "The Velo will eat 'em!"

We all shook hands and they were pleased when I said that an hour's practice would make it fair for all. By now we had sorted out someone for each corner and Tony had got a red flag to start us off. It was to be a Grand Prix start, that is, with engines running, for it was obvious to me that neither of the two lads really knew much about it, for, although the bikes were big bikes compared to mine, it was a bit like a big unfit man of say fifteen stone, climbing in the boxing ring with a really good welter weight; at least, that is what it looked like to me. At 10.20 a.m. all was ready and by then quite a good few of the lads had turned up and, as yet, the challengers hadn't heard the Velo run, but both had been looking at it and they weren't looking very happy. Anyway, the chap on the rattly Matchless took off fast and instead of going slowly round to view the circuit he overshot the first bend and only just missed the oil drum marking the other end of it, then he almost lost control and got tangled up in a gorse bush. The Norton rider, seeing this, took off more slowly and went very steadily round the circuit. They had agreed to practice till 11.00 a.m., then start the race. By the way they were going round it was very obvious to me that neither of these two chaps really knew what they were doing, for watching them, I could tell that they had no experience in riding under power on the racing line. I didn't start my Velo up until 10.40 a.m., as I knew that really, they had bitten off more than they could chew. I'll endeavour to explain. Picture a circuit roughly in the shape of an oval with straight sides, but, looking at it in your mind's eye, the left side has a couple of curves in it. Now, to go through the bends fast, one must go down the left-hand side in order to go through the bends in the straightest possible line, so in actual riding, one ends up going up the straights from inside on the bend you have just come out from, then in a straight line for the outer edge of the circuit for the next bend and so on. Neither of the two riders had attempted to do this, so I knew that they just didn't have the experience to drive into a corner with throttle on. I, on the other hand, had a few thousand miles of practice through the Wolds, and I knew that it takes time and high concentration to get it right. Even then, a knowledge of the circuit is essential. So I took off in third gear and went very steadily round the circuit. The two riders had pulled in and were having a chat and both were looking at the Matchless, so, taking advantage of this, I started to speed up. By the time I'd done a few laps I'd got it sorted out, and knew the correct line through the bends. The squiggle bit down the straight I was taking in a straight line and by now my mates were cheering me on and generally enjoying themselves. I did one last lap and really moved, everyone, including the other two riders, was watching and along the straights I was close to the 100 m.p.h. mark. I pulled in just before the start and my pals all came across and all were very impressed with the Velo. I knew that one or two of them didn't know quite what to make of it, as it was a new experience for them. The other two riders started up and did one more lap; the Norton was again smoking like a British two-stroke, so when they pulled by me I asked the Norton rider if he had plenty of oil in. He said he'd filled it up before he left home, even so, there was room for a about a pint in the tank. I told him I had some if he wanted it, but he said it would be all right.

At 11.00 a.m. the starter lined us up on a thick chalked line, asked if we were ready and, seeing that we all were, he dropped the flag. On sheer power, the Norton got to the top of the circuit first. I could hardly see the corner for smoke as he shut off. I had taken the racing line and I was only about five lengths behind him when he reached the corner. His approach placed him in the centre of the track, so, gently easing off, I waited for him to drift out, as I knew he would, then, opening up, I shot by on the inside, coming out of the second bend dead on the racing line. As I shot past the starting line a big cheer went up as I flew past them with the Norton about five lengths behind. After three or four laps I had broken well clear, in fact I was nearer to lapping the Matchless than the Norton was to catching me. My mates by now had placed themselves round the bends on the inside for safety, the starter and the three timekeepers, as there was one for each rider, were still of course all at the starting line. The distance was to be for ten laps, and by lap five I'd lapped the Matchless, in fact I went by him up the straight like a rocket and one lap later, he'd pulled in with a slipping clutch. By lap seven, my pals were literally jumping up down in excitement. I, of course, was really moving now, and at one end of the circuit I was taking both bends in top with the outside footrest a few thou off the ground. On lap eight I was rapidly overhauling the smoking Norton, and on lap nine, I lapped him in the same bend that I'd got by him on the first lap. My mate were going barmy with pleasure. The Norton stopped at the starting line so I shut off as well, and slowly now, went back to the start. When I pulled up I was surprised to see that quite a few strangers had come in to see what was going on.

As I stopped my engine a crowd of my pals came over and I received far more praise than I deserved, as it had been very easy.

"Hell, I wouldn't have missed this for anything," said one chap. "I wouldn't believe it if I hadn't seen it. A 250 making a 500 and 350 look sick. Bloody marvellous, George. That bike's a wonder and you can really ride it." Just then, my challenger came up.

"Well, you won all right, but it wasn't fair..." That is as far as he got, for the chap who had just been so ecstatic over my performance butted in with a vengeance.

"Not fair! Not fair! I'll say it wasn't fair. A 250 against a 350 and a 500! Not fair! Pay up, you conniving so and so. George on his 250 has made you look a right prat, so pay up!" Everyone was cheering and shouting, to hear this lot anyone would think I'd just won the lightweight TT. It was a terrific atmosphere and the next moment and without further comment twenty pounds was slapped into my hand. The Norton was now dripping oil from the camshaft drive tube and the rocker box, and the Matchless, which may as well have not been there, had all but burnt his clutch. Tony was laughing as he said,

"I bet he won't be saying a lot after this," And quite a few cameras were clicking. The next day I took the MOV to work, for I knew that the lads would like that, for by lunchtime a big crowd had gathered in the car park round the Velo, and to my surprise, five women from the office had come down to see the bike and it wasn't long before they were having their photos taken with me and the Velo.

"A big victory smile, please!" shouted one lady, but somehow, I didn't get a picture, only from my pal Tony. From this and other stories, the Velo was becoming a legend, but at this time I didn't realise that there was more to come, and a dream ride wasn't far off.

Chapter Forty-Three
A New Honda and a Sidecar

On arriving home from work on a Friday night, I found that Ivy was upset because she had been kept waiting twice that day whilst trying to catch a bus. It had put her all behind and for once the dinner wasn't ready: a rare occasion.

I'd had many complaints from Ivy about this before, and I could see that she was really annoyed, but this time, I meant to do something about it. Her birthday was in two weeks' time so now was the time to do it. So, on Saturday afternoon I went along to Brandish & Sons, Coventry's only Honda agent and at this time the Japs were fighting to get a foothold in the market, so every Honda at this time was like a show bike. The finish and attention to detail, without any doubt, made Honda the best bargain in Great Britain.

When I walked into Brandish's of course they all knew me, and were surprised to see me looking very hard at a Honda 50cc Scooterete. After a good look at it I spoke to the salesman and found out that the price with a full comprehensive insurance policy and a tank full of petrol was £87.17s.6d: a wonderful buy. That included two driving mirrors, a flasher set, number plates, as there was one front and rear then, a tool kit, a spare plug and a very detailed driver's handbook in English. Knowing me, the salesman let me try one. It was poetry in motion without any doubt at all. Apart from my Velo, it was the sweetest running engine I'd ever heard. It was so quiet that at a few yards away, you couldn't hear it running. Ivy had kept her driving licence up from driving the Morris 8HP so she could of course ride one of these using the same licence. I ordered one for the following Friday complete with two saddlebags and a chrome backguard carrier with four elastics with hooked ends.

"Please don't let me down," I said. "It's my wife's birthday present."

"It will be ready for you after 12.00 a.m. on Friday, sir, without a doubt."

So, on Friday, Ivy's birthday, I told a white lie. I told her that I was to pick a car up, so someone would pick me up. Not an unusual event in my job, so she didn't suspect anything. During the week, Ivy said,

"Why won't you tell me what you are buying for my birthday? I might not like it."

"If you don't," I said. "I'll have it for myself."

She looked more puzzled than ever, then started to giggle.

"What's the joke?" I asked.

"I can't imagine you in black underwear."

"Very funny," I replied. "But this will be a little bit better than that."

Friday morning a tinsmith from our works, who only lived two roads away, picked me up and, as Ivy was still in bed that morning, I was able to sneak out with my riding gear without her seeing me. At Brandish's all was ready and so was I, for I'd taken a drop of Redex with me, some to go in the oil and the rest in the petrol.

"What a lovely present, does your wife know?" asked the salesman as I handed over the cash.

"She hasn't a clue," I answered.

"You should get a big kiss for that, sir," said the salesman with a big grin. Well, I started up the little engine by pushing the kickstart lever with my hand and in just a few seconds it was ticking over without the choke. I let the oil get well round and of course I'd put in the Redex as protection, so off I set and the little bike was as smooth as silk. It just purred all the way home, as you can be sure that I'd let it rev freely and kept it off load. When I got home it was so quiet that I was able to ride it right into our drive and no one heard it arrive. Pushing it through our gates I went in home.

"You're late tonight," remarked Ivy, for normally I got home for five on Fridays, and it was now 6.15 p.m.

"Where have you been?" asked Ivy. "I hope you haven't been looking at another bike!"

"Come outside and see your present," I said.

"Outside?" Ivy's voice had gone up an octave. "Whatever is it?"

I caught hold of her hand and pulled her outside. Then she saw the bike. She stopped dead, her face all flushed and, placing her hands on her face, she said,

"Oh darling, it's lovely – but I can't ride that!"

"Get on," I said. "It's dead easy. It has a semi-automatic clutch, you can't go wrong." Well, within minutes Ivy was going up and down our road. We lived in big cul-de-sac so the traffic was limited. However, during the next ten minutes Ivy had vanished and I was just about to get the Enfield out, when she came up the road in top gear, beaming all over her face, and as she stopped and switched off the engine she said,

"Darling, this is the best present you've ever bought me. It's lovely."

So started Ivy's life on her Hondas. She had three altogether and although the next two were okay, they were OHC against the OHV of the first one, the birthday bike was the best of the lot. She did thirty-two thousand miles on it and in all weathers. Ivy was never held up for transport again. In fact she used to see the people looking at her enviously when she went flying past the bus queues. It was also a very handy transport for Ivy to cart the two lads about with and later, the daughter, too, became a passenger.

About three or four weeks after Ivy had got her Honda, I was in Alf Holland's buying some cadmium bolts for the Enfield and just casually, I asked Bernard, who was serving me, if he knew where I might pick up a chair for the Enfield.

"What a pity you didn't mention it sooner," said Bernard. "The chap who went out two minutes ago has one for sale and it's nearly new, but don't worry, we know roughly where he lives." So, ten minutes later found me knocking on doors in search of him. Bernard was a road out, but in the end I found him. The sidecar and chassis were a Watsonian Sports in black with brown leather upholstery and a heavy-duty weather hood that had never been used in the rain. In fact, it had only done just over a thousand miles and the tyre bore that out. Even the Avon tyre and size numbers were in gold letters and the wheel had a full alloy trim, a very nice job. Apparently he'd bought the chair and chassis new from Brandish's to take his girl out who liked dressing up and wouldn't ride pillion. The bike he had when he met his girl was a 350 MAC Velo which now lay collecting dust in his garage but the bike that the chair had been on was a 600cc Panther and he was now using it solo.

"What have you taken the chair off for?" I asked.

"My girl's left me and I'm selling the Panther on Saturday, as I've got a good price for it, but he doesn't want the chair. That's why I'm selling it separately."

"I see, and the Velo?"

"Oh, don't mention the Velo," he said. "That's a very sore point. I changed the oil on it and I didn't know you had to bleed the system and I've scrapped it. It needs a new engine, so if I sell the Panther and you buy the chair I might get one, but they don't come cheap."

"Well now, this could be lucky for both of us. I know that you don't know me, but my job is a competition mechanic at Standard Triumph and before that I did fifteen years at Elliott's Garage as bike mechanic. Also, on top of that, I've got two of the best Velos in the country. They are my favourite bikes and Velos know me. Ask the Holland brothers. They'll tell you, so don't despair. If I do your bike, we could make a deal. Are you interested?"

"Now I know where I've seen you before. Of course, Elliott's! They've always done my bikes for me,"

"Well, it would have been me who repaired them then."

His eyes lit up. "I am interested," he said. "They want nearly £200 for an engine,"

"How much are you asking for your chair and chassis?"

"Well, it's nearly new. I was hoping to get about £120 for it. It cost me £175 and I've got the receipts,"

"Then we have a deal and it should break about even." A big smile came on his face and he said,

"You're not George that 'Velo fellow', are you?"

"That's what they call me," I said, and we shook hands on it.

"I know Velo prices so well that if you like, we'll have a recap to see what it may cost, then you can ring Velos or whoever and check for yourself." I went over to the Velo and tried the engine. It was solid.

"It's seized in the bore as well."

"Yes, it locked up on me in Hearsal Lane. I had to push it home."

So I wrote down all the prices of the parts that would need to be replaced, that was piston and liner, big end assembly, offside bearings, nearside bearings, gaskets and the oil pump to be checked after stripping. The parts came to sixty-three pounds.

"Yes, we would be about even," I said. "I'll do it for the price of your chair and should the oil pump be damaged I'll do it all for the price of your chair, how is that?"

"Brilliant," he replied. "I was told the parts alone would cost eighty-five pounds, so yes, it's a deal."

So, two days later, a mate at work collected the MAC for me in his brother's 10CWT van and I soon got cracking on it as I had nearly all the bits in my spares. When I collected the Velo engine, there was a complete MAC flywheel assembly and the main bearings and plenty of shims, pistons, little ends, rockers, I'd got stacks of parts so now was a good opportunity to put them to good use. A week later I was kicking up his MAC. It started third kick. I'd done what I told him I'd do and had all the old bits in a box and, to play it safe, I'd put Shell oil in it with Redex and Redex in the fuel, but just to make certain it was right, I did twenty miles on it in order to retighten the head and reset the tappets etc., and by the time I'd finished it and generally gone over the bike, it was a very smooth machine.

I rang him on the Monday night and told him the good news and he collect it the next night. I fitted the sidecar to my Enfield on the following afternoon, after collecting the fittings from Geoff at Hearsal Lane. The chap was really chuffed with his Velo, and he said that it had never run so well. The chair fitted on a treat and after I'd done my mod to the chassis down tube, it was a very nice outfit, but strange to say, I needed to find a Meteor twin-drum front brake to make it safe, but I'd got another Velo customer and a very nice combo for a few days' work; not bad.

Chapter Forty-Four
A Scott, a Fire, and the Enfield is Boosted Up

The sidecar was an immediate success and a warm and very comfortable ride. All my family liked it, and when winter came, it made my journeys to and from work much safer, as a combo, when set up correctly, is safer than the average car, though not of course a four-wheel-drive vehicle. I'd only had the chair on for a couple of weeks, when a customer at work came in to see how the work was progressing on his TR3A Rally car, for it was one of my 'spare' jobs. He was very pleased at the progress on his car and on opening the boot he said,

"Could you make use of this? It's brand new, I've never used it."

It was a Lucas 7" flame thrower.

"Many thanks," I said. "This can go on my combo outfit,"

And when I'd changed the bulb from twelve volt to six volt, I mounted it between the bike and the chair and it was a cracking light to drive on, away from traffic.

That weekend was a lucky one for me. In fact the whole week was, for I received a phone call at work from my friend Geoff Holland. He had an Enfield Meteor to spare and it had a twin-drum front wheel which he knew that I wanted, so that night, I collected and fitted it to my Enfield, for I had both cables and the lever as well, and when I checked the two lots of brake linings, both sides had almost new shoes and springs fitted, so I now had a very good combo. After I'd got this all fitted up and tested, and I'd better mention how much safer it had made the outfit as the stopping power was now very good, about forty-five per cent better in fact, I was wondering if it would be worthwhile to do away with the Y junction on the cylinder heads and fit two separate carburettors instead, for as it was, there was one

Amal carburettor feeding both cylinders via the Y junction. Back in the 40s and 50s, the golden rule for tuning was, 'one pot, one carb, one pipe', for it wasn't until later that the idea of a four into two, then two into one, if done very accurately, was a collective source for power. On a bike such as the Enfield, of course, then the old method should be an improvement as any mechanic would tell you; one carb feeding two pots via a Y junction is always a trap for uneven carburation, for the discrepancy caused from the machining of the junction and the heads nearly always gives a different plug reading. In other words, to make it simple, one would be very lucky to have a Y junction with one carb and get both mixtures correct by the plug colour. I suppose for the average chap it was near enough, but I was never satisfied with near enough, hence my pondering whether to convert it or not, for having explained all this, ironically mine wasn't too bad, but with the chair on it, it had amplified the problem somewhat. For although the Enfield 500 Twin was a very good bike, it had never been designed for tuning as there wasn't any room to fit bigger inlet valves (a must if you want extra power).

I was still pondering whether or not to do this, when two young chaps came up with two-thirds of a Scott 500cc motorcycle in the back of a van.

"Are you George the Velo man?" asked the older of the two, and when I told him that I was, he asked me if I would look at the Scott that they had bought as a non-runner. I did so and at once, I could see that it had been done by someone who, to be blunt, hadn't a clue.

"How much did you give for this?" I asked.

"We gave twenty-five pounds for it to a chap in Nuneaton. He said that he hadn't got the time to finish it, but it's got a lot of new bits on it!"

"Yes, and by the look of it, all the wrong bits as well. The carb – that's wrong, the silencer – that's wrong. Where's the rest of it?" I asked.

"Here in this box," said the older one.

"Well, it's going to cost more than you gave for it to get it going. My advice is to take it back and tell him what I said, because there is a lot of work here and you'll need another carb and the right silencer just for starters, so go and see him."

I felt sorry for them, for they had bought a pup of unknown origin. Who knows what one might find on a bike like that? However, two hours later they were back. The man they had bought it off had spent the money on a push-bike, so they were stuck with it.

"Would you buy it?" one of them asked.

"I don't really want it. It would probably cost too much to do up," I replied. "And I doubt if you would get more than fifteen pounds for it like that. He saw you coming, lads."

The two lads thanked me and drove off. An hour later they were back again and when I went out to them, the older one said,

"My dad says that we've learnt a hard lesson and if you want it, he said to let you have it for the fifteen pounds and be shot of it." Well, I didn't have to have it of course, but I was sorry for them and it was worth fifteen even as bits, so I said,

"Have you got the logbook for it?" The logbook was brought out in seconds and after checking the engine number and frame number I took their names and addresses and gave them the fifteen pounds and got a receipt for it. The older of these two lads now owns the big Kawasaki motorcycle shop and workshop in Nuneaton and Atherstone. When they had gone, Ivy came out and, looking at this dilapidated heap of motorcycle metal, she said,

"Don't tell me that you've taken that on to repair!"

"No, of course not," I replied. "I've just bought it."

Ivy glared, shook her head and went back inside. I guessed, by the look of it, she must have thought I was mad. It even made me think at the time. Even so, after a few weeks and about ten visits up to Alf Holland's, I was ready to start it up, for Alf's had got all the bits I needed, including the crankcase seals, which were gone.

By the time I'd sorted it all out, the two lads would have spent a fortune on it, if they had attempted it. I spent twenty-three pounds on it and a rebuild with new piston rings and gaskets, carb, silencer and a lot of bits and pieces, and nearly all new bolts and nuts, etc. and a new rear drive chain which I already had. The engine started second kick and it was nice and quiet. Of course, I'd need to move the silencer to find the best position, and of course to retune the carb, but save for that and a pulling down of the cylinder heads after a good warming up, the engine was very smooth and steady. As you may or may not know, a two-stroke 'lives or dies' on the exhaust pipe, so it was critical for any two-stroke to be any good that the exhaust must have no leaks of any sort, and the back pressure area of the exhaust is also critical, but get it right and you've got yourself a goer, for a twin water cooled two-stroke 500cc, when done right, was a goer. For instance, the acceleration was far superior to any valve bike of any make, also, being a two-stroke it was in a way similar to a four-stroke cylinder, for it had the same power stroke with only two pots. I could fill a whole chapter on this subject, but because this basically my own story, there is a lot more to be told.

At work, just a week before I completed the work on the Scott, the chap who had challenged me on the Velo bought himself a 125cc Francis Barnett motorcycle, for he too was fed up with waiting for buses. Usually in our thirty-minute lunch break at midday, I used to clean off my bike with a paraffin rag, then with an oily rag to stop rust. This particular day I was doing just that when our friend came out with a tin and a two inch paintbrush and proceeded to wash down his muddy engine. Almost at once, I said to him,

"Is that SPB you're using?"

"It is, so what?" came the reply.

"Only that one spark from your mag and up goes your bike, for it's the fumes that ignite."

"You don't half come out with some statements," he said. I was cleaning my MAC at the time and our auto-electrician was with me, Bill Handley. Bill turned to our ignorant friend and said,

"He's dead right, you know. I bet you daren't call his bluff," And before we could stop him, he had kicked his engine over. There was a puff and a flash and the whole of his engine was alight. Seconds later the tin he was holding ignited as well. He threw it away from him and the SPB from the tin went all over the bike and in one second the whole machine was engulfed in flames.

"Move my bike, Bill," I yelled as I ran for the crash shop to get a CO_2 fire extinguisher. I ran as fast as I could, but it was too late for his bike. It had been very badly burned by the time I got back. I put the fire out, but not before it had scrapped his bike and burnt a three-foot hole in the motorcycle shed roof. Well, I won't go into all the remarks he had to face over this. Of course, the management was furious about it, and we believed at the time that the fact that he'd lost his bike was punishment enough, but he also got a good ticking off from the workshop superintendent. But to the lads the real crunch came two weeks later, when they found out that the bike was only insured third party with no fire or theft covering, and even months after, if ever he got a bit cocky, some bright spark would make a remark such as, "Seen any good fires lately?" It always did the trick. I felt sorry for him and offered him the Scott, but he wasn't really bothered about replacing his bike as he was now getting a lift in a car; but we got on quite well after I'd bought his riding coat off him, and I promised him that if he ever wanted another bike, I'd build him one at a very low cost. This seemed to bury the hatchet, for after that there was no backbiting or hard feeling and we got on very well.

Having now had time to think about whether or not to fit up the Enfield with twin carbs, I decided to have a go. I was pretty sure that it wouldn't improve their performance a lot, as larger inlet valves couldn't be fitted in these cylinder heads, for they weren't made for it. However, I did know that the power output would be improved, so because it was now a combo, it would be a worthwhile job to do. At least I should be able to get both cylinders spot on as far as carburation was concerned and possibly get them pulling better on the mega if at all possible, so this is what I decided to do. Obtaining two suitable carbs for the job wasn't a problem. Alf Holland had two new ones and I got them for a very reasonable price, as Geoff sold them to me as disused stock and shop soiled. I also got the throttle cables, cable junction box and two cutaway slides as old stock. So the next weekend I got stuck in to the conversion, which was a straightforward job, for I had the needle and jet size in the original carb to follow. The throttles and air chokes had the cables going into their junction boxes; these of course I had to make up to pattern, as no such cables could be bought intact. I fitted a large 'swill pot' between the two carbs, feeding both, making sure that it was forward of the carb bodies to avoid swill or spluttering on take off. The whole job went very well, and by Saturday night at around 8.00 p.m., I was ready for a start up. To my delight the engine fired on the first turnover. It was running slightly too fast, but after adjusting the slide stop screw and cables it wasn't long before a very nice even tickover was produced. By the use of a $^3/_8$" rubber pipe about two feet long, I could listen to the air being sucked in on both carbs. The tune of course, is to get both carbs dead even, and of course, with the engine being in very good shape, it was very easy to do. I gave the bike a trial run and it definitely pulled better. The acceleration had improved too, and at 65 m.p.h. the exhaust note was very hard and healthy, good enough to try and get it on the mega, a job for later on. For now I was very satisfied, so I decided I'd go and watch a bit of TV for a change.

A week later, I'd got two very good second-hand megas from Geoff, these being a pair off a 500cc AJS twin, a right and left hand, so it didn't take long to make up two sliding fixing plates in order to adjust the megas in or out on the exhaust pipe to affect the right tune. But first of all, after fitting, the correct mixture setting had to be found by needle and jets. Neither were very far out and after three attempts I got a very good plug reading, so all that was now left to do, was to find a good hill, then, by moving the megas either in or out from their sliding brackets, I was rewarded by a very good pulling power and on the correct mixture. So I completed the tune, as one was very limited on an Enfield Twin, for as I mentioned, it wasn't built with this in mind. However, the outfit was now a very good one and I was pleased with my efforts. It was an improvement on the rest and that's what tuning is all about.

The following Sunday I'd arranged to take my apprentice with me and go for a Cotswolds run starting at 6.00 a.m. and doing about 150 miles or so. My apprentice was all dressed up and waiting by his house as I arrived at two minutes to six. He was very excited as I swung the outfit round and waited while he got into the sidecar. His mum gave a wave from the bedroom window.

"My mum thinks we're mad," he said, "but I've been looking forward to this all week." And believe me, we had a very good run as the weather was good and the bike with my passenger in the snug sidecar, ran and sounded better than ever. For sure, its pulling power was a lot crisper, also the pick up was very good and I ran it around 60-65 m.p.h.. Accelerating to retain the power band up hills, and the whole outfit ran beautifully. We got out in a lay-by, for we had both brought coffee and biscuits. My passenger was thrilled to bits and he told me that he was definitely going to save up and get a bike. I grinned, as he was a very nice lad, and it looked as if I'd found another convert. We arrived back home about 11.30 a.m., having done 168 miles of very good combo riding. His mum came out and thanked me for taking him. Also, she said that since her son had worked with me, he couldn't wait to get to work. Later this lad got the 'Apprentice of the Year' award, and later still, became a 'gaffer' on a very well-paid job.

Chapter Forty-Five

The Velo and the Enfield at the Isle of Man

A few weeks later my pal Tony asked me if I would hang on to the Scott for him, as he had tried it and liked it very much as it was in good order and of course a very good goer. I told him yes, he could have it any time he wanted it, so that satisfied him, for he'd just paid a good sum out for two lovely ponies for his two daughters and he would have the Scott later on. After all, it had been Tony who had sent the two lads up to me with the Scott, in the first place. I offered to let him have it and pay later, but he said he'd wait till later as someone owed him about £300 for a job he'd done. I think the chap that owed him had got wife trouble. However, the tax on the Scott ran out the next week as I'd only taxed it for six months, so I told him it was there when he wanted it. A week later, Tony reminded me that we had an extra week's holiday this year, as a handful of us, and I was one of them, had sacrificed some time last year for the firm's benefit. No one minded this for most of the Competition lads would do almost anything for the honour of the firm, for the firm of Standard Triumph was a wonderful firm to work for, and I and a lot more appreciated it.

"What about you and I going to the Isle of Man for the TT? If we applied now, we would be sure to get it, and besides," And his eyes lit up, "just imagine the Velo on the island! It would be the ultimate test. What about it?"

"It isn't good enough," I replied. "It needs a six-speed gearbox. It would be useless up Snaefell. A bike needs to be built for the Isle of Man and the MOV isn't."

"I know all that, but damn it, you won't be riding it in the TT, but you could take it round the course. You know you'd love that, besides, let me ride the Enfield solo and I'll have all our gear in the panniers leaving you free to have a go." Before I could reply Tony cut me short. "We'll split everything fifty-fifty, but I'll pay the extra insurance on the Enfield myself and on a full policy for the job."

"And what will Maureen say?" I asked.

"No problem this year," replied Tony. "I've already told her we're going." I looked at Tony and he was smiling all over his face.

"All the lads know," he said, "and there isn't one of them that thinks you won't go. I'm sure Ivy will understand you probably won't get another chance,"

"We'd better go, then. I'll see Ivy about it tonight. In the meantime, I'd better take the chair off the Enfield, so that you can ride it around for a bit."

So the arrangements were made. After a debate with Ivy, she told me to be very careful, and to get it out of my system, for she knew that it was something I'd always wanted to do, particularly with a bike like the Velo. Well, a chap I knew who went quite often to the TT gave me an address for digs close to where he stayed at Ramsey, so I wrote and got us fixed up, so all the arrangements were made and our gear all sorted and packed into the two large leather panniers on the Enfield.

The year was 1969 and the weather was perfect and our journey to Liverpool was a good one. We had made very good time and had ridden between 60-70 m.p.h. all the way, where we could, and both bikes were running very well. Tony was very happy on the Enfield, as he remarked that he'd like to keep it! The sea crossing was rough and we had to lash both bikes to the steel bulkheads just for safety. The petrol had been drained as a fire precaution, a shipping rule for all bikes. On reaching the island there was a petrol pump on the quayside where we could fill up. We were told that it was very good fuel, just for bikes, so we both filled our tanks and slowly set off in search of our digs. We found the address quite easily and there was even a cover for the bikes, like a huge carport. The landlady was a honey and brought us tea in bed all the week. After a nice chat with our charming landlady, we decided to introduce ourselves to the circuit and hopefully get a lap or two in as an introduction to the circuit, for it was the sort of circuit that took a lot of getting used to. For instance, when Geoff Duke first went out to check over the circuit, he took a fortnight to view it and get it all weighed up, but it paid off as on his very first practice lap on the works Norton, he surprised everyone by making a very fast time.

Well, Tony and I had been discussing 'Mad Sunday', that is, the Sunday after the racing when the circuit is left open for the public to 'have a go', as you are only allowed to go round one way, the same as the bikes, and the police were present to stop any cars coming on or cutting across the circuit from the many side roads. To ride on the circuit on 'Mad Sunday' was, as it said 'mad', for with amateurs on bikes, some of whom hadn't a clue, the TT course on 'Mad Sunday' was really a cocktail for death. However, I wasn't an amateur, and I'd got a racing bike tailor-made for me, so if I didn't take the chance on the Sunday, I wouldn't get another one. I was going to be very careful, but nevertheless I was going to take it on and have a go, and hopefully, get in a fast lap, just for the hell of it. As Tony had said, it would be the ultimate test for me and for the Velo. The actual TT week was great and although my Velo was outclassed by the machinery of the day, I would have loved to have had a go. I also know that I wouldn't have disgraced myself, in fact, I was soon to prove just that, despite the fact that the Velo only had a four-speed gearbox. However, after the races, Tony and I went gently round trying hard to learn the course. Prior to 'Mad Sunday' I carefully checked over both bikes and, apart from the main chain on the Enfield requiring a slight adjustment, everything else was fine. The Enfield chain did get a little oil from the crankcase breathing tube, but putting a drop of thick oil on the chain, say once a week, was enough to keep it quite happy. The chain and chain oiler on the Velo were crack on and needed no attention, other than to top up the oiler. So, after checking the tyre pressures and a run over with the oil can on all cables, both bikes were ready to go. Tony was to follow me round at his own pace, for obviously, the Enfield couldn't get round bends like the Velo. Even so, I bet it would shine up the mountain, for I knew that it was Snaefel where the Velo would be lost for gearing, as I'd already found out that, as I had predicted to Tony, third was too low and top was too high. I needed that £600 six-speed gearbox. At the Isle of Man at any TT, you will find some of the world's best bikes and riders, as it is the Mecca for all motorcyclists, and some of the wonderful contraptions and specials you see are there in abundance. Also, there are some very good riders there, who, like me, aren't able to race but would love to have a go, hence 'Mad Sunday'.

At the top of Bray Hill where the start is, great crowds gather to see these various machines that have come just to tackle the world's most demanding motorcycle circuit, for it has everything and also, with one lap measuring thirty-seven and three-quarter miles, there is so much to remember, and to remember it is a must if one is to get round at a reasonable speed. That is, of course, if one is able to, for there are so many riders on it, you are lucky to be able to get a clear run. When Tony and I arrived at the start, both machines were received with complimentary remarks and I was asked on more than one occasion if my Velo was a vintage works racer. I hung about for a clear run to take off and after about five minutes or so I got my chance.

"See you later, Tone!" I yelled and pushed off amongst the cheers.

The Velo, being all warmed up, went off like a rocket and at this moment, I wished my old friend Arthur Taylor could have seen this, for again I was to rely on Arthur's 'secret springs' which I know were a big advantage. The megaphonics when the throttle was slammed shut were better than some of the TT racers, and the large crowd at the bottom clapped and yelled their approval as the Velo, with me crouched low, went roaring by. About two miles further on, as I came sweeping out of a right-hander, a chap came out from my left, and running into the road, to slow me down. I braked and changed down with a cacophony of megaphonics 'wow-wowing' behind me. Taking the next right-hand cautiously I could see why I was slowed down, for a Dommy Norton that had taken off just before me had gone into the bend too fast, lost control and had gone down a grassy ditch into a stream. The rider was just being helped away from his bike, as there were plenty of people on most of the bends. This of course was the real danger of 'Mad Sunday', so I decided to just go when I could, but also, not to take any chances, for a good rider I might be, and I had a great bike, but I didn't know enough of this circuit to really have a go, so easy does it every time. About five miles further on, I came across the two bikes that had taken off before me, and I didn't intend to be held up where I could see to go. Besides, I was on a racer, I must have the edge, so where I could go, I would. I was gaining well, and one of the riders heard or saw me coming, as both increased their speed as I drew close. We were approaching the Highlander, the fastest part of the course, so on going through Crosby, I hammered on and took both of these two 500cc bikes in one sweep.

I knew by past experience through the many dices in the Wolds, that this manoeuvre had caught them on the hop, for like most of these similar incidents, the ones being overtaken speed up, but usually only for a short run, as most riders couldn't equal the Velo through the bends. I didn't hang about, and by the time I'd got to the Highlander, both bikes were well to my rear. By the time I'd got to Greeba Bridge, I'd lost them as I'd reached over 100 m.p.h. and was going well. At Ballacraine, I'd caught up with a 500cc Matchless, he too, on hearing my approach turned up the hammer, and two bends further on, he almost ran out of road in his endeavour to stay in front. I was enjoying this, and my big front stopper was a bonus here, for I had to keep using it, as I approached these bends. I was grinning to myself now, and I was really set to have a go. I was riding well and I felt very confident, for the Velo was built for this and I'd got stacks of Cotswolds practice and it was all paying off. I was right at the rear of the Matchless just before a series of bends, and by timing my move very carefully, I passed this bike on the inside, as he misjudged one of the bends and slightly overshot; I'd just realised we were at Doran's Bend. I was going well, and by the time I'd got to Ballaugh Bridge, I'd taken three more machines, and it was here that I very nearly lost it, because I was at Ballaugh Bridge a split second before I knew it, but on a fast bike a split second can spell disaster, and it very nearly did. The approach to Ballaugh, because of my lack of knowledge of the course, was taken too fast, with the result that the Velo shot into the air with shouts of "Oh!" and "Ah!" from the crowd at the bridge. I was forced to push the bike over in mid air, and by a stroke of luck, we managed to stay on the road, but only just, as I found myself running along the kerb at great velocity. People gathered at Ballaugh to be thrilled. Well, the Velo had certainly done that. I felt the blood run to my head as I gained control of my bucking Velo just 1" from the verge. I shot off still aboard, but it had been too close to repeat. 'Watch it,' I told myself, or it could be my last ride, but all the same, the incident had sharpened me up. I was now one hundred per cent on what I was doing.

Quarry Bends were getting close and I knew that a classy rider could take all three in a straight line. I was hoping to find that line, ready for the next lap. I had gone down Sulby Straight in a bit of a turmoil; it was critical to know this course, for one must be ever watchful on every bend. Quarry Bends were only just ahead, I slowed down, for to drop a clanger here would mean disaster, for at Quarry Bends there is no fencing, just a very big drop and on to very big rocks. On going through these three bends, I began to realise just where the approach would have to be, in order to go through in a straight line, but there was no room for error, for at speed, there wouldn't be enough room to rerun the line, for one could very easily go over the drop. I was very pleased to tackle this part of the course all alone, as I could give full concentration to the road, and not to other riders. This was a very spectacular part of the course, for now I was about to tackle the mountain. This, I knew, was where I was going to be struggling, for I knew that the only thing to do was to go steady, and above all, not to over rev, hence the need for a six-speed gearbox. In 1969, the powers-that-be governing motorcycle road racing hadn't then passed a law governing the gearboxes to six gears, and during the race, it was amazing to see and hear the 125cc Kawasakis screaming round at 100 m.p.h. with their multi-type gearboxes. I believe they had six double acting gears, making the box a twelve speeder. The rider had a huge rev counter in front of him and with one eye on the road, and the other on his rev counter, regardless of the gear he was in, the rev band must be maintained to keep the screaming engine on the power band, the revs being between eighteen thousand and twenty-three thousand, an incredible engine. So here was I, about to struggle up with only four gears and revs of around 6,000 to 7,000, but here we were, change down, and get the right line. On some of these bends, the racing line could still be vaguely seen, particularly on the tarred surface, as the weather was hot, and the softer tar showed up the line. Even so, I caught and passed a 350cc BSA in lovely condition. He heard the Velo coming and waved me by just before the Ramsey Hairpin. I waved back, then with two perfectly timed gear changes, cranked over and roared round the hairpin amongst a load of cheering. Roaring away up the mountain, I had to be very careful not to over rev, as I'd guessed third was too low and top was too high, so it could only be a controlled climb in third, then second for the bends. The engine was great, I had the power all right, if I'd had the gears, I could have gone up like a rocket. It is now that I could see how important it was for the gearing on all occasions to be correct. Before I reached the Jim Guthrie

Memorial, I was aware of two big bikes coming up fast. One was an International Norton and the other was a Vincent Black Lightning, both having a go. As they got close, I pulled in to my left and waved them on, both waved back as they went by. Both of these bikes were in lovely condition. It looked as if they were prepared for it like I was.

I listened to these two beauties as they slowly pulled away and by the time I got to the Bungalow, the Velo was running very well and I was rapidly gaining on three more bikes in front of me. If I remember it right, one was a Rudge Ulster 500cc that had just passed a 350cc AJS and a 350cc Honda. I too took the AJS and the Honda in my pursuit of the big Rudge. The Rudge rider knew I was there and he too was determined to stay in front, for he was hammering on very well. But I was a better rider than the man on the Rudge, for he wasn't lining up for the bends correctly. On the approach to Brandish Corner, he slackened off whereas I hammered on, having gone over the outside of the road to get the racing line which I got, and it was a shaken Rudge rider that saw me roar by at over 70 m.p.h. and I was right over. There was a crowd at Brandish and they must have loved this, for it was a highlight to see overtaking on a bend. A rider has to be fully confident of himself and his bike to do it, and I was. I could hear the cheers as I shot by, then immediately gunned to my left in order to line up for Windy Corner, the next right hander. Here, I very nearly overdid it. I went through Windy like a bat out of hell. I remember seeing two chaps sitting on the fence on the apex of the corner, and on my approach, for on my line I was going straight for them at great velocity, they both fell off the fence backwards! I must have taken Windy at around 90 m.p.h., for I'd put a good distance between me and the Rudge, but as I came out of the corner, the rear tyre started to slowly slide towards the grass verge. I realised at once that I had one chance. I pulled slightly left, and eased myself over to the nearside and kept the hammer on; it was the only way out, and it paid off. Looking back I think that my tyre tread had filled up with wet tar, enough to override the grip. However, I made it, and looking back, I could see that it had done enough to make the Rudge rider give up, for he was fully upright and he had shut off. I could tell by the distance I was pulling away from him. I must admit, I'd got carried away and I'd never ever gone through a corner at such a speed. It said a lot for the Velo and its two tyres. But when the adrenaline runs it's a case of your heart ruling your head. I'd felt a judder on my left foot as I came out of the slide, and looking down, there was a clump of soil and grass on my toecap that I'd taken out of the bank; you can't get much closer than that. I still kept up a cracking pace, taking two more riders as I did so and, completing the first lap and also cooling off a bit, I was all set for the second.

The second lap was taking longer, for not only did I encounter more bikes, but also in the wrong places, so I took advantage of this to study and try to remember the many bends and corners. The only clear part that I got on lap two, was again down the mountain, where large crowds had gathered. I came down very well and took three big bikes just before Brandish corner, so called after Coventry's Walter Brandish, who apparently ran out of brakes and went straight on, but survived all in one piece. So, at Brandish again, I'd got the right line, and at a very fast rate, went through both Brandish and Windy with the crowds cheering and waving like mad, and at Windy Corner, a chap held up a large sheet of cardboard with the words in chalk, 'the best'. I had to grin; the Velo was doing it here, just as it did in the Wolds. The atmosphere was wonderful. As I started my third lap, again I got a big cheer. I looked at my watch, as there wasn't another bike in sight, and this time, I really did fly down Bray Hill, with crowds waving and cheering me on. Two miles further on, again I came across four riders who immediately flattened out and waved me by, but this time, I reached Glen Helen before I encountered another rider. I was going very much faster through the bends now, as a lot of them reflected in my memory, and of course, for the same reason, I was getting a better line. Again I caught up three more riders, but I was really moving and, on hearing the Velo, these three pulled over and waved me by; this was great. At Kirk Michel, I caught up with a chap on a 350 Cammy Velo using Castrol R. I had smelt it a good two miles before I'd caught up with him. I shot by as he braked for a bend, then he too, having someone to follow, took off after me. By the time I'd got to Ballaugh Bridge, I was pulling away from the Cammy and I took Ballaugh very well and on the correct line, with yet again mad cheers from the crowd, and this was where I saw the last of the Cammy, as I was going very well and I meant to keep a 'bat on'. The mountain climb was taken much better because I was now able to anticipate the bends better, get my change done sooner, and so, keeping the revs on the power curve, and of course, making full use of the road, I got up the mountain a lot quicker, for now I didn't see another bike, and to my utter delight, I took the famous Quarry Bends in a straight line, going very fast. There were a dozen people around in Quarry Bends, all waiting and watching, and I shot through amid cheers and clicking cameras. The descent too was fast, with no riders in my way, I was going great, and again, I took Brandish and Windy very fast and both on the racing line, but this time, to my surprise, the crowds at both corners were all standing up and I could hear the cheers and see all the enthusiastic waving; these people were genuinely appreciating my effort, and again at Windy Corner, the same chap was holding up his cardboard with '*the best*' printed on it in chalk. This time, I gave him a wave as the Velo roared by.

By now I'd got that wonderful feeling that I first encountered on the HRD, but it was now much stronger, for this was my bike. I'd built it and it was my moment of sheer ecstasy; the Velo was good enough for the Isle Of Man, and here I was proving it.

But I mustn't slow down now, for I knew I was doing very well. I glanced down at my engine; it was running like a watch – old Arthur, bless him, would have loved to see this. However, dreams over, I shot on and as I shot over the starting line, I looked at my watch. By gum! I was very, very pleased, for I'd just done a lap in the time of just under twenty-eight minutes. At a rough guess that was over 82 m.p.h. and on the ultimate of courses. I shut off and, amidst a load of cheering people, I pulled in and stopped my engine. This was it, for to get another free lap like this one, would be almost an impossibility, so I didn't intend to attempt it; I'd done enough. I was immediately surrounded by very enthusiastic crowds.

"Brilliant!" someone shouted, and everyone was talking at once, as I received many slaps on the back and people clamoured to see my 'dream machine', for now that's what it was; one of the best. I parked the Velo and checked the oil in the oil tank. It hadn't moved and the engine, apart from some whitish dust from the mountain, was oil tight and had ran like a watch. I took out my twin platinum point own-brewed spark plug, and the mixture reading was spot on, a nice lightish brown, just trying to go darker, absolutely perfect for racing, for one must remember that for long hard runs, it's death for the valves and pistons if too lean a mixture is used, but here it was spot on. My exhaust pipe was only straw in colour for the first foot on leaving the head, showing again a perfect burn. Yes, I was at this moment in time, a very happy man. My only regret was that I wished Ivy and my family had been there to see it.

About twenty minutes later, Tony arrived on the Enfield and he too had enjoyed himself, as he had two slow laps and enjoyed watching the various bikes having a go. No, he hadn't seen me at all, for he'd pulled in at one or two places, but he felt sure that it was the Velo's megaphonics that he had heard at Glen Helen. I must have gone by on one of his stops. The Enfield had ran very well, said Tony, and had made easy running of the mountain. Both of us were elated as we swapped yarns. Of course, I mentioned my near crash at Windy Corner, but he grinned, as someone who saw us together had already told him that his mate on his Velo was delighting the crowd and also doing his best to rip up Windy Corner!

At night, most of the riders who had been having a go round the course all met at the pub on Douglas Head, so Tony and I decided that we would join in the fun. But when Tony and I arrived, I was very surprised at our reception, for all looked round as we pulled in, and immediately started clapping.

"Great riding, mate," said one chap. "That's one hell of a bike," And immediately, we were surrounded by people. One young lady came up to me as I sat on the Velo, and smiling all over her face, and with a glass of port in her hand said,

"Ah, this is the man," And, giving me a big kiss in front of all added, "Your riding has thrilled me better than all the stars. You were wonderful." I was ecstatic and of course I thanked her very much, for it was a highlight of my motorcycling life. It had all come together on the magic Isle Of Man. They cleared a spot for the Velo where all could see, and someone put a pint of bitter shandy in my hand, for they had asked Tony what I drank, and they all drank my health and I theirs. I could have got a fabulous price for the Velo right then, for there were people there in evening dress and some very wealthy people came over to us for a chat and of course, to have a closer look at the Velo. How many times I was asked if it was a work's 'puka' racer I don't know. What I did know, was that all this, was like a dream. I couldn't have been much happier if I'd won the lightweight TT. I was by this time like a man in a trance. At 11.45 p.m. two very happy chaps arrived back at their digs. Our landlady had waited up for us and had prepared for us a lovely steak and kidney pie supper, for she too had been watching and was at Windy Corner.

In turn, we had bought her a big box of chocolates, for she really had given us some lovely meals and with tea in bed, we had had a wonderful week, and the weather, too, had been fabulous.

Monday saw Tony and I pouring our surplus petrol into our landlady's petrol tank on her car, for a bike must be empty before going on board the ferry. The crossing this time was much calmer and quicker, but at Liverpool where we filled up with fuel, about fifty odd riders followed Tony and I as we crossed Liverpool and not one rider tried to overtake. I told Tony afterwards, it was probably in respect of my last lap, for it had certainly caused a stir, but whatever the reason, it was a wonderful send-off, as we sounded like a squadron of aircraft as we all went thundering along, with crowds of people all staring at us as we went by. The journey home was good, but there was one little incident that was a bit funny, only Tony didn't enjoy it much, and that happened when, about halfway home, we pulled into a cafe for a couple of sandwiches and tea and cake. As we pulled in to stop, the front wheel of the Enfield dropped into a fairly deep pot hole. There was a plop, as the nearside fork leg top shot off under the hydraulic pressure in the fork leg. The cap shot up into the air and the oil in the leg covered Tony, much to his disgust at the time. However, there was a garage only 100 yards away, where I got a pint of 20SAE oil for the forks and a small tube of Stag Jointing Cement to seal the threads on the cap. Other than this, the whole trip had been a huge success and it was one holiday I'd never forget.

I'd bought Ivy a classy single row of pearls, which she still has to this day, and of course, I'd bought presents for the kids and a TT tie for myself, as I considered that I'd earned it. Back at work, the lads couldn't hear enough and two days later, the artist in our offices had done a huge drawing, and it was very good, of me airborne on the Velo, with clouds and seagulls looking at me in indignation and Tony on the Enfield all dripping with oil. A perfect end to a perfect trip.

Chapter Forty-Six
The Velo Tackles the Triumphs

A few weeks later, after our exploits on the Isle of Man, Tony and I had just been about got back to earth, all the stories had been told and retold, the chair was back on the Enfield and I'd also had the cylinder head off the MOV and reground in the valve seats and checked it all through. One Monday morning, I was going to work on my combo and had just got onto the A45 Birmingham Road, when a Triumph motorcycle tester came by me with a Mini Cooper very closely following behind. The Mini then pulled out and overtook the tester and almost immediately pulled back in again, cutting the tester up in doing so. I could clearly see the bike wobble as the rider was forced to brake hard and just for a moment I thought he was going to lose it, as blue smoke shot up from his rear tyre when the wheel locked up. However, he held it well and quickly recovered and tore after the stupid Mini driver who by now had got his foot down. Well, it didn't take the Triumph long to catch up with him and drawing alongside, the Triumph rider stood up on his footrests and then, as he went by he brought his left fist down very hard onto the Mini's roof. The Mini driver almost lost control as the car went from left to right along the road. The Triumph looked back but the Mini driver had been taught a lesson and was dropping back. In the meantime I had pushed on and at around 70 m.p.h. I too overtook the Mini rider and shook my fist in the air, for this man had all but been the cause of a nasty accident and he knew it, for he had now shut right off, and was rapidly dropping back.

Two days later I went to work on my MOV, as a new chap had started on the Monday and, as a motorcyclist himself, he had asked me to show him my Velo. Again as I entered the A45 I did so just as the same tester who had hit the roof of the Mini went by, so naturally I followed him up as we were both going the same way. When he realised that I was behind him, he opened up and the 500cc Triumph he was riding was soon at 90 m.p.h. with me still behind him. I was still there when he turned left off the A45 for the Triumph works which were just off the A45. He gave me a wave and I waved back and carried on to my right turn for our works.

Back at work, one of our lads who we had passed in his car came over to me and said,

"You and that tester were moving a bit this morning. It woke me up when you two shot by and the exhaust note from your Velo was fantastic. What was going on?"

"Nothing really," I said. "I was just catching him up and seeing me there he took off, so I followed him up."

"It looked to me as if you were both having a go," said this chap.

"But they'll be watching you. They don't like being passed on their own ground as it were, so watch out!"

"Thanks, I will. But the old Velo can hold its own," I replied.

Well, about three weeks later on again I had gone to work on the MOV and when leaving work I was going to call in at Alf's, so I had gone straight down the A45 instead of my usual way through Allesley Village. But as I slowed up for the first traffic island, two Triumph testers came alongside and one shouted,

"What is it, a 350?"

"No, a 250," I yelled back. He grinned and shouted,

"See you!" And they both took off. The Velo had just about warmed up by now and I instinctively followed them up, no real reason – I just couldn't resist it, so off all three of us shot. It wasn't long before they realised that I was there, so they opened up with the intention of leaving me behind. We had got clear of the traffic by now and all three of us were going along like bats out of hell, in line astern. We reached speeds of 90 and 95 m.p.h. and on the approach to the second traffic island, and using my big front stopper, I got by both and took off, lying almost flat on the tank. I'd done it now and there was no turning back.

'What the hell am I doing?' I thought. 'I must be mad, taking on two 500 bikes.' But it was too late; I was now committed. I had to see it through. I thought of Arthur Taylor and his 'desmo springs'. It was all or nothing now and a long straight road, but to my delight I was actually pulling away very slightly and 112 m.p.h. was fluctuating on the speedo – the Velo was simply flying. By now we were coming up to the third island at Baginton. I should of course have gone left at the second island where I took the two Triumphs, but instead I was three and a half miles further on risking a blow up, and for what! As we got closer to the Baginton traffic island I shot a glance back over my shoulder. It was only a glance at this speed, but what I saw caused me to shut off and slow down. I was by this time about seventy yards in front of the nearest bike and the nearest bike had clouds of blue smoke belching out of its offside exhaust pipe. Yes, the engine had blown and the race was over.

I pulled in at once and stopped my engine. The two Triumph testers did the same and the sound of the smoking Triumph was like a bag of nails; it was finished. The second Triumph had been a good hundred yards further back. It was a remarkable feat to say the least. The chap with the blown engine said,

"I'm in the shit now. That was a Grand Prix engine that I've just blown up. I never dreamt you would get by us and stay there. You can tell your mates you've just blown up the Triumph, but if I tell our gaffer that a 250 did this..." And he touched the bike with his boot. "He'll never believe it." The Velo was fine and even on the Isle of Man it hadn't gone faster. This was its swansong, as it was never to go faster again. It had proved to be one hell of a bike and of course, I was even more proud of it still.

"I'll come in to your works, tomorrow. I'd like a picture of that bike." So we shook hands and we all went right round the island and headed back, me to Alf's and the two Triumphs back to the works. On my way to Alf's I could hardly believe what had just happened, as my mind was still in a whirl. It had been so incredible. A 250 blowing up a 500 twin, but I'd just done it!

At Alf's, I told my two mates Geoff and Bernard what I'd just done.

"Bloody hell!" said Geoff. "You're not going to live this down. It will spread like wildfire! Congratulations! It's a remarkable achievement." And he shook my hand very strongly. Geoff went on to say that if Velos hadn't been folding up my engine might have gone into production, for it had just been announced that the Velocette Motorcycle Company was to finish. A very bitter blow; it was to be the end of an era. I must go and see them before this took place and find out why.

Chapter Forty-Seven

The Last of Velocettes and I Miss a Gem!

The MOV was still running beautifully despite its fastest run, even the tappets were on song and I knew that Arthur Taylor's desmo springs had paid off. Arthur I know, would have loved this story so I hope his loved ones will enjoy it too, for without Arthur, my beloved Velo wouldn't have been so famous. The next day I again went to work on my MOV and having only told my pal Tom McCulloch what had happened, I knew that the two Triumph lads were coming in at lunchtime, so I'd decided I'd let them tell it.

So, it came as a big surprise to me, when the chap who saw me 'having a go' as he thought, came up and said,

"You're a dark horse. What about the Triumphs last night? Aren't you going to tell us about it?" I was flabbergasted, for I'd only told Tom and I knew that he wouldn't talk.

"How did you get to know?" I asked. "I've only told my mate Tom."

"Ah hah," he said, touching his nose, "a real bird told me, and she lives next door to one of them and she works right here in the office and I brought her to work today, because her husband has taken the car." So I told him the story just as it happened, and in minutes it had gone right through the department. I had one or two slaps on the back over it and the only chap who wasn't pleased was my challenger friend of Honiley Airport saga. His reply was, "He'll end up in a box, the way he's going on." But by all accounts it was the topic of the week and when the two men in question came in on two brand new 500 twins, then all could see just what the Velo had taken on and they also got the story from the horse's mouth. The rider of the bike that blew up told us that the cylinders had blued with heat, proving that the engine had been too tight to run so fast, for it's very doubtful that if the Triumph had done more miles that I'd ever have achieved it, but that's what happened and here proving it were the two riders. Nevertheless, they had a job to take in the fact that it was a 250 that had done it.

About two weeks after this, I was stationary at the traffic light junction at the top of Hearsal Lane, near Alf's, when the speed cop who had pulled me in to look at my combo, which I was on now, came alongside, and as the lights changed he said,

"Blown any good Triumphs up lately?" Yes, even the police knew about it and there was no doubt that the Velo was well-known. I'd have to watch it, for a speedster is usually caught. I also wondered if the Velo's former owner ever got to know, and if he did, what he thought about it. The following weekend I went to Velos on the MOV. I didn't really want anything, only to find out why they were closing up. I was very lucky, for in the service department was Mr P. Goodman, who owned Velocette. I made it my business to talk with him and to say how very, very sorry I was to hear the sad news. He was very kind and explained just why it was to be. During the war all motorcycle and car factories had been on war work, their machines were worn out and the death blow was from our own Government, as there weren't sufficient funds to pay for new machinery, as Great Britain had all but spent out. On the other hand, Germany and Japan were getting help from their rulers and as the Japs' cost of living (on rice) was far cheaper than ours, their recovery was better in many ways than our own. Don't forget that we owed America millions of dollars and, as Mr Goodman had said, for us to compete against the Japs at the price that they could produce them, our prices would have been approximately three or even four times higher, so who, other than lads like me would be able to afford to buy them? They only had to see how well they were finished, to know that with our worn out machines it was an impossibility, the end of an era, and I'm not ashamed to say I shed quite a few tears over it, but I'm very proud to have played a big part in it, for some of my greatest moments had been on motorcycles and in particular, on my beloved Velocette.

Mr Goodman told me to come next week as there would be a big sell-out in the next two weeks. It was very sad. I never thought I'd see this day and it was a very unhappy Velo rider that went slowly back to Coventry that day.

The following week, I was just about to start out for Velos on my combo when one of my neighbours asked if I could help as he couldn't start his car. I wish now that I had made an excuse and left for Velos. As it was I stopped to help, and found his points were covered in oil. Twenty minutes later his engine was running but the delay had cost me the last Mark VIII Velocette to leave the production line, for a dealer was just loading it into his van when I got there. It was a bike I'd have given my eye teeth for, as it was the finest bike that Velo had ever made. Just try to buy one today and you will see, so just like Velos themselves, my luck too, had just ran out. I got a lot of bits and pieces very cheap, but to miss the last Mark VIII – I daren't think of it in case I burst out in tears and I'm not joking, for I had visited Velocettes for the very last time and I was very downhearted.

Chapter Forty-Eight

The End of an Era

The fact that the end of British bikes was upon us, was only just sinking in and I was devastated. Life without them wouldn't be the same; it was the end of an era. But it was my era and it would affect me as I'd grown up in it, it was my life or at least, it had been and I didn't like the thought of Japanese bikes taking over from the British. To me and many like me it was like a kick in the teeth, after all, we had just been at war with Japan and now they were taking over the British bike industry. I just couldn't stomach it. I wished now that I'd bought up the two Velos in Gray's showroom, for Velos were about to become very hard to find and, of course, quite costly too. Also, with the closure of Velocettes, all the spares seemed to vanish as dealers around the country took stock of the situation. Of course, spares were still available but not in as many dealers as before and the longer it went on, the more scarce and costly they became. I was very pleased that I had a fair supply.

I was still repairing British bikes at home, but I didn't see many Velos. People were storing them up, for, as classic bikes, they would become valuable. But of course Velocettes weren't on their own, for many other firms were also closing up. There was BSA, Ariel, AJS, HRD, Frances Barnett, James, Excelsior, Norton, Matchless, Panther, OK Supreme, Royal Enfield and many subsidiary firms that were suppliers for the British motorcycle industry. While all this was happening, the Japanese bikes were slowly taking over. Familiar names now were then just getting known and two things sold the Japanese bikes: the finish, which was excellent, and the price, which was very good, making a Jap bike a good buy. A different type of motorcycle was here an alloy oil drip-free machine and a model to suit nearly all tastes. The little two-stroke 'reed-valve' engines were brilliant, for they went like the clappers, far faster bikes than the old

British two-stroke, for as you will most likely be aware, the old British two-strokes were nearly all a petrol-oil mix for lubrication, whereas the Japanese were a straight petrol with an oil injection system, making the blue smoke from a two-stroke a thing of the past. The larger machines too were very good, OHC being a standard procedure on nearly all models, making a very potent bike for all, and at the right price. But, once the market was sold, then up went the prices; today a beautiful bike can be bought – if you have the money.

I'm pleased to say that there were still old British diehards like me, who kept the British bikes still rolling, but we knew that our days were numbered, and that the Japanese bikes had all but taken over. After repairing a couple of Jap bikes at home, I'd decided that in future, I was only going to repair British bikes. Rightly or wrongly I was too old to change, so my mind was made up: I'd stay British on bikes until the end. The British bikes, like myself, had a good code on the road, we always gave each other a wave and we always stopped to help another British rider if they had broken down. I didn't go out on many fast runs those days, for one thing, many more cars were on the road, which made it dicey, to say the least, also, I was spending a bit more time at home, even if it was in the garage, as Ivy has just pointed out to me! But one run I did almost ended in disaster, for this Sunday, although I'd gone out early, about 5.30 a.m., I came across another Velo rider in trouble, so I stopped to help him. He'd lost his spark, and although it didn't take me long to get it back for him, as his mag pick-up brush had stuck, I was really too late going back, with the result that I was getting into the traffic. On the approach to Stoneleigh Hill, at Stoneleigh in Warwickshire, I approached it from the Leamington side, and as I came over the brow, I suppose I was doing around 60 m.p.h.. On the other side of the brow, which was steeper, half a dozen cars were stuck behind an older Morris Oxford with L-plates on, that had stalled its engine just before the hill top. As I shot over, an Austin car at the back had just started to pull out onto his offside of the road, but when I appeared, he quickly pulled in again and stopped. Only, he only half pulled in, as the white line marking the road centre was halfway under his car. I was going too fast to stop, and I knew instinctively that it was going to be bloody close, for on my left was a solid stone wall, and I knew that if I hit it at this speed, I was finished. So, making myself as small as possible, I roared through at full bore, making certain that I didn't hit the wall.

Well, I missed the wall, but just caught the car, at least I hit his outside mirror with my right shoulder, and, with a shooting pain in my arm, I smashed the mirror to pieces, but I was through.

I didn't even attempt to stop, after all, his car was on my side of the road. The fault was his and he knew it. The idiot could have killed me, so, rightly so in my book, I left him sitting in it; it just may have taught him a lesson. I had a black shoulder for weeks. I was lucky I hadn't broken it, and I must admit, that it was this incident that made me decide that I'd done my last very fast run. Besides, I was no longer a young man. In fact, I was getting to be more like a veteran each day, and so was the Velo. But it wasn't going to end my Cotswold runs, for these I loved, and I'd carry on for my pleasure, for as long as I could. There must be many Cotswold people who will remember the Velo and its rider all in black, except for a white helmet with 'Velocette' in gold across the front and the red rose of England underneath, roaring through every summer and even in the winter if the weather allowed (very sorry if I woke you). I always went steadily through towns or villages, but of course, on a Sunday morning, the sharp staccato note of a single cylinder tuned engine is always distinctive, again, I apologise if I woke you, but your Wolds helped to keep me alive. Also, I enjoyed some of my greatest moments amongst them. One chap who admired me and the Velo always came to see me at home about a week or so before Christmas and the next time he came, he asked the same question that he'd asked for years. The question was,

"When are you going to sell me your 350 vintage?" Like me, he just loved Velos, but had never been in a position to afford one, but he loved my 1929 Cammy. When he asked me this question this time, Ivy was there, and turning to me, she said,

"Just why don't you let him have it? You never use it, anyway!" So, in a weak moment, I gave way and let him have my 1929 Cammy MKI. It made his Christmas, but I knew I'd done wrong as soon as I'd said it. One doesn't sell a vintage when one is a Velo man, but I did, and I should not have done it. However, the last I heard of it, he'd made a glass case for it and it was in his lounge as his prize possession. No doubt it is still there, worth far more now than ever before. The Scott too, I had promised my old mate Tony Stringer that one day he could have it, so I went mad and fulfilled my promise. No doubt I'd made two of my good mates very happy. About five years before I finished work, I gave my Enfield twin on solo form to my son Bob, who later sold it to get a car – the old story.

About this time I too started to use the car to go to and fro for work, but not out of choice. The fact was, that my daughter had started work at an office which I passed daily, so it was for this reason that I used the car as it saved her waiting for buses. This left me with my beloved Velo and I thought I'd got it forever, for I had great plans for after I retired from work, to go on my usual Cotswold runs. Only this time there was to be no real speeding, also, I had found that I had a high percentage of lead in my blood, through the years I'd spent on engines. Later, this, in turn, turned to leukaemia of the blood, so with all the costs and commitments etc., we got through a lot of cash. In other words, I was snookered, for it became a fight for life. As our funds started to run out, I was forced to sell my dream machine; it broke my heart, for at Brooklands race circuit on July 4th at a Sothebys sale, my Velo went for £3,000. The year was 1987. When I walked away from it, I couldn't speak. I was all choked up. No, it wasn't as bad as losing one's dog or cat, after all they are God's gifts, living souls, but my Velo had been my brain child, and with all the rides I'd done on it, it came as a very bitter blow, as I'd had it for thirty-two and a half years.

Now by this time, I was starting to win my fight for life. For one thing, I'd never smoked, a very important point, secondly, I didn't have drugs or chemotherapy; it was all done by herbs. The herbs came from Austria. Fortunately for me, we have a very dear friend in Austria, who got me the thirty-six herbs that make up the cure for leukaemia and it worked, for I made a full recovery. The Velo went to the Rochester Motorcycle Museum, and as far as I know is still there, so I'll put down the details of my old Velo, so if any of you go there, then you'll know what to look for. They are as follows: Reg No. FKV 393; Eng No. MOV 6234; Frame No. 3282. There is if you check, a rather strange element here, for 393 added up comes to 15. 6234 also makes 15, and so too does 3282, does this make my lucky number 15? It certainly makes one think, for I had a charmed life on the Velo and at no time did I ever feel unsafe. At least, I have some wonderful memories of my old bike, and my handiwork is still able to give pleasure to thousands of people. After all, it isn't everyone who has a 'special' that ends up in a museum.

Chapter Forty-Nine
A Can-Amm Bombardier is Made Good

But my motorcycling days were not quite over, for as I got better and gained strength, my darling wife and our lovely German Shepherd bitch were at last getting back on our feet and I had a very strong urge to work on a bike once more. So, after talking it over with Ivy, it was agreed that I could have £400 to buy a suitable machine for a strip and a rebuild, so my interest was rekindled to find a bike. Of course, a Velo would have been ideal, but as I've already said, Velos were hard to find and also quite costly, so the search was on. I never even thought of a Jap bike. I was a British motorcycle mechanic so there was no way I'd do up a Jap bike, the interest just wasn't there. I found a very suitable candidate in the form of an Army bike. The bike was a Can-Amm Bombardier, it had an Austrian Rotax 248cc two-stroke disc-valve engine, a five-speed gearbox, a very strong multi-plate clutch, a very strong cradled frame with a pair of strong telescopic forks. Almost the same as the Norton road holder forks. The engine took four-star petrol and it had an oil injection system which was excellent. The oil was contained in the wide top rail of the frame.

The big advantage of the two-stroke single cylinder engine was its disc-valve, for it was the only two-stroke to give full engine braking, for on the closing of the throttle, the disc-valve in the crankcase closed up and acted as a brake, just the same as a four-stroke valve engine. But with a two-stroke we had the advantage of a very good acceleration, giving the rider the best of both worlds, a very nice machine.

This bike was ideal, for it was in very good order throughout. It hadn't been dropped or knocked about and best of all, it had only done 2,010 miles. This bike would be a good buy if the price was right. It would also be a challenge, for I knew very little about it. After a bit of haggling, I got it for £395, delivered with all the army papers to go with it. So I'd got myself another bike and a big grin was already spreading over my face. It was a big heavy bike for a 250, but the engine was a good one and being a two-stroke and a five-speed box, it had plenty of power as the engine was a Rotax competition engine and had a very large finned cylinder and cylinder head, all alloy and in heat-resisting black, a very impressive layout. The control cables were extra heavy and very nicely made, the wheels were of a heavy type, having a 3.25 x 19 front and a 400 x 18 on the rear. The rear suspension was very good, having a five-point adjustment to suit all, and the strong pivoting arm could be lubricated. The carburettor was a German 'Bing' one and the tuned exhaust system was one of the best I'd ever seen. Do you remember me mentioning that a two-stroke lives or dies on its exhaust pipe? Well, on the silencer, impregnated in the metal it read thus: *in no circumstances must this exhaust system be altered.* Truly a very good buy and all in army colours. It was only made as a one-seater like my Velo, but the seat was big and strong and with its beautiful suspension, it was without any doubt, the most comfortable machine I'd ever ridden.

In my conversion of the Velo, I hadn't kept a written record, but I didn't intend to do the same with this one, so right from the word go, I got it all down, so if anyone out there wants any information, yours truly can give it and I will leave instructions for me to be contacted through the publishers for this reason, as a little help can save you pounds and hours of work. I don't intend to cover all the details here, that put it right, but there are one or two interesting things that I am sure are well worth a mention.

The Can-Amm Bombardier is a universal armed-forces machine built in Toronto in Canada, but it is a bit of a hybrid, for it had an Austrian power unit with a gearbox and clutch, the frame and forks were I believe, made by Norton Motorcycles, and it was very well done, being webbed at all the joints for extra strength. My old 500cc Twin Royal Enfield was a good strong bike, but this one was even tougher, for it was designed not only as a road bike, but was extra strong everywhere for heavy cross-country work. The fuel tank held three and a half gallons, either four star as preferred, but *not* unleaded, as this would have damaged the piston. The electrics were all Suzuki, but altogether a very nice piece of very strong and reliable motorcycle. On receiving the bike as it was delivered free of charge, I was told that possibly there would be a carburation problem, as the machine had been set up and used in the Canadian Rockies, so I knew it was in for just the sort of work I enjoyed. The first job was to make a strong wooden cradle for it in order to get both wheels off the ground and make work easier. The next job was to get the whole lot thoroughly cleaned up, to see just what I'd got, for if one wants to learn about a strange piece of machinery, the first thing to do is to clean it, one can learn a lot that way. But prior to this I'd put a gallon of four star in the tank with a drop of Redex, topped up the two-stroke oil and attempted to start it. The kickstart and gear shift was on the left, but the engine didn't want to know, just a splutter and then a wet plug. It was obvious that spark, timing and carburation would all have to be gone into to find out why. The civilian agent for these machines was Armstrong Motorcycles, Motorcycle Works, Jubilee Crescent, Velame, Bolton, B41 60F. Tel. 01204-396984. I've put this in, for it's just possible that it may be of use to someone. However, I got the correct timing but as for the carburation, I was on my own, for they didn't deal with it, as it varied as to where the bike was run, so the next phone call would have to be to the Bing Carburettor Company in Germany, an excellent firm to deal with, so again, I'll put down their address, it is: Ftitz Huntermyre, G.M.B.H. Bing Vergaser-Fabrik, Senefelderstab 7 – Postfack 8500 Nurberg 13, West Germany.

Well, I'd only just about got started on this work, when to my horror, my right leg started to swell as if it had been blown up by an air pump. I mention this as it has a bearing on this story a bit further on. What I'd got was a thrombosis (blood clot), obviously a legacy from my leukaemia that I'd only just got over. Had I known then what I know now, I'd have given myself plenty of Vitamin E, but I didn't know, so at the hospital I was put on Warfarin (rat poison) to thin the blood. The treatment should have been for six weeks only, but a cock-up left me on it for twelve weeks. By this time I was looking and feeling ill again, for now I'd got a poisoned system as well. Now, whether this had any bearing on my next problem I'll never really know, for by now I'd developed an acute prostate gland problem. I then, thinking I needed liquid, drank a whole bottle of lemonade for good measure, only to lie in agony and rolling about like a pregnant woman about to give birth. Ivy, on seeing this, quickly sent for the ambulance, and in twenty minutes I was rushed off to hospital. At the hospital I was worked on at once, there was a doctor, a matron and a staff nurse, all working on me and it didn't take them long to get me drained off. After I was made comfortable, I was told that in another twenty-four hours I would have been dead, with a burst bladder. So now I was to have my operation on my prostate gland, so I just laid back and waited to be dealt with. I was lucky in this respect, as the operation was to be done with a laser beam, no surgery, but even so, I lost four pints of blood. I refused blood on two accounts, one, if I'd had just one pint of blood from a smoker, it could have brought on the leukaemia again. Secondly, and most importantly, it is against God's law. Ask Paul Michael Glaser,

'Give blood, spread AIDS.' It makes sense.

I had four and a half bottles of glucose from a drip and after my 'op', I couldn't even lift my head from the pillow, but in two days, I was up and helping to serve tea and coffee in the wards. I made a very good recovery. I was then sixty-five years of age, but a lot fitter and more active than many men some ten years younger than me, but I'd also kept myself fit all my life, now it was paying off. So now that I was out of pain, and my leg almost back to normal, my thoughts were on my latest project. All I had to do now was my prostate exercises and then eat the right things like honey and yoghurt, then get myself in shape. The five days I was in hospital, I dreamt of the Cotswolds air and my many rides on the Velo. My surgeon at the Coventry Hospital was Mr Blacklock, and I publicly thank him for a wonderful job. I had obviously met a true craftsman.

Back home I found it very hard to keep off the bike, but I knew that I had to rest for at least three to four weeks and Ivy made sure that I did. I was feeling very good, and although I had lost about a stone and a half I was eager to get cracking, so I kept up all my exercises and all the daily water drinking and when I was able, I took our faithful dog on some country walks to get my strength back. Also, I'd had plenty of time to think, so I'd worked out a few of the problems. The carburation would have to be worked out on the bike, so it was going to a bit of trial and error, as of course, the exhaust couldn't be altered.

Chapter Fifty
A Bit of Reverse Tuning

With the tuned exhaust system already there, the problem was tuning in the carburettor to the exhaust. I must admit that it took a bit longer than I thought, for a two-stroke isn't as easy as a four-stroke when it comes to tuning in reverse.

So, first I got the ignition timing spot on and a nice fat blue spark to go with it. I could now really get stuck in, boy, it was great just to be alive. Well, after a couple of weeks and several jets and different settings I started to get a result. Two days later it was firing up first kick, even from cold. Now I was grinning again, so it was another box of chocs for Ivy, as I'd always done this when I had won, but it wasn't over yet, as you will see.

I was now in the same position with the Bombardier as I had been with the Velo. I wanted a run prior to the MOT, but I wasn't going to get one, so I had to get the best result possible, get it through the MOT, then get it re-registered and taxed, then, and only then would I be able to sort it out on a run. A few days later, I'd got a good spark plug reading, light brown, so I took it for its MOT. Of course, it passed first call, for after all, it was almost a new bike, so now, after it had been taxed with its new civvy no. 0494 GVC, I could at last take it for a run. So the next morning, the weather being fine, I'd decided to go round the big 'green block' as I called it, a distance of just three miles there and back, but it was just right to go round as a test course, for it was fairly flat having only one hill, but with a few sharp bends and about a mile long straight, just right for testing.

On the road to and from the MOT station the bike had run very well; the only adjustment I had to make, was that the tickover was too slow but a one-third turn of the throttle cable adjuster soon put that right. The engine was well-balanced and was very smooth, the acceleration was very good as it usually is in a two-stroke, and despite the higher riding position, the machine handling was very good and so too were both brakes. The suspension was a dream, comfort being paramount, just right for me after my ordeal, so, armed with three spare plugs, a plug spanner and a small screwdriver for the carburettor, I was all set to go.

But although I wasn't going far I put my gear on, for the danger is always there, the distance doesn't matter. The engine fired up first kick, so after a two-minute warm up, I took off and it was great to be back in the saddle. I knew that this was the finest tonic I could have. I'd put in a lot of work on the bike, and I'd eliminated every snag that I could see, but as I've said before, the test run is always the deciding factor. I did a couple of laps, as it were, round the block, then pulled in and checked the plug, the reading was slightly rich, but at least it was on the safe side. So, weakening off the mixture screw by about a quarter of a turn, I did two more laps, but this time, I opened it up a bit, for on the first two laps, I hadn't exceeded 55 m.p.h., for I must first make sure that all was well and that the machine handled well. It did, so now I could move a bit. At 70 m.p.h. the engine was as smooth as silk the rev counter was reading about 5,000 so it was running well within its limits, for its top revs were around 10,000, the rev counters top reading was 11,000. I was enjoying this test run very much, what a lovely bike to ride. One could sit on it all day and not feel fatigued, as I did later on and proved it. Anyway, after checking the plug once more, I was delighted to see that it was about perfect and the performance gave witness to it. The acceleration up to fifty was faster than the Velo, being a two-stroke with the correct gearing, as the five-speed box was a boon and, like the Velo, the gear changes were nice and positive, the clutch too was brilliant, light in action and very, very smooth.

Yes, I liked it very much, for it had made a nice bike, so different to the old Velo, but as a bike, it was in my opinion, one of the best value for money that I could have got, after all, it was all but new. In bottom and second gear, the front wheel came up easily if too much throttle was used, and even in third, one could get a lift if you accelerated hard. I know that on my way home from the test and having got the carburation spot on, I couldn't resist a big wheelie when coming up our road. Of course, Ivy spotted it, and when I got in, she said,

"Hello Evil Knievil, are you satisfied now?"

Yes I was, I told her, it was a big success and I was feeling great, the best tonic I could have had. The next day, our very best friend, Werner Keene came up to see us, and he had brought me a present in the form of a Scott chain oiler. I was delighted, as I didn't expect it and certainly, he couldn't have got me a better present. I treated Werner like a son, we both love him very much, for a finer lad would be very hard to find. His mother is the Austrian lady who saved my life by getting me the herbs from Austria where Werner's parents now live. Werner was so impressed with the Bombardier that he asked me if I could get him one. I told him that I would certainly try, as I said, we looked on Werner as a son. So, the next day, I fitted on the chain oiler and it was a huge success, a must on a good bike, and well worth the cost and the effort involved fitting it. The following day turned out hot, so, with tools in my rucksack, I decided to go a longer run and get the setting right on my new chain oiler. Looking at my log of the Bombardier, I see that the date was 7.9.88 and that the temperature in Coventry on that day was 78°F. The intention was to complete a thirty to fifty mile run and get the chain oiler set right, so, with tools and three spare plugs, two of them softer, in case of any oil up taking place and a Mars Bar just in case, I set off.

I stopped three or four times in the first ten miles in order to regulate the chain oiler as it was too rich, and, having got it right, I took off again to enjoy the ride. Between Knowle and Warwick, and without warning, the engine cut out dead. I knew right away that the spark had gone, for if it had been fuel, there would have been spluttering etc., but in any case, I'd put two gallons with Redex into the petrol tank, so I knew I had stacks of fuel. Before I set out, I'd told Ivy just where I was going, just in case, but just then I'd better make a quick check on the sparks, and sure enough, it was completely dead. The ignition was a coil-cum-rotary mag with no points, just a magnetic signal, an excellent system, so the cause could take a bit of finding and if I was to try and sort it out here, it could take too long and Ivy would be worrying herself sick. It rather looked to me as if the coil was dead, for on the check that I made, there was no life at all, so, because I was anxious for Ivy, rather than taking a chance and stripping out the coil box, which could take quite a time, I decided to push it back home, as at the time, I thought that that would be quickest and in any case, if the coil had gone, then I would have wasted my time, so I might as well start pushing. So, removing my riding suit jacket and crash hat and gloves, I put them in the two large leather panniers that I'd taken time to fit on the bike. Well, at least I could ride it downhill; so off I went. I was just 9.7 miles from home, as I'd zeroed the trip before I started. By and large it wasn't too bad. The heat was the problem, so using all my know-how I got down to it. About an hour and a half later, Ivy knew I was in trouble, for I had said that I would be back within the hour. Ivy knew that I would keep my promise, as I knew too well how anxious she would be. So, one and a half hours after I'd left, Ivy swung into action. She notified the police who, in view of my previous illness and recent operation (this was just six weeks after leaving hospital) , got out the helicopter; and of course, I knew nothing about it, So, except for the heat and the fact that after six miles or so my calf muscles were tightening up, I was doing okay. But I had now reached a very steep hill with a sharp bend halfway up, but just before this hill was a wide grass verge with a large oak tree growing on it, making a cool, shady spot for me to rest, which I did, pushing my now very heavy bike into the shade, where I all but went to sleep, for I fully cooled off and rested for twenty minutes.

While I lay on the grass with my riding jacket holding up as a pillow, I heard the helicopter overhead. Of course, they didn't see me, and neither did I know that it was me they were searching for, so, quite unconcerned, I started off up this very steep hill. Halfway up I could only do a few steps, then stop with the front brake on to stop the bike rolling back. A couple of cars came by but they were car men, they'd never lived with a bike, they didn't know what it was all about! So slowly, I finally got to the top of the hill only to sink down again to rest, for I was by now feeling distressed, so I had yet another ten minutes rest in order to get my breath back. By now I was using every trick in the book. I'd already put another ten pounds of air into the tyres to eliminate drag, and keeping the bike upright to ease the weight, on reaching a slope I ran the bike forward and side-saddled keeping very low again to eliminate drag and it was in this way that I finally got back. About half a mile from home, I passed a friend's house, so I called in and they gave me a large lemonade and a couple of biscuits. The lemonade came just right, for I was now drying out and my mouth had gone dry. I was reluctant to put a pebble under my tongue to keep the saliva going, in case I swallowed it, but after ten minutes the lemonade gave me the extra boost I needed to reach home.

Back home, Ivy notified the police and thank goodness we weren't charged for it, so after a bath and a change of clothes I laid in our garden all the rest of the day, with Zara, our dog, lying down with me. I slept for nine hours that night, but it had proved my recovery, as apart from my aching calves I had no after-effects. In fact, after a hearty breakfast, I couldn't wait to get down to the trouble that had robbed my otherwise perfect bike of its spark. On stripping out the coil box, I soon found out why; in fact, had I stripped it out on the road, it would have saved me a big push, for all that it was, was human error. Someone had packed the coil box with chassis grease instead of Lanolin grease. The result was, because of the hot day and of course, my longer run, the grease in the coil box had melted and shorted out the coil action to earth. It was as easy as that. The coil was fine, so, washing the lot out with hot detergent water, the spark was back and it fired up first kick. The idea of filling the coil box with Lanolin grease was to make it waterproof, but as I wasn't going to run it in the rough, I didn't repack it, as that now wasn't necessary in its civilian lifestyle.

So we were back to square one, and I set out to do the test again, but before I went, Ivy came out with two Mars Bars, just in case, but she knew that I wouldn't attempt to push it again, so off I went. The engine ran like a watch, and never missed a beat. Of course, I did the same run that I'd intended to do the day before, just for the hell of it, but this time it was cooler and there was no grease in the coil box.

The old Bombardier was now flying along, and on a humpback bridge that I could see over, I took it a steady 50 m.p.h.. There were two couples sitting on the bridge, and when the old bike got air bounce, there were yells and shouts. Again I was enjoying myself. I might not be young any more, but I can still ride a bike and right now I was fully enjoying it. When the bike touched down it was fantastic, there was no shock wave, the whole bike just floated up and down twice, then back to normal. Had I been on the Velo, I'd have been fighting to stay on. This old army bike was great: big, strong, reliable, quite fast, but oh, how lovely and comfortable. It was like an armchair on wheels. I tell you, I loved this and it suited me fine, a bit of comfort in my old age and still on a bike. The grin was still there, I was living again.

Chapter Fifty-One
Another Bombardier is Brought Back to Life

By now, I'd made a few enquiries for Werner to get him a Bombardier, as he liked mine so much, but they weren't too easy to come by at the time. However, I did find one. It had been in the rough, as it was scratched all over and would need to be stripped. The mileage was only 4718 so even though it had been roughed up a bit, at this low mileage, it was a good buy. I bargained with them and my superior knowledge won the day, for I got it for £245 having got £55 knocked off the original price. Needless to say, my friend Werner was delighted, especially when I told him I'd do it all up like mine.

Of course, I now knew the model quite well and although his needed a lot more work than mine did, I wouldn't be struggling, for I now knew the job. So, as with mine, I made a log and got cracking. There was a lot of work, including a respray and a lot of little jobs. Altogether I'd done seventy-three separate jobs, but Werner had got himself a very nice bike.

Whilst I was doing Werner's bike, I'd already made an all-alloy bracket to lower the front guard down over the front wheel, for as they were on the Bombardier, they were fastened under the fork leg with about fourteen inches clearance to disperse mud etc., so I was going to fit them close to the wheel, so that the water would be kept down, for as it was now, the rain coming off the front tyre was spraying the bike and the rider. So this I did on both bikes, and it was a very good move, particularly with a strong rubber mud flap on the bottom, for already, Can Amms had a plastic type flap at the forward top end of the guard, but after my alteration, it was a very good water stopper. I also fitted panniers on Werner's bike, for the strong steel pannier frames were already on as a part of the bike, but could be taken off if desired.

Werner too, supplied another Scott chain oiler for his bike which I fitted with no bother. That weekend, Werner came to see his now posh-looking bike. It had come up well and looked newer than mine on account of its respray, and when Werner saw it, his eyes lit up and he embraced me just like a son would. Also, he'd brought me another present and the same for himself. It was a pair of anti-theft clamps that anchored round the fork legs and a chrome vanadium steel clamp just under half an inch thick that slides through into the very strong lock and so clamps the front wheel and locks it solid. The only way to pinch the bike would be to lift it on to a van or pick-up, but at least we'd made it as difficult as possible and both bikes were now well equipped. The large flashers and a large twelve-volt system made the Bombardier a first-class bike and a lot stronger than any other bike that I've ever seen, and that includes the Harleys.

The Bombardier averaged between 50-75 m.p.g. according to the traffic and speed, but a more reliable bike you would have a job to find, for it was made for a very tough job, and believe me, it's got a lot going for it.

Werner was delighted with his. He used it daily for work and it never let him down as maintenance is simple and there is a long flute tube in the silencer that can be taken out for cleaning, keeping the over square two-stroke happy. This model would be a very good globe-trotter.

If anyone reading this has been inspired to get a bike, I'll tell you truthfully, a Bombardier is a very strong contestant. For a kick-off, they don't cost the earth to buy, they are the strongest of all bikes, their design is brilliant, the mechanics second to none, the road holding too is very good and I think I've said it all about the comfort and the suspension, so don't pay the earth for a Jap bike, first go on the search and don't buy something you can't afford. I tell you, you would have a real problem to find a bike as good as the Bombardier for the price. Try for yourself and you'll find out that I'm right. I hope my advice and my experiences will help you make a good choice, so good luck to you, and remember, the right bike can be a joy for life. I know, I spent half of mine on my beloved Velo. For a young man with a wife or girlfriend who may be thinking that the Bombardier is only a one-seater, don't let that put you off, for there are plenty of good second-hand dual seats around for a few pounds. As for the fitting, easy – just make a strong cradle to fit the bike and adapt the seat to fit it for the rear frame is ideal for a pair of suitable footrests, the five-speed gearbox being ideal for the extra weight and as for the engine, well, being a two-stroke, it would laugh at it and don't forget, best of all, you'd have engine braking. Another way of finding a decent bike is to go to a Sotheby's sale, yes of course there are expensive bikes there, but there are also some very good buys at reasonable prices and the good part of it is, that one usually gets the history of the machine to go with it. To get into a Sotheby's sale one must write for a catalogue which is also your entrance fee, where everything that is for sale will be clearly marked and priced and the history given or any other information relevant to the article. It's a very good day out even if you don't buy anything and no one is going to pressurise you into doing that. It's a far better proposition than going to a second-hand bike dealer, for very few dealers ever bother about history or past owners. To most, a second-hand bike means a meal ticket and that's all. You can buy a load of trouble as many of you reading this have probably already done, so don't buy in haste, 'easy does it every time'. Far better to go to an army sale or a Sotheby's sale than risk a clapped-out doctored job from a shady dealer. Sorry dealers, I'm not running you all down, of course, some dealers are very good, but none come cheap, so the choice is yours.

So in case anyone would like Sotheby's address, it is as follows: Sotheby's, 34-35 New Bond Street, London, W1A 2AA. All connecting addresses and information will be sent to you for all other venues. If one should buy privately, then the same thing goes, find out about the history and if you can't and you're not a mechanic or maybe you're not sure, then don't buy. Be like the dealers: if it doesn't suit you or your pocket, then forget it. Another one will come along, so be patient. A good bike is well worth waiting for and remember, there is a lot of rubbish about, so don't buy it.

I had only a few rides on the Bombardier, for one thing, we had used up most of our savings as I hadn't worked for three and a half years. It's not too bad to tax a car and bike if you're earning, stop earning and the picture soon changes. So we decided to sell the house, which was paid for and find a small bungalow by the sea for our retirement. The Bombardier came in very handy for this as its cheap running costs compared to the car won every time. However, once we had made the move, funds were still too tight for me to run around on my bike so I wasn't too surprised when Werner rang up and asked me if I wanted to sell it. He wanted it for his wife, Angelique, they would then have a matching pair, a very wise move.

Chapter Fifty-Two
My Last Ride on the Bombardier

Well, I could see that I wasn't going to use it a lot and the tax, insurance and MOT had all run out five months before, and as I said, Werner was like another son to us, and not only that, but it couldn't go to a better owner, for Werner was like me, one could eat food off Werner's bike or car, for they were immaculate in every way. In fact, he was more fussy than myself, so we decided to let him have it.

Angelique at this time, had got a 125cc Honda and had just got a top secretarial job at Harley Davidson UK and wanted to drop the Jap bike before starting there. The arrangements were for them both to come up in their car and one of them to ride it back, for both were riders and drivers. However, I thought it a bit much for Angelique to take a strange machine through the Welsh mountains, so I rang them up and told them that I would bring it down on the following Friday, which they agreed to. Well, I soon got the bike sorted out and running. It started second kick even after standing for a few months, so with the MOT and tax all done and a short fourteen-day insurance, come Friday, I was all set to go. Friday came all right and so did the Welsh weather. It was pouring down and when it rains in Wales – I don't think I need to say any more. The date was 5th October 1990, and I started out about 2.00 p.m., and if anything, it was raining even harder and I knew I was in for a tough ride. But I'd got the right bike for it. It was built to take all this and through the mountains I was very pleased to be on such a machine. The sheer volume of water was pouring off the mountains and onto the road in torrents, bringing with it small boulders and a lot of loose shale. I had to dodge rocks and sometimes go across the road to avoid small waterfalls on the road. The lack of traffic was the only good thing and for the first seventy miles, I only came across about eight or nine cars and most of them were all steamed up and were only going slowly. I, too, wasn't doing more than about 45 m.p.h. for the conditions were deadly. I thought to myself, 'How would Angelique get on in this lot, and her not knowing the way?'

I had two or three slides on the shale, but my riding ability soon ironed them out, and I didn't stop until I'd got to the M54 leading on to the M6. So, at a pull-in along the M54, I stopped for a look at the bike and a Mars Bar. Despite the rain, the rear chain was oiled and the bike was running like a watch. I wasn't cold, my gloves were in plastic covers and my old Mark VIII goggles hadn't steamed up. I was doing fine and so was the old bike. But when I reached the M6 I had a shock, for all lanes were at saturation point. All traffic had come to a halt. Of course! What a clot I was! It was Friday, and all the weekenders were out.

Well, it's no use being on a bike if you don't make use of it, so, with headlamp now on main beam, I proceeded between the cars on my way to Coventry. Some drivers had a 'dog in the manager' attitude, for on seeing me coming, they ran across my path to stop me, but the Bombardier had got a trials bike steering lock so I had no problem dropping into second or bottom and just riding across the rear of them. One silly ass shouted,

"Why you and not me?"

I replied, "You're not in my class. I'm a rider, that's why." So, slowly but surely, I made my way into the Midlands. By now, the rain had eased a bit, but it was still raining well. At the Corley service station, there was a queue of cars about a mile long all along the hard shoulder for fuel, as most were running out, so now I had to use my wits again. So, without any hesitation, I dropped a gear and, lifting up the front wheel, I dived for the pump and got it. I turned to the driver I'd got in front of.

"Sorry chum, despatches," I said.

"Carry on," he replied. "I wouldn't dream of holding up the army."

"Many thanks. I appreciate it," I replied.

Well, I put three pounds worth of fuel in the tank and pushed the bike clear of the pump.

"Carry on, sir," I called out and dashed in to pay for my fuel. Again in the kiosk, I cried out in a loud voice, "No. 5 pump, three pounds, despatches, can't stop," and ran out to the bike. Of course, it fired first kick, and as I shot out of the petrol station with my front wheel lifting, a big cheer went up. I was through.

So, still riding between the stationary or, to be accurate, almost stationary cars, as a bit of movement was now evident, I slowly made my way down onto the A45 Birmingham Road.

Once there, and although the traffic was heavy, and it was still raining well, the traffic was still moving at about 50 m.p.h., so it wasn't long before I arrived at Coventry, but I was now in the works evening traffic, so I still had to ride with great caution, for cars in the wet, particularly when going slow, soon steam up, making the vision very bad, as many car drivers haven't got the sense to open nearside and offside windows about an inch so that the airstream can clear the glass, so never ride in the wet without your headlight being on and above all, keep your distance and stay alive. On arriving safely at our friends' house, they were very relieved to see me and, despite the rain, I was glad that it was I who had ridden it down. After all, it was my swansong on the Bombardier, and somehow it seemed right, for it had all started and finished in Coventry, just fifty-two years ago, I'd done fifty-two years on British bikes, and now you can enjoy it too, for I really hope that this book has been a source of enjoyment for you as for me. Some of my best moments were achieved on British bikes, hence this story.

Chapter Fifty-Three
The Story Ends

Looking back at all those years, one wonders where have they all gone, for when one is young, one never dreams of getting old. I know I thought I was here forever, but, like millions before me, when one gets old, one knows that it isn't to be. That's when one looks back at the great days, the days of your youth and vigour. Don't abuse it; it's precious and it all goes too quickly. I didn't mention many of the other bikes that I owned during all that time, simply because those bikes were ordinary standard machines that I used as everyday transport, but I had one more Velo MAC in standard form, one Model G 350cc OHV Royal Enfield, one CO Enfield, the Army Model G, one 125cc Francis Barnett, one Triumph 500cc single 1928, one 350 SV Enfield 1925 and a 350cc Lewis, that I should have kept, for, like the Rudge, it was a racer and would be worth a packet today. I also bought my son Bob a new Honda 50cc Sports as his first bike, a cracking little model, a great bike on the ice. Also, I bought a smashed Honda 125cc and rebuilt and sold it after using it for a month. Also, I bought another smashed-up bike, a Kawasaki 90cc reed valve six-speed two-stroke, which when done went like the clappers. Werner had that off me, and he enjoyed it very much. I only ever lost on one bike out of all the bikes that I owned and that was a 1000cc V Twin AJS combo, the very first ride I had. A milk float hit me coming out of a side road and it bowled me over and I was trapped under the bike. That I let my pals Geoff and Bernard Holland have for spares, as both the frame of the bike and the sidecar chassis were both scrap, but I got clear with a slight cut on my face and a bruised right leg. Now, at seventy-three, in the year of 1995, I look back and wish I could do it all again, for there is no way I would have missed my fifty-two years on British bikes. I've written a poem

about my MOV Velo, so I'll finish my story by putting in the last few
lines of my poem. It reads thus:

Blokes will look at my bike in the days when I'm gone,
They may even wonder what sort of a rider sat on.
But when the wind's in the willows and over Cotswolds high
    ground,
Comes a lovely high note, a mechanical sound.
It's the sound of my Velo, truly in song,
And a big smile on my face as we both glide along.

by George John Hylands – that 'Velo Fellow'